The
Loneliness
of
Children

The Loneliness of Children

BY

JOHN KILLINGER

The Vanguard Press
New York

ACKNOWLEDGMENTS

For their kind permission to reprint material in this book, acknowledgment is made to the following:

Adolescence: The Crisis of Adjustment by Simon Myerson; published by George Allen & Unwin Ltd. Reprinted by permission of George Allen & Unwin Ltd.

Adolescent Sexuality in Contemporary America by Robert Sorenson; published by the World Publishing Co. Copyright © 1973, 1974 by Robert C. Sorenson. Reprinted by permission of the World Publishing Co. % Harry N. Abrams, Inc.

How Children Fail by John Holt; published by Pitman Publishing Corporation. Copyright © 1964 by Pitman Publishing Corporation. Reprinted by permission of Fearon Pitman Publishers, Inc.

A Circle of Quiet by Madeleine L'Engle; published by Farrar, Straus & Giroux, Inc. Copyright © 1972 by Madeleine L'Engle Franklin. Reprinted by permission of Farrar, Straus & Giroux, Inc.

The Needs of Children by Mia Kellmer Pringle; reprinted by permission of Schocken Books Inc. and Hutchinson Publishing Group Ltd. Copyright © 1974 by National Children's Bureau.

CHILDREN OF CRISIS: Vol. II, *Migrants, Sharecroppers, Mountaineers* by Robert Coles; published by Little, Brown and Company in association with the Atlantic Monthly Press, 1972. Reprinted by permission of Little, Brown and Company.

Childhood and Society by Erik Erikson; published by W. W. Norton and Company, Inc. Reprinted by permission of W. W. Norton & Company, Inc.

Confrontation with Youth by Rocco D'Angelo; Monograph No. AA-11, 1976, published by Ohio State University Press. Reprinted by permission of Rocco D'Angelo, Ph.D.

v

For our sons
ERIC and KRISTER
with love and gratitude
for our life
together

CONTENTS

INTRODUCTION

Parents today are more sensitive to the needs of their children than were the parents of any previous generation. They give more thought to their children's welfare, lavish more money on their education and entertainment, and spend more time with them than parents of fifty years ago would have dreamed of doing. Because of this, they assume that the children ought to be happy and well adjusted to life. It rarely occurs to them that little Susie or Joey could be lonely, afraid, or starved for affection.

It had not occurred to me — until one day about six years ago.

Searching for something in my thirteen-year-old son's briefcase, I came upon a crumpled note he had written to himself. It said: "I am still going to run away." I was stunned. The boy had always been the most unremittingly cheerful human being I had ever known. He had been an object of love since he was a mere gleam in his parents' eyes. The note seemed crazy, ill-founded, impossible; yet it was real, and signaled something deep inside our son that for some reason or other had never been voiced to us.

This book was conceived on the day I discovered that note. If my son was lonely, I thought, with all the love and attention he had received, what about other children, children whose parents are less devoted to them? Somebody needed to delve into their minds and say what they were feeling. I wrote myself a note to this effect, so that I wouldn't forget it, and left it on my desk.

I talked with my son, and he shared with me some of the feelings that had led to the cryptic message in his briefcase.

I forgot the note on my desk.

Then something happened that brought it back to my attention with a vengeance.

It was Saturday morning. I was just finishing my first cup of coffee when the phone rang.

The voice on the line was choked with emotion. At first it was not clear. Then I made out the words, "John, help me."

It was the architect who had designed our house several years earlier. When I asked what was wrong, he said, "My son committed suicide."

I couldn't believe it. The boy was a leading student at the finest prep school in the city. He had recently won a merit scholarship. His name was in the papers. He was popular with his classmates.

I sat in the parents' living room as they picked over their memories of recent months.

There had been no clue, no forewarning. The boy had been quiet, but he had said nothing of loneliness or unhappiness. The parents had suspected nothing.

As they talked, one possible answer emerged. For several years, the boy had had an interest in military strategy. He had saved his money for a trip to a university campus where hundreds of people — mostly adults — gathered annually to play war games. He had made the trip only a few weeks before his death. When he returned home, he seemed unusually introspective, and didn't want to talk about the games.

I asked what the games were like.

"Oh, they have boards and maps and computers," said the father. "It's mostly nuclear stuff. They plan strategy for knocking out major cities, retaliating against enemy attacks — that sort of thing."

I wondered. Had it all been too much for his young mind — the talk of conflict, wholesale destruction, nuclear fallout? Had it fascinated him at first, and then overpowered him?

For days I couldn't get the image of the boy out of my mind. I kept recalling a quotation from Charles Dickens's *Oliver Twist:* "What could one poor child do?"

I went back to the note on my desk.

This time I would not forget. Someone had to say something about the loneliness of children, about the special problems of being a child in today's world. Not necessarily of being a child from the ghetto or a child with a physical handicap or even an abused child. There were plenty of books on these subjects. But of being a child at all, a normal child, whose parents may even genuinely care about the feelings of their offspring.

I began to talk with children, and to listen to their side of things. I questioned young people and adults about their childhoods. I interviewed school teachers, nursery workers, psychologists. Friends who work in orphanages and reformatories tape-recorded interviews for me, so I could compare the statements of children in those places with the statements of ordinary children. Teachers in numerous schools obligingly supplied me with essays their classes had written on life and loneliness.

Eventually the picture began to come in strong and clear: Childhood is a very difficult time of life. For many children, it is filled with fears, anxieties, and confusion. Even those who are happiest experience occasional feelings of doubt and rejection. To be a child is to be vulnerable, to be open to misunderstandings and, even from loving parents, misuse.

Adults often forget how hard it is to be a child. They recall some of the more dramatic events or moments in their childhoods — spankings, conflicts, disappointments. But these are often viewed through a mist of romance and sentimentality, while numerous other feelings of rejection and suffering have been allowed to slip away completely.

I hope the evidence in this book will help to recover some of those lost feelings. Maybe, if we can remember what childhood was really like, we will be more careful about the feelings of our own children. We will be more sympathetic about their separation-anxieties, their self-doubts, their school worries, their inability to make smooth transitions from one stage of childhood life to another. We may even love them more.

One more thing.

Loneliness is a feeling, a mood. It can mean the state of being alone, separate, isolated. It can also imply alienation or rejection, which involves the feelings of others toward the one who is lonely or alone. And the existentialist literature of this century suggests that loneliness may even be a metaphysical quality, a sense of homelessness in the universe, of not belonging anywhere. One finds this latter manifestation in the writings of Camus, in which people are essentially strangers in the world.

I have resisted the temptation to try to define what I mean when I speak of the "loneliness of children." I much prefer that the reader build up a composite portrait of it for him- or herself. In this way the reader will understand it, will feel it, and will know it is not something that can be limited to the simple terms of a definition. I want the reader to experience the many-sidedness of children's loneliness — the multiple ways in which they feel assaults on their personalities, their dignity, their well-being. In the end, when the book has been finished and laid aside, that many-sidedness should appear. It should form like a sadness in the heart. But it should come also with a resolution — that we will do everything in our power to make things better for children.

The
Loneliness
of
Children

1

The Ordeal of Infancy

When do children first begin to experience loneliness? Some say it is when they are made to sleep in their own rooms at night, and are afraid of the dark. Others contend it is the first time they become lost or separated from a parent, say in a shopping center or a theater. Still others think it has to do with the first faint recognition of mortality, the budding suspicion that people die the way birds and animals do.

The truth is, children probably have their first taste of loneliness the moment they leave their mother's wombs, before they are even conscious of their feelings.

They do not know it is loneliness they are feeling. Their minds have not begun to distinguish between acceptance and nonacceptance, love and hate, inside and outside. But somewhere deep inside their tiny psyches they are already registering sensations of pleasure and pain, comfort and discomfort. They know their warm, previously safe little worlds are in upheaval, that they are being expelled from the only existence they have ever known.

For nine months the fetus has been gently cradled in the amniotic fluid of the womb. Temperature and pressure have remained absolutely constant. Feeding has occurred naturally and continuously, without interruption. Then suddenly, almost without warning, this Nirvana-like existence comes to an abrupt end. The uterus, which has been such a peaceful home, starts a series of violent contractions, forcing the fetus headfirst through the birth canal. The supply of oxygen from the mother becomes greatly reduced. The head pushes repeatedly against the hard pelvic bone until the bone eventually gives way, permitting the head to exit, and leaving it with a permanent swelling beneath the scalp known as the *caput succedaneum*. The lungs fill with air, massaging the small heart into motion, and the two cavities momentarily compete with each other for space in the infant chest. Like a once dormant but now vitalized pumping house, the body begins to respond to its environment, and the heaving thoracic muscles force oxygen in and out of the lungs and send blood coursing through the body.

We seldom think about the shock of this experience for the newborn child, for we do not generally regard fetuses as sentient, feeling creatures. Yet the infant's central nervous system is highly developed by the time of birth. So is its cutaneous nervous system, the sense of touch. Even at the preconscious level, the child doubtless experiences an amount of trauma commensurate with the dramatic rearrangement of its life as it passes from intero-uterine to extero-uterine existence.

If you would put yourself in the child's place, imagine having this nightmare:

> You are being pushed, shoved, pummeled on your way through some strange elastic chute. Your whole world is in upheaval, as though an earthquake, a hurricane, and a nuclear explosion were all occurring simultaneously. There is a blinding light, and you feel alien creatures pulling at you, upending you, poking gleaming instruments at you.
>
> You begin to cry, to scream. It is something you have never done before, but now you cannot help doing it. You gasp for breath. Your chest is heaving.
>
> The horrible creatures have clapped you into a cart and are wheeling you through lighted tunnels to some unknown destination. You do not want to go. How will you ever retrace your way? You scream and struggle, but to no avail. You are powerless against them.

For days you are poked and prodded by strangers. They are giants, and often they lift you and handle you brusquely, peremptorily, against your will. They place strange objects in your mouth. They roll you in a cloth that feels rough and foreign to your body. Sometimes they carry you through the long tunnels into great rooms where you are handled by other strangers.

You cry frequently, for you understand nothing. You want the awful nightmare to end, but it doesn't. You begin to despair of ever returning to your normal state of consciousness.

This is the way birth must seem to an infant — like a nightmare. Everything is new and different. It is the kind of experience that can only be described as cataclysmic or world-shaking. Even though it is not at the time articulated into consciousness, its effects are bound to be enormous and long-lasting.

Otto Rank, a psychoanalyst, was so impressed by the consequences of this trauma that he developed his entire counseling procedure around it. In analysis, he said, the patient is in actuality struggling for rebirth, for a new entry into the world without the complications of life entailed in the first entry. Even though the patient doesn't know it, he or she unconsciously associates personal problems with the original upheaval and displacement from the protection of the womb. Therefore, says Rank, the essential task of analysis

is really neither more nor less than allowing the patient to repeat with better success in the analysis the separation from the mother. But this is by no means to be taken metaphorically in any way — not even in the psychological sense. For in the analytic situation the patient repeats, biologically, as it were, the period of pregnancy, and at the conclusion of the analysis — *i.e.*, the re-separation from the substitute object — he repeats his own birth for the most part quite faithfully in all its details. *The analysis finally turns out to be a belated accomplishment of the incompleted mastery of the birth trauma.*[1]

What this suggests is that loneliness in children is ontological. It is tied up with their beings from the moment they are born. It has physiological and neurological origins that can never be totally erased. Regardless of how well children are treated or how much they are loved by their parents, they will continue all their lives, in varying degrees, to experience personal anxieties and uncertainties related to the shock of being born.

Arthur Janov, the developer of Primal Therapy, strongly concurs with Rank's theory. "Birth Primals," he says — therapy sessions in which patients are encouraged to relive early experiences that were either unconscious at the time or later repressed — , "leave little question as to the powerful effect of early physical trauma on later general behavior. I lay such stress on birth trauma not because it alone 'causes' neurosis, but because looking back from the point of view of birth primals we can see what a tremendous impact these traumas have in terms of laying down stored tension."[2]

Janov thinks that people who have had hard births of various kinds — breech births, premature births, cord strangulations, births with excessive labor times — are most likely to reveal psychological tensions or abnormalities in later life. The treatment Janov prescribes for these persons is a dramatic re-enactment or re-envisioning of the birth experience itself. They assume fetal positions on the floor and, responding to suggestions from a therapist, attempt to recapture long-dormant or unconscious emotions until they have gone through a psychological re-birthing.

In *The Feeling Child,* Janov includes a remarkable verbatim from a man who underwent a primal. The man, an actor, had come to Janov complaining of sexual impotence and of occasionally waking at night with the feeling that he was a woman. In analysis, he mentioned that he had been born three weeks prematurely. Janov deduced that this was somehow related to the impotence and the feeling of being a woman. The latter feeling, Janov thought, was probably an identification with the man's mother, an intermediate step toward becoming once more the baby in her womb.

In the primal, the man actually "regressed" to the fetal stage and re-experienced birth. But he also acted out his mother's role in the birth. Here are his words:

> I sank deeper and yet earlier into my birth. Now I felt even smaller, something very primitive, like in the pictures of the fetus at six or seven months I had seen in the book *A Child Is Born*. I felt almost as tiny as a rat. But something was happening. There was no me. I was feeling that I was her. That these quivers and spasms were really her and that she was trying to force me into existence. I didn't want it! I hated it! Terror! Screams! I only had known myself as *her*. At least that's where I was at when the spasms struck. So that I felt there was something new about her I was becoming aware of. Before I had only known her from this tube that went from the middle of me to her and from the warm liquid of her I had lived in. Now I had to know her from the outer limits of me, and yet even with the quivering and spasms, I couldn't tell where I left off and she began. . . . But why did I have to learn this? Why? . . . The spasms and the flopping increased, and I found that to survive soon I would have to assume and feel that it *was* me. . . . I was scared I might die. I had to be me if I was going to stay alive. I had to get out and be my own boss from then on. Now it was me, really me coming out. I screamed and screamed. I felt my neck choking, and I was still a tiny, undeveloped thing. Something was around my neck, and I could feel my head coming through an opening into cold. I was choking on fluids and there were hands around my neck. A big gasp — and then a terrible pain in my chest. My chest was going up and down, and with each movement — terrible pain. . . . I screamed and screamed with each new gasp. I never asked for this. Why do I have

5

to do this? It was so painful being out — alive, breathing.
. . . I lay there for a long time screaming, wheezing, hoping
I could keep up with the air going into my body, feeling
great pain in my lungs with each new breath.[3]

Was the man hallucinating or did he actually relive
the experience of his birth? Janov thinks the latter, and cites
as evidence the fact that the man immediately began to take
responsibility for his life in ways he never had before.

Some French pediatricians and psychologists have
begun to apply theories about the birth trauma to therapy
for patients still in their childhood — some as young as six
months old. At this point, the treatment is usually limited to
children who show signs of hypertension and abnormal
levels of anxiety. Instead of prescribing tranquilizers for
the children, as pediatricians in this country frequently do,
the doctors suggest physical therapy aimed at re-enacting the
birth experience and successfully "separating" infants from
their mothers.

At clinics in Pau and Cagnes-sur-mer, for example,
children are treated in small, ovoid-shaped rooms reminiscent of their mothers' wombs. Each room contains a bath in
which the water is maintained at 98.6° Fahrenheit, the temperature of the human body. The walls of the room are
bathed in violet light similar to the light thought to be perceived by unborn children when their mothers are sunbath-
ing; the light is shaded toward the red end of the spectrum
to stimulate apathetic children, toward the blue end to calm
the hyperactive. A strange, almost musical sound is broadcast
into the room. It is the sound of the child's mother's voice
reading a children's story; only it is distorted on an 8,ooo-
Herz frequency to sound as it might to a child still in the
uterus. As the child is soothingly bathed and massaged, the
scents of lavender, thyme, and marjoram are introduced into
the room, and the recorded voice of the mother becomes
gradually normalized until it is fully recognizable.

Drs. Alfred Thomatis and Anne-Marie Saurel, who

operate these particular clinics, say they have had revolutionary results with children suffering from a variety of psychological problems such as anorexia, hyperactivity, and apathy. The children appear to undergo a kind of "sonic rebirth" and re-emerge into the world with healthier, happier attitudes than before.

There is no widespread agreement among psychologists and analysts about the value of this kind of therapy. But there is a growing consensus about the profound shock produced in the infant's system by the changeover from interouterine to extero-uterine life. It is entirely possible, most doctors agree, that the birthing process is able to leave children with residual psychological damage fully as devastating as the physical handicaps with which some are born. And one of the most significant aspects of this damage is the sense of abandonment or forlornness produced subconsciously in the child's mind as a result of being physically ejected from the placid residence in the mother's womb.

The Importance of Fondling

It does not take a genius to see what the newborn child needs most when he or she is expelled from the security of the womb. To replace the oxygenation and circulation of the blood formerly provided by the mother's body, there must be new work done by the child's own lungs and heart. For the constant temperature of the mother's body there must be substituted heated space and/or some form of body clothing. There must be some new supply of nourishment to replace the internal feeding that occurred in the mother's womb. And — no less important — the child needs a continuation of the gentle cradling and physical assurance to which he or she became accustomed during nine months in the amniotic fluid of the womb.

Too often, in our culture, there has been a failure to recognize this last need. The idea of a sanitary nursery and the strict discipline of infants has frequently taken precedence over the natural inclinations of mothers to keep the newborn at their sides, where the infants could continue to enjoy constant physical contact and take food whenever they expressed the desire for it. Until World War II, the most important child-care manuals expressly forbade mothers to rock their children, on the theory that too much fondling would spoil the children and leave them with high dependency levels. And until even very recent years, nearly all hospitals made it rigid practice to separate mother and child at birth, returning the child to the mother only at limited intervals, primarily for nursing. In many hospitals — most of them, unfortunately — this is still the rule.

Children need fondling, touching, cradling. They need the feel of flesh upon flesh, the sense of the mother's warm presence, the sound of her loving voice. This is the source of their security. It is the only real therapy they have, in the early hours and days after birth, to overcome the trauma of entering the world. If they are deprived of it, the trauma is likely to be more intense and prolonged, and later healing more difficult.

What the newborn child has a right to expect, says Ashley Montagu, is a continuancy of the peaceful life he or she experienced before expulsion from the uterus. What the child receives is often another matter:

> The moment it is born, the cord is cut or clamped, the child is exhibited to its mother, and then it is taken away by a nurse to a babyroom called the nursery, so called presumably because the one thing that is not done in it is the nursing of the baby. Here it is weighed, measured, its physical and any other traits recorded, a number is put around its wrist, and it is then put in a crib to howl away to its heart's discontent.
>
> The two people who need each other at this time, more than they will at any other in their lives, are separated from one another, prevented from continuing the development of a symbiotic relationship which is so critically necessary for the further development of both of them.[4]

It was by observing animals that Montagu first came to realize how significant is the contact between mother and baby. He had always supposed that when a horse licks a colt or a cat licks a kitten it is in order to clean the afterbirth from the newborn. Then he discovered that this is not the purpose at all — that what the mother animal is really doing is massaging and stimulating the offspring's vital organs. Without this subcutaneous stimulation performed by licking, baby animals often fail to stand, and subsequently die. This discovery in turn led Montagu to understand that certain critical functions are also served when human mothers cradle and nurse their babies. These are related to the deep psychophysical needs of children following birth — especially the needs for consolation and reassurance.

For years, the death rate of infants placed in foundling homes shortly after birth was nearly one hundred percent. The children almost invariably developed a form of atrophy known as *marasmus,* or "wasting away," in which their physical progress became retarded and they eventually ceased to eat or to respond to other persons. Doctors attributed the deaths to some nameless childhood disease. Then it was discovered that if nurses only violated the rules and fondled the children when they fed, bathed, and clothed them, the children did not develop marasmus. It was as simple as that — the children were dying of neglect.

R. A. Spitz, who has done extensive study among institution babies, doubts whether any kind of institutionalized care is able to meet children's needs, even when nurses attempt to provide minimal fondling and love for the children. His investigations have revealed that a large percentage of such babies are deficient in motor development, even in such simple things as learning to sit, stand, or walk alone. They also tend very easily to become listless, to take food or regurgitate it with equal ease, and to lose weight when they should be gaining.[5]

Experiments with rhesus monkeys, which exhibit profound similarities to human beings, confirm Spitz's findings.

Monkeys removed from their mothers at birth and placed in a cage with a furry, inanimate substitute progress better than monkeys deprived of a mother-figure altogether, which often sicken and die. But monkeys left with their mothers develop normally, and are much healthier and quicker than monkeys raised with a substitute.

Children simply have a strong need for love in the early months of extero-uterine life — the strongest, perhaps, they will ever have. And during this period they are unable to receive love except in its most practical, nonverbal form — as touching, caressing, cradling, and soothing. They may never realize, in later years, that they have received this kind of love. But their psyches, which are so busily receiving impressions and forming attitudes toward the world, will know and remember.

Children and Working Mothers

The need children have for their mothers immediately after birth does not suddenly go away when they are six months or a year old. It continues with little abatement through the first three years of their lives.

"It is difficult for a baby to get used to living outside mother's body," says Hiag Akmakjian in *The Natural Way to Raise a Healthy Child.* "After birth — and to a lesser extent throughout early childhood — the mother acts as a protective shield, a tough psychological skin between the baby and the world that enables him or her to become accustomed to stimuli and demands, growing stronger in the process, finally taking over without outside aid."[6]

If the shield or protective skin is removed too early, the child's system cannot respond adequately to its environment. The stimuli are overwhelming, producing a sense of anxiety that may well become permanent in the child's makeup.

John Bowlby, R. A. Spitz, and others have in recent years made important studies of the attachment and separation patterns in children's lives. These studies indicate that the small child is attached to one figure, the mother or an adequate mother-surrogate, more than to any others in its life, and that deprivation of this figure, especially in the first three years of the child's existence, can lead to serious psychological maladjustments not only in childhood but throughout life.

Bowlby's experiments show that young children are upset by even brief separations from the important parent. Their distress follows a basic sequence. When a child notices its mother's absence, it first reacts with *protest,* usually in the form of crying or tantrums. If the crying fails to bring the mother back, the child then falls into *despair* of her return, though the protest is continued intermittently in hopes that she may still reappear. Eventually, if the mother does not come back, despair gives way to *detachment,* a form of emotional self-protection equivalent to an adult's decision not to expect anything in order not to be disappointed. The final stage, detachment, is abandoned if the mother returns within a reasonable length of time and attachment to the mother is resumed. If the periods are prolonged, however, the child may adopt a permanent internal posture of detachment and forever despair of having or maintaining attachment relationships. Some children learn to fake excitement at reunion with the parent, but at a deeper level remain skeptical of the parent's faithfulness and maintain a perpetual uneasiness about the relationship.[7]

After the age of three, children experience much less distress when left by the major parent. This age coincides, interestingly, with the nearly full development of the human brain. At birth, the brain has an average volume of 330 cubic centimeters. When the child is three, the average volume is 960 cubic centimeters, only 240 cubic centimeters short of full maturity. It has increased in size nearly three times since birth, and has but another fifth of its growth to go. Investigations indicate that three-year-olds whose mothers leave them usually understand that the parent will return; until that age, and especially until about two years and nine months, they are as uncertain of reunion as they were at the age of one year.

It is impossible to assess the extent of the damage done to tender psyches as a consequence of being left by the mother or mother-surrogate. The feelings of despair and detachment as described by Bowlby may lead to a more or less permanent state of anxiety or to a sense of personal rejection which not even psychoanalysis can overcome. This is hard news at a time in history when many mothers must work outside the home for economic reasons and when other women are determined to rise above the "captivity" of motherhood as soon as possible after the births of their children. But the choice is clearly between the children's needs and their own.

Mikey, age 3½, is an unfortunate example. I met Mikey during a visit to a day-care center for preschool children. He was a beautiful child with blond hair and enormous blue eyes. Mikey would hardly talk. He simply stood and stared. The other children were quite kinetic, but he seemed to be an onlooker, not a participant. The one word he kept saying over and over was "Mother." I asked if he missed his mother. He finally shook his head yes. "Where is she?" I asked. "Workin'," he said. It was the only other word he would say. From then on it was only "Mother."

I asked the attendant how long he had been at the center. She said he began coming when he was two and a half. At first he had thrown terrible fits every time his mother left him. Sometimes they lasted for an hour or more. Then the protests had begun well before the mother left home with him, sometimes starting when he had to get out of bed and eat breakfast. Eventually, however, he had despaired of avoiding the separation, so had begun to accept it stoically, without crying. Did he run to greet his mother when she came in the afternoons? Not any more, said the attendant; he seemed as indifferent to her coming as to her going. Yet he spoke her name over and over, day in and day out. It was like an echo that had not yet died away.

One can only speculate, in a case like this, that the child's ability to form deep and lasting attachments to other persons may well be impaired for life. He will not blame the mother. Small children do not question the right of adults to behave as they do. He will blame himself. He will believe he is not good enough, not worthy enough, to command his mother's attention. And even after he matures and knows better he will still feel unworthy.

Latest figures indicate that approximately one-third of U.S. women with children under three work outside the home at least part of the time. More than fifty percent of those with school-age children work at least part of the time. One-sixth of all the children in America live in single-parent homes where the parent must be employed outside the home.

Urie Bronfenbrenner, a child-development authority at Cornell University, raises the question, "Who is caring for America's children?" Bronfenbrenner and other psychologists fear that television has now become the major babysitter in our culture. By the time children are a year old, they are being parked in front of the TV set for entertainment while parents do housework, run errands, or, when the children are a little older, go to work. Their primary relationships are not to caring adults but to a two-dimensional screen filled with noisy cartoons, high-pressure ads, unreal adventure stories, and mindless quiz programs.

Every child, says Bronfenbrenner, needs to spend a substantial amount of time with at least one person who is devoted to it. "I mean there has to be at least one person who has an irrational involvement with that child, someone who thinks that kid is more important than other people's kids, someone who's in love with him and whom he loves in return. A colleague of mine once said, 'You can't pay a woman to do what a mother will do for free.' If you substitute 'person' for 'mother' I'd agree. You can't pay for an irrational commitment. And yet a child needs that. He needs somebody who will not just be there certain hours and then say, 'I'm off now, I work nine to five.' Notice I said at least one person. One really isn't enough."[8]

The Ongoing Need

Bowlby's attachment-separation experiments show that children at the ages of two years and nine months to three years pass a magic threshold that permits them to begin to be absent from the major parent without harmful effects. Left in a room alone, they will not try to follow the mothers when the mothers leave, especially if they are engaged at playing with some object. They may even be venturesome enough, at the age of three, to wander off from the major parent themselves.

But the need for touching and stroking does not end when this new plateau of independence has been reached. On the contrary, the need persists for years. In some children, it never entirely abates. Touching and cradling continue to be important nonverbal symbols capable of recalling and reconstituting the feelings of security the children experienced as babies in their mothers' wombs and later in their arms. If the symbols cease before the children are ready, anxiety is bound to follow.

Many adults are troubled by a sense of loneliness or rejection that owes more to childhood deprivation than to anything happening to them in the adult world. That is the real tragedy. It is bad enough for children to suffer. But children who suffer usually become adults who suffer.

Here are two examples.

Susan L., a 31-year-old secretary, went to her priest, and eventually to a psychiatrist, complaining of depression and loneliness. She was active in church and was constantly thrown with people in her work, yet never seemed to feel that people cared for her.

"Maybe I try too hard," she said, "and frighten people away. God knows, I want to be friends. I want to have a circle of people around me. But apparently I don't know how. Other people seem to do it without trying. I never could, even in high school."

With the help of the psychiatrist, Susan was soon in contact with her childhood feelings, and recalled thinking then that there was something wrong with her because her parents never touched her. She had seen friends' mothers and fathers embracing them, patting them, caressing them, and wondered why she was so repulsive to her own parents that they never wanted to treat her in a similar manner.

"My father did hold me on his knee and kiss me when I was very small," she said, "— maybe two or three. But then he stopped. I remember feeling puzzled, and thinking I had done something terribly wrong so that he didn't want me anymore, and refused to let me climb in his lap the way he once did." Her mother, as far as she was able to recall, had never shown any physical affection toward her, even in those early years.

The father, suggested the psychiatrist, may have been Victorian in his sexual upbringing and regarded it as improper to fondle a daughter after she had passed the age of three. That could have explained the sudden cessation of outward affection. But no excuse could be offered for the mother's behavior. Susan was simply unfortunate in having missed the kind of physical stroking and attentiveness that are so natural between parents and children when the parents freely enjoy their children, and that serve to assure the children that the world is accepting and loving toward them. Understanding this as an adult would probably help to ameliorate Susan's feelings of social inadequacy, but it would never completely eliminate her sense of loneliness or alienation. That was too deeply ingrained in her psyche; it was part of her ontological posture toward the world.

The second example is a former student of mine, Robert M., who is now a chaplain in the U.S. Armed Forces.

Robert is a pleasant-appearing man in his mid-thirties, highly articulate, very compulsive about his work, and filled with anger toward the military bureaucracy, most authority figures, and his parents. His mother, a prostitute, placed him in an orphanage when he was two years old. Seven years later, she withdrew him to come and live with her and a man, not Robert's father, whom she had married. The man was an alcoholic. During drinking bouts he would become violent, beating both the mother and Robert. At fourteen, Robert left home. Working at various jobs, he put himself through high school and college. He married, attended seminary, became a minister, and subsequently entered the military chaplaincy.

Today, after twelve years in service, Robert is professionally successful and highly respected by his colleagues. But he is still at war with the world that made him suffer so much as a child. He has had therapy, and speaks of having achieved a reconciliation with his past. Yet the anger clearly effervesces just below the surface. He is extremely competitive, and constantly compares himself and his work with others and their work, for he expects to be accepted only on his merits. He is a likable man, but he has great difficulty liking himself. Life is still "red in tooth and claw" for him, despite his years of training and analysis. He may *know* what his problem is — know it mentally or intellectually — but he cannot shake the memory of years of loneliness and alienation. He cannot, as a grown man, give himself a past filled with all the care and affection he missed.

Nor can any adult. That is the terrible pity. There is no "second time around" for any of us. We may talk about having a second childhood, but even that will not replace an unfortunate first childhood. This is why it is important that our children have a good childhood now, full of love and gentleness and touching. There will be no second chance.

2

The Threat of Separation

In his book *The Uses of Enchantment,* Bruno Bettelheim has taken an absorbing look at the important psychological truths enshrined in fairy tales. These tales owe their popularity, says Bettelheim, to the fact that they embody our strongest hopes and fears. And many of them, he points out, deal with the universal childhood fear of being separated from one's parents.

"Hansel and Gretel" is a good example. The boy and girl are taken into the forest and "lost" there because the parents can no longer provide food for them. As the mother represents the source of all food to children, it is she who is considered at fault for the abandonment. The witch's house, on the other hand, made of gingerbread and sweets, symbolizes the deceptive attractiveness of the evil world, which consumes little children who are not protected by parents. But the story is an encouraging one because it shows what clever, intelligent children can do to save themselves when they are abandoned by parents; they can trick the witch into her own oven and enjoy the good things of the world without paying an ultimate price for them.

"There is no greater threat in life," says Bettelheim, "than that we will be deserted, left all alone. Psychoanalysis has named this — man's greatest fear — separation anxiety; and the younger we are, the more excruciating is our anxiety when we feel deserted, for the young child actually perishes when not adequately protected and taken care of."[1]

Jeanette W. was 15 months old when her older sister was stricken with polio and the mother had to leave Jeanette in the care of a friend in order to be with the sister in the hospital. Jeanette, a bright child, had been talking in sentences since she was 12 months old. Garrulous and happy, she had "chatted like a magpie." The incomprehensible separation from her mother traumatized her so severely that she ceased speaking altogether, and did not resume until six months after her mother's return. For a long time after that she was very difficult to understand.

Stuart Sutherland, a British psychologist, has told in *Breakdown* the story of his mental collapse precipitated by the unfaithfulness of his wife with a best friend. In psychoanalysis, he recalled this experience from his infancy:

> When I was two years old and my brother was born, the nurse told my mother not to see me for a fortnight. My mother obeyed the nurse rather than her own instincts and, so I am told for I have no memories of that period, I sat outside her locked bedroom door and howled for fourteen days.[2]

Although Sutherland himself was cautious about drawing a connection between his childhood trauma and his inability to handle his wife's infidelity, there can be little doubt of the relationship. Betrayal by his wife touched the deeper note of unresolved betrayal by his mother, evoking in midlife a sense of psychological impairment far beyond the degree of immediate causation.

Bettelheim underscores the connection between childhood fears and continuing apprehension in adulthood. Separation anxiety, he says, is not restricted to a particular period of development. Once the child has been marked by it, he or she may suffer throughout life. This is one reason fairy tales are appreciated by adults as much as by children — the assurance they give is needed in maturity as much as in infancy. The shining promise, the one we all seek, is that we shall never be deserted.

Bettelheim cites the Turkish fairy tale of Iskender, whose mother has the father set him adrift in a casket on the ocean. A green bird rescues him from this and many subsequent dangers, each time reassuring him, "Know that you are never deserted." This, says Bettelheim, is "the ultimate consolation, the one that is implied in the common fairy-tale ending, 'And they lived happily ever after.' "[3]

An Imagined Danger

Freud said that *darkness* and *loneliness* are the primary agitators of separation anxiety. In either case, he said, it is separation from a meaningful adult that matters, not the phobia of the thing in itself. For example, he once heard a child who was afraid of darkness call out, "Auntie, talk to me, I'm frightened." "But what good will that do?" asked the aunt. "You can't see me." To which the child replied: "If someone talks, it gets lighter." "The longing felt *in* the darkness," said Freud — to be near the aunt — "is thus transformed into fear *of* the darkness."[4]

Once, when our children were small, the family was exploring the mazelike pathways through great bushes and outcroppings of rocks along a high point near Fuenterrabia, in Spain. One of our sons, who was eight, had bravely gone off by himself. During a lull in our chatter, a small voice from several yards away said, "Keep talking, so I'll know where I am."

That is perhaps what it is all about: "Keep talking, so I'll know where I am." Even when children are feeling adventurous, they wish to know where the adults in their lives are. It is their way of feeling secure in the midst of insecurities. The parents are their reference points, and they soon become uneasy when they cannot locate those points.

I have been amazed, on occasions when I have asked

entire classrooms of young children to describe a time or times in their lives when they experienced the anxiety of loneliness, to see how large a percentage of the children would speak of an occasion when they felt the panic of separation from their parents in a market or other public place. Here are examples of what some third and fourth graders said:

> On one spring break we went to Florida. This was the first time I had been to Florida. We went to Disneyworld. I got lost from my parents. I was very scared, frightened, lonely. A lady came up to me and asked me if I was lost. I said, "yes." She asked me what my mother looked like. I told her. Finally we found them. I was happy then, and very releaved.

> I listened for a baby but there was none. So I looked in the baby section, no Mom! Just then I thought about if Mom had left the store! I hurried up to the front. I saw my mother leaving so I followed her and didn't tell her about getting lost!

> One day I went with my mother to Giant Foods. We were getting ready to check out when all of the sudden I could not find mom. I started crying; it was about the fifth time that day. I looked all over the store but I could not find her. I was only 3 years old. I could not stand it. I said to myself, "I've sometimes dreamed how it would feel to be lost, but I never dreamed it would be this bad!" A man asked, "What's the matter?" I was crying so hard I could not talk. My mom came and got me. I hugged her all the way to the checkout counter. I asked her where had she been all the time? She said the checkout counter. She had been in front of me all the time.

Infantile anxiety, Freud observed, has very little to do with real danger.[5] None of the children cited above was in any true jeopardy. In fact, small children are usually oblivious to danger until trained to avert it. They will dart into a busy street, stand on a cliff, climb out on a limb, walk into a deep surf, with no apprehension whatsoever. As Freud says, we may *wish* children did come into the world provided with more fear of natural dangers. But they do not.

What *does* frighten the child is to be separated from the mother or other important adult, and darkness, loneliness, and other anxiety-producing experiences merely become metaphors for this basic phobia. Freud even insisted that every adult phobia could be traced back to a childhood anxiety. "Infantile phobias are not merely prototypes of those which appear later in anxiety-hysteria," he said, "but they are a direct preliminary condition and prelude of them. Every hysterical phobia can be traced back to a childish dread, of which it is a continuation even if it has a different content and must be called by a different name."[6]

Here is the situation, then: All anxieties (as opposed to fears aroused by actual danger) are extensions of the basic anxiety-producing fact, separation from the favorite parent. Because the newborn child is still very much organically related to the mother, loss of the mother during the period from birth to three years old is catastrophic to the infant, and will have permanently damaging effect. *This loss can be actual or imagined; the result will be the same in the child.* After three, the loss will be less catastrophic, for the child's socialization process is then under way, but it will still be severe. If the child's trust in the mother or caretaker's presence has been impaired in early childhood, the sense of apprehension or anxiety will continue strongly throughout childhood into adulthood, expressing or disguising itself in various kinds of phobias and anxieties.

The Empty House

I have already mentioned that United States figures now indicate that over half the mothers with school-age children and one-third the mothers with preschool-age children are employed outside the home. Recent surveys in Great

Britain indicate that the figures are almost as bad there: 46 percent of all married women work outside the home and 26 percent of all women with children under four are working mothers.[7]

It isn't any wonder that psychologists are worried about the phenomenon of the "empty house" and what it will do to present generations of infants and children.

Dr. Benjamin Spock, the famous child-care expert, has expressed vigorous concern about the problem: "I myself believe," he says, "that the government should pay a salary to parents to the extent that they stay at home to care for their preschool children, for children should not be deprived of the parental attention which creates security and sound character just because of the family's financial needs. More specifically, it would be worth the cost to a nation to prevent the serious neglect of some children which is the main cause of the character defects that result in poor application in school, truancy, delinquency, and, in adulthood, irresponsibility and petty criminality."[8]

Many children I have interviewed — those old enough to reflect on such matters — view the empty house as a symbol of their separation anxiety, one that amplifies all the feelings of loneliness and parental rejection they may have experienced from other causes.

Gerald S., a boy of twelve, said that his mother had gone back to work when he was seven. From that time on, he and his sister Gena, three years older, had come in from school to an empty house. Whenever there was deep snow and the schools were closed, they remained home alone, because the father had chains on his tires and always managed to get the mother to work. Asked to describe how he felt on coming into the house alone, he replied: "Oh, it's not so bad, I guess. It's quiet. I turn on the TV. That keeps me company. Sometimes I bring friends home, and sometimes Gena's here." Did he ever miss his mother or father? "I guess. Yeah, I do miss them." Did he ever feel there was anything personal in their not being there? "Well, you know how you feel sometimes. Like maybe — Well, you feel sorta funny when you go to another guy's house and his mom's there. You maybe sorta wonder if your own mom cares about you. But I'm sure she does. And we can have extra things because she works. That's nice."

Bronfenbrenner believes that the empty house is invariably a predictor of some kind of trouble in the child's psychiatric history, "whether the problem is reading difficulties, truancy, dropping out, drug addiction, or childhood depression." He also thinks that the undesirable traits of youth culture today are directly traceable to the empty house:

> Sometimes children are alone for hours with nothing but television. The TV isn't going to care for them. What happens? The kids find other kids who are coming home to empty houses. They create a peer-group culture, and it's likely to be an ugly culture — a culture of destroy, of break, of act out. The essence of it is *anomie,* a social and emotional disintegration, inside and outside. Frightening as it may be, this screaming for help isn't occurring just among a small minority of children. Hardly a school in the country doesn't have a problem with vandalism and violence. Think what that suggests. A major institution, charged with preparing the next generation for adult life, is a focus of aimless destruction.[9]

Anson W., a school principal, agrees. His school has been "hit" three times in the past four months, with damage running to more than $14,000. He is convinced it is his own students who are responsible. "The trouble is," he says, "they don't have any parents. They're out on the streets at all hours, riding around with older kids, drinking beer, turning on with drugs. School is a prison to them. They haven't been taught to respect anything." Do they come from bad sections of the city? "Some of them, but not all, by any means. I can show you where some of them live. They live in hundred-and-fifty-thousand-dollar houses with live-in maids and cooks. Their mamas are out getting their hair done, going to parties, playing tennis, taking trips — never home. The maids raise them. They're just as bad as the ones [children] from the slums."

Many teachers verify this picture of the upper class empty house where the mother is too involved with social life to spend time with the children and therefore delegates the responsibility to servants who are not suitable surrogates.

A first-grade teacher told me about correcting one of her pupils at lunch one day for the way the girl was behaving over her meal. "What would your mother think if she saw you eating like that?" she asked the girl. "I never eat with my mother," the girl replied. Subsequent questions revealed that the girl had always eaten with the maid in the kitchen, leaving her parents free to "dine" at a later hour.

A high school teacher said that she often heard tales from her students of wild weekends when parents went away to Bermuda or San Juan, leaving servants "in charge" of the children; the children invited friends in, drank heavily, and then spent the night in sexual orgies. One student's parents, she said, had gone to Europe for a month, leaving him in the care of the maid, who had exercised no supervision whatsoever; he spent the entire time partying, carousing, and driving his parents' car recklessly through the city at night.

We tend to appraise such stories in terms of the general breakdown of traditional society or of the irresponsibility of today's youth. But the first and most immediate price is in terms of the individual youth's loneliness and sense of neglect. Magistrates and judges say there are as many empty, aimless lives among the young people in suburbia as there are in any ghetto in the inner city. Crime has become a way of life for many of them, not only to support drug habits, but as a means of overcoming boredom or identifying with peers who are looking for a few kicks. Sometimes the young people are consciously or unconsciously rebelling against the respectable image of their parents, for they know the emptiness of their parents' existence and contemn their middle-class hedonism, their ego-centeredness in the family, and their hypocrisy about moral values.

In the second volume of *Children of Crisis,* dealing with the way of life among migrants, sharecroppers, and mountaineers, Robert Coles talked about the loneliness and alienation experienced by children of the very poor because of their sheer exhaustion from poverty and migrancy. But sometimes the children of the rich feel just as lonely from a surfeit of material advantages unaccompanied by genuine caring from the parents who provide them. At least the families of the poor are normally together in the evenings and take their meals together. Poverty provides a kind of solidarity that wealth, on the other hand, dissipates. Siblings in poor families are also given certain responsibilities of caring for the young in the family, whereas in some well-to-do families the caring is left to professionals or tends to be nonexistent. So it is fully as possible for rich kids to complain about the empty-house syndrome as it is for children of the lower middle class and lower class.

A Cozy Place to Hide

Children whose attachment needs have not been met and who are therefore much more sensitive to separation as a reality with which they must live often develop attachments to special places where they can shut out the world. Well-cared for children may also acquire special places as havens from noise, responsibility, or siblings, but lonely children tend to regard such places quite differently. They see them as indispensable retreats, as fortifications, as inviolable sanctuaries.

Kevin J., a 13-year-old, says he has had a succession of such places since he was five and his parents divorced. The first was a large cardboard box in a basement fruit room. Then he and his brother and mother moved to a small house on the edge of town and he discovered a ravine in a field behind the house; it became his favorite hiding place and "fort." When he was about ten, Kevin felt the insufficiency of the ravine ("It really wasn't very deep, and people could see me in it") and abandoned it for an attic space in the house, which he could reach via a pull-down set of stairs in the upstairs hallway.

Sally N., a quiet, retiring eight-year-old, has a large wooden box in the storage room of her home. It was placed there when she was very small to keep her toys in. She likes to get into the box, hollow out a space by moving the toys to the sides, and crouch there for what seems to her like hours, playing with her dolls and imagining a happy world. Sometimes when her mother calls her she doesn't answer, thinking she is safe in her private place.

Harold R., a shy boy of six in a home where there is constant bickering between his parents, likes to retire to a field next to the family garden and burrow into the high weeds. Sometimes he plays games while doing this, imagining that he is a soldier crawling through the jungle, or an animal playing in a passageway under the earth. He likes the cool feeling of the damp weeds and grass, he says; it is like "another world."

In every case, such places can be described as womb-like. They offer the children the illusion of the kind of protection and sanctity they experienced in the intero-uterine period of their existence. Key factors are the shape of the hiding place (boxlike, hollowed out, a burrow, a ravine), its coziness, its secrecy and privateness from adults who would not understand, and its imagined inviolability. These spots are veritable kingdoms to the children, places where they can reorder life as they would like it to be, where fantasy counts more than reality. Whether the home is empty in the real sense, because parents are working or absent for another reason, or in the psychological sense, as bereft of love and understanding, the secret place becomes a home within the home, deflecting harm and shutting in warmth and dreams of self-worth.

Separation as a Form of Death

We normally regard expulsion from the uterus as the beginning of life. Children's ages are counted from the moment of birth, not the supposed time of conception. We talk about Tuesday's Child, Wednesday's Child, and so on, as if everything began at the moment of arrival into the world.

But it is equally possible to regard the separation from the amniotic sac and the mother's womb as a kind of death. The infant "dies" to the intero-uterine existence and begins to live an extero-uterine life. Something is given up, left behind, abandoned. Part of the problem of childhood life is the fact that this is so. If the psychological filaments binding the child to the safe and pleasant life of the womb are not successfully cut in the early months of life, so that the child learns to face the world and the future with equanimity and at least a modest sense of adventure, then the child will spend the rest of his or her life longing at times for the Nirvana-like existence that was left behind, and may in fact, if the filaments are too strong and pressing, become genuinely neurotic or psychotic.

Even if the child has been loved and cared for by one or both parents, separation from a meaningful adult will also amount to a kind of death, even when it is for very brief periods. That is the character of separation. It is like enduring a death. It entails a certain amount of grieving or mourning. When the child is rejoined to the parent, the grieving is ended; but it may be started up again after a brief interval by another time of separation.

As Bowlby notes, "Young children are upset by even brief separations. Older children are upset by longer ones. Adults are upset whenever a separation is prolonged or permanent, as in bereavement."[10] The point is that to a young child who is as yet inexperienced about such matters even a short separation may seem permanent, an actual bereave-

27

ment. Gradually the child learns better, and is able to endure separations more stoically, realizing that they will pass.

Yet there is a sadness even then, for the child who is learning the character of temporary separations is also gradually learning the truth of life, that to live is to live toward permanent separations. I remember the wistfulness with which our children celebrated their birthdays during adolescence. There would be characteristic excitement as the time of a birthday approached, and much banter around the dinner table about presents, spankings, cakes, and wishes. Then, when the day finally arrived, the child would seem lost in reverie, unable to reach the level of excitement shared by other members of the family. There would be a faraway look in his eyes, a remoteness in his responses. Once I questioned one of them about his mood. "Oh, I don't know," he replied. "I guess I'm a little sad, when you come down to it. I want to grow up but I don't. I want things to stay the same." Later he admitted that he had presentiments of death. Not for himself so much as death in general. Death first for his parents. Then for himself, in due time. Life was moving inexorably toward separation.

Some children actually come to identify separation with death, fearing that the meaningful parent will die while they are apart. Myra P., a housewife, recalls that she was obsessed by this fear during her first year or two of school. Her mother was older than her friends' mothers, and somehow she thought this meant her mother was about ready to die. She became convinced that the death would occur while she was in school. Therefore she dreaded going to school each day, and spent many uncomfortable hours grieving about her mother's passing, expecting to return home in the afternoon and find her dead or to learn she had died and been taken away. "It was terrible," says Myra. "My fear overrode everything else I remember about those early months in school. I knew my mother was going to die while I was away."

Nelson M., a professor, recalls his inability to distinguish between absence and death when he was a small child: "At the age of four, I was dressed up by my mother and sent to a wedding in the home next door. I had no idea what a wedding was about. There were a lot of strange people there. My childish mind did not comprehend what was transpiring, and I was alarmed when I was told that the groom was taking the bride away. The bride was my friend. I had seen her in that home every time I was there. I suppose I thought marriage was like a death or something, and the groom was going to kill my friend. I was incensed at this, and wanted to kill him. I couldn't understand why the bride's mother was so happy, or why everybody else seemed so jolly. I went home feeling very frustrated and lonely, supposing I would never see Edith again. That strange man was going to do away with her, and nobody seemed interested in stopping him. The spell of my grief hung over me for days, and was not shaken, I am sure, until I saw her back again on a visit."

The Harm Done by Threats

Even if children learn to distinguish between separation and actual death, so that they are no longer completely morbid about temporary parting, they continue to regard any threat of separation as though it had an air of permanency about it. This is particularly true when the threat involves unknown factors with which the children have not previously had some experience, such as some dark, mysterious stranger who, it is said, will take a child away if the child does not behave as its parent wishes.

Ann H., now in her forties, vividly recalls the terror she felt whenever her mother told her she must be good or the "buggerman" would get her. "I didn't know what a 'buggerman' was, but I imagined someone big and dark and sinister who would sweep me away forever if I didn't do exactly as my mother wanted." She had nightmares about the buggerman, in which she was cut off from her parents by the portentous figure and could never get back to them. Did she ever tell her mother about the nightmares? "No. I suppose I thought that I must not tell, or it would actually happen. Maybe I believed, subconsciously, that my mother was in league with the buggerman and would tell on me if I mentioned the dreams."

Parents have of course used such threats against children since time immemorial, and often think very little about doing so. It is one of the behavior modification methods passed on from generation to generation unless some sensitive parent along the way remembers the damage done to his or her own sensibilities and refuses to use it, breaking the chain.

Bowlby feels that of even greater consequence in disturbing the child is a threat to abandon the child, for the child fears separation even more than the loss of love.

"A threat to abandon a child," he says, "can be expressed in a variety of ways. One is that if a child is not good he will be sent away, for example, to a reformatory or to a school for bad boys, or that he will be taken off by a policeman. A second is that mother or father will go away and leave him. A third, which plays on the same anxiety, is that if a child is not good his mother or father will be made ill, or even die. A fourth, probably of great importance, is an impulsive angry threat to desert the family, made usually by a parent in a state of despair and coupled often with a threat to commit suicide." [11]

The "reformatory threat" is extremely common. One woman I talked with, Susan H., testified to having lived in mortal dread of being sent to a reform school by her mother, who used the threat often. "I loved my older sister," she said, "who was married and lived in another state. Often, when she would come to visit, I would cry as she left, and be unable to talk. She and mama thought it was because I would miss her, but that wasn't it at all. I was afraid I would be sent to reform school before she got back and would never see her again."

A young man, Frederick S., remembers having stayed

in the house for days when he was a small boy of perhaps four or five years, afraid he would be taken away if he ventured out. He had been playing by the roadside when he had seen a Greyhound bus approaching. Stepping out on the curb, as he had seen grownups do, he waved to the driver to stop the bus. The driver pulled the bus to a halt, opening the door as he did so, and the boy, fearful of what he had done, fled and hid in some bushes. Later, Frederick told his mother about the incident. "You shouldn't have done that," she scolded. "Why, the police will come and get you for that!" Terrified, Frederick hid behind the bed in his father's room until evening; and even though he ventured out at suppertime, he prudently remained indoors for several days, lest the same busdriver see him or the police arrive and find him.

John Y.'s parents argued constantly when he was a boy, and his father, he recalls, was particularly irritable. Sometimes it made him physically ill when they argued, and he would run outside and vomit in the yard. His mother, perhaps sensing how upset the arguing made him, learned to use it as a control method. Whenever she wished to make him be quiet, she would say to him, "Now Johnny, you must be very quiet or you will upset your daddy and he will go away and leave us." The boy lived for several years under the impression that if his parents ever divorced it would be his fault. He became extremely quiet and introverted as a result, for he never wished to do anything that would cause his father to go away.

Though parents seldom mean such threats when they use them, and possibly intend them even as a form of teasing, children have no way of realizing this. To them, the threats are real, made in deadly earnest. A particularly headstrong or rebellious child may defy the parent to produce the consequences of a threat, but most children internalize the message and live in dread of its fulfillment. This is the evidence given in a book called *Four Years Old in an Urban Community,* a study by J. and E. Newson of seven hundred children and parents in Nottingham, England. The Newsons cite a fairly typical case of a mother who threatened her four-year-old, was tested by the child, and had to partially carry through her threat:

> I used to threaten him with the Harley Road Boys' Home, which isn't a Home any more; and since then, I haven't been able to do it; but I can always say I shall go downtown and see about it, you know. And Ian says, "Well, if I'm going with Stuart (7) it won't matter"; so I say, "Well, you'll go to different ones — he'll go to one Home, and *you'll* go to another." But it really got him worried, you know, and I really got him ready one day and I thought I'll take him a walk round, *as if* I was going, you know, and he really *was* worried. In fact, I had to bring him home, he started to cry. He saw I was in earnest about it — he *thought* I was, anyway. And now I've only got to threaten him. I say "It won't take me long to get you ready." [12]

The Newson study reported that 27 percent of the parents interviewed admitted using threats of abandonment as a means of controlling their children's behavior. Assuming that many parents were probably embarrassed to admit they had used such threats, the real figure is probably closer to 40 percent. Many parents who did use threats said they knew it was wrong but used them anyway, especially in moments of special tiredness or irritability.

Bowlby considers such threats as producing incalculable damage in children's psyches: "Threats to abandon the home and/or to commit suicide, made perhaps only at rare intervals but with an angry vehemence, are likely to have an effect entirely out of proportion to their frequency. Their effect, moreover, is magnified should the parent, father or mother, subsequently be so ashamed of having made such a threat that he or she cannot acknowledge either what was said or how frightening it must have been to the child. In such families the child has no opportunity to check his inevitable fears against the real risks, whatever they may be." [13] In the latter case, even psychiatric help is complicated by the fact that the parents usually attempt to conceal their having made such threats, attributing them instead to the child's guilty conscience or fantasy world.

The long-term effects of such threats are graphically illustrated in the situation of Jonathan D., a highly touted professional person, who was offered an attractive position in another city. At first there seemed no question of his taking it; it was the kind of job every person in his profession hopes for. But the decision did not come easily. Jonathan counseled with numerous friends and business associates before making it. Finally he accepted. Then, a few days later, he reversed himself and said he would not come. He was in great agitation. His normally buoyant sense of self-worth plummeted. He felt uncertain about his future, his ability, even his sanity. "My compass has gone haywire," he said; "I feel hysterical, out of my mind. I should have gone to that job. I don't even know why I turned it down."

Jonathan sought the help of a competent analyst.

The first sessions with the analyst were spent rehearsing contemporary material—Jonathan's encounter with the job opportunity, his emotions as he was making the decision first to go and then not to go, his feelings about his present position, the people he worked with, and so on. The analyst worked slowly, patiently, allowing Jonathan to release a great head of steam he had built up over the present crisis. Then the analyst began to ask questions about Jonathan's childhood — about his siblings and their relationship — about his mother and father, and how he felt about them. Jonathan returned home after each session greatly stimulated by the psychoanalytical process. He ruminated constantly on his childhood and returned eagerly to following sessions with new bits of information he had dredged up out of his memory.

Jonathan is a complex person and there were several strands worth pursuing in his analysis. But the one thing the analysis finally centered on as etiologically significant in Jonathan's recent decision-indecision was the threat that hung over his head for several years during his childhood. His parents were temperamentally unsuited to each other and spent most of their time together quarreling. The father usually terminated the quarrels by threatening to get a divorce and sending the mother back to live at her father's house. When the frightened child finally got up the nerve to ask his mother what would happen to him if the parents divorced — he thought he was about six when this occurred — she said he would probably be sent to military school. From then on, whenever he heard his parents quarreling, it spelled only one thing to him — having to leave home and go to military school. Military school became the great menace of his life. He knew he would not get along there, that the other boys would pick on him, that he would not like wearing a uniform, that he would be very lonely, that he would not be able to please the teachers and officers, that, in short, it would all be miserable for him. Three or four times, during these years of anguish, the family drove past a military school on the way to visit the mother's home in another city. Jonathan cringed whenever he saw the place; he thought it looked like a prison camp. Once or twice his father even mentioned that it would probably be good for Jonathan to go to such a school, unwittingly reinforcing Jonathan's fear.

From the analysis, Jonathan was satisfied that the paralysis he experienced with regard to the move to another job and city was directly related to his fear in childhood of being sent to military school. Now in middle age, and having lived in the same home for nearly fifteen years, he felt deeply and inexplicably threatened by the thought of moving. He knew the new position was much better than his present one, and that his family would adapt beautifully to the move, but something inside was constricting and forcing him to remain where he was. After the analysis had focused on the episode of the military-school threat, he felt noticeably relieved, and his old sense of self-worth and confidence returned. He even believed he would then be capable of making a move.

Being Left with Others

Few parents, even the most conscientious, are able to remain with their children constantly through childhood. They must occasionally leave the children with relatives or friends while performing certain missions on which the children cannot be taken. If children are normally loved and well cared for, and if sufficient preparation is made in their minds for these times, the occasions should not be traumatic. But they are often remembered by children as times of considerable uneasiness, and children who have never been properly fondled and loved usually recall them as occasions of enormous anxiety.

William P., a teacher, recalls:

> Several times, when I was a child of three or four, I was left in the care of an elderly woman who lived two doors from our home. Usually it was for only an hour or two, while my mother went to the doctor or while she and my father made a brief trip to a nearby town. Mrs. Hornsby was the kindest, sweetest soul imaginable, and I normally enjoyed visiting her in the presence of my mother. But the moment I was left with her I became exceedingly anxious, fearful that I would never see my mother again. Mrs. Hornsby tried to think of imaginative games to keep me entertained and divert my attention from my absent parent, but she was never successful for very long. She would point out things in the funny papers that she bet I had not noticed, or play checkers with me, or play hide-and-seek about the house, but my attention never digressed from my mother's having left me and gone away; in fact, I think the games and diversions may have had the opposite effect from the one intended, and made me all the more suspicious that my mother would not be coming back.

David H. was often left in a similar manner with his aunt and uncle, who had a large grandfather's clock in their living room. To this day, many years later, he remembers the monotonous ticking of that clock as he waited, waited, waited for his parents' return, and cannot bear to hear a clock ticking, for it reminds him of the great anxiety he experienced on those early occasions.

Eight-year-old Donnie T. wrote this about a recent experience:

> I was very lonely when my Mom went to the hospital to get my baby sister. The babysitter stayed at my house. I wanted to go to the hospital too but Mom said "No, you cannot go, somebody has got to stay here and get things ready for the new baby." I went to a restaurant to eat with Dad one night, and we had pizza. It was very good. I also had a Coke and Dad had a beer. He let me taste the beer. Then I had to go home while he went to see my new baby sister, because I could not go in. I missed my Mom and worried about her a lot.

Children's parents, after all, have been their world. Separation destroys that world. The entire sense of reality, or way of perceiving the external environment, must be rebuilt; yet children are ill-equipped to do this. Later, perhaps, when they are older, they will have developed coping mechanisms. But as children they have had no prior experience of world construction — none at least that helps them to deal with a trauma of this proportion and suddenness. They feel not only deserted but devastated.

If the Child Must Be Hospitalized

More than 60 percent of all children must be hospitalized for overnight or longer at least once before the age of ten. This represents another problem to a child's sense of well-being, for hospitals can be cold and forbidding places.

C. M. Fagin, in a study of two groups of 30 children each, aged 18 to 48 months, found a high rate of disturbance in the children whose parents did not remain with them during the hospital stay. In follow-up visits to the mothers one week after the stay, and again one month later, the mothers almost unanimously reported a high degree of emotional tension in the children, coupled with a noticeably high sense of dependency; the children became quickly upset whenever the mothers left them, even for very brief periods.[14]

Cicely R., a 17-year-old, recalls her period in the hospital to have her appendix removed; she was nine at the time.

> I remember mom waiting in the room with me until after they gave me the pentothal or whatever it was to make me sleepy. I wasn't aware when she left. That made me feel good. Dad would have been there too if he could, but he had this big business deal and couldn't leave the office. I don't think I was really scared. I just hurt and they said the doctor would take care of it, and I believed them. The part I didn't like was when mom and dad went home that night after it was over. I felt like this big iron door clanged shut when they walked out, and I was in a dungeon or something and couldn't go with them. I didn't know what would happen to me. I had never been away from them at night that I could remember. It wasn't too bad, I guess, but I didn't like it. I used to have bad dreams about it sometimes.

One reason for children's fears connected with hospital separation is the automatic association many of them make between hospitalization and death. In stories and television programs they see people dying in hospitals, and assume there is a better than even chance that that is what happens to people who sleep in hospitals. Normal separation anxiety, then, which to the child can make almost any absence seem more or less permanent, gives way to hyperanxiety in which the child is convinced of the separation's utter finality.

Bard V., a usually ebullient 11-year-old, was thus concerned about his hospitalization for treatment of a lymph gland infection:

> I was really glad when the doctor came in and said I could go home the next day. Boy! I didn't know if I would ever get out of that place. It was nice, but you know how it is, you worry a lot about what's going to happen to you and whether everything will be OK and all that. I hoped I would be OK and I was, thank goodness. But I still worried.

Bard even confessed that he worried for several days after he went home, lest he have to go back to the hospital again. He couldn't believe he had been reprieved.

Children do not usually talk to parents about fears of this kind unless the parents are sensitive to signs of anxiety and pick up on them in conversation. Even then the children are likely to deny that they harbor fears or misgivings. But children usually know very little about anatomy and physiology, and their imaginations can concoct exotic and freakish outcomes to their situations. When young Portnoy, in Phillip Roth's novel *Portnoy's Complaint,* has a recessed testicle and imagines it is floating loose through his body and will probably go to his heart and kill him, it is a brilliantly comic scene; but it is entirely possible for a child to conceive of such a bizarre eventuality and to despair secretly of surviving so innocent an ailment. It never hurts for the parent to be as assuring as possible, in a comprehensive way, for he or she never knows when the words will be gratefully received by an overactive imagination.

Not all children react negatively to hospitalization, of course, even when left alone overnight. Rick M. was born with an eye problem and had four corrective operations by the time he was five, the first occurring when he was only eight months old. The doctor insisted he be hospitalized the night before the operation, which is not always a wise procedure in the case of such a small child. There were no private facilities in the pediatrics wing of the hospital, and Rick's mother and father could not remain with him beyond eight o'clock in the evening. Rick's father still remembers the empty, lost feeling he and his wife experienced as they walked out of the hospital and went to dinner at a nearby restaurant; it was the first time they had been separated from their baby. But the child had been extremely sociable since his first weeks of life, and already had many adult relationships. Perhaps this prepared him for the experience, and it did not seem to be a bad one for him. He showed no reluctance to enter the hospital again a year later for another operation.

Some hospital administrators know enough about the psychology of separation or have enough instinctive humanity to wish to provide places for parents of small children to remain with the children. Wherever this is true, children show much less anxiety and, in certain kinds of cases, even heal faster than children in hospitals where separation is the rule. Fagin's study referred to above concentrated on two groups, one consisting of children who had to remain alone in hospitals and the other of children whose parents stayed with them. While the children who remained alone showed aftersigns of emotional upheaval and increased dependency, the children whose parents stayed with them displayed no such signs. In some cases among the latter, parents indicated that they believed the hospitalization to have been a good experience for both children and parents, as it provided an opportunity for closeness and growth in relationship.

Sensitive doctors and attendants can also be helpful in making hospital stays positive experiences for young children. When Rick M. was hospitalized at the age of five for his fourth and final eye operation, he had a kind and thoughtful anesthetist, who came to see him the night before the operation. The man asked him how he felt about the operation, and whether he had any questions about what would happen. In the course of an animated conversation, the anesthetist discovered that Rick was very fond of Batman and Robin, who appeared daily on a television serial. The next morning, when the sleeping child was wheeled back to his room from the surgery, two packages of bubblegum containing Batman cards were taped neatly to the palm of his small right hand!

The Trauma of School

The largest single problem of separation anxiety among children undoubtedly occurs at the age when they must begin their educational experience outside the home. Until then, most children spend the majority of their time in the environment of either a parent or a relatively constant figure who serves as a parent-substitute. With the arrival of school age, however, they must be taken away from this figure, sometimes almost forcibly, and placed in another environment for long hours every day. It is a natural moment in the individuation process for some children, but a very traumatic one for others. In any event, it represents a major alteration in the lifestyle of every child.

"It is easy to forget just how radical is the adjustment required of the five- or six-year-old," says Martin Herbert in his massive study *Problems of Childhood.* "For long periods each weekday, the child is removed from the familiar, comfortable routine of his home, from a playful existence with a nurturant mother near at hand, and is plunged into the more exacting disciplines and the hurly-burly of school life. During these hours there is no appeal to mother's protection and comfort; the mantle of authority has been handed over to strangers." [15]

The crunch comes, Herbert maintains, when the child finds he has been transferred from a relatively "closed" system, where he understood the rules and routines, to an "open" one, where everything is strange and he is subject, at least for several weeks, to the unexpected, the unpredictable,

and oftentimes the un[...]
attention, and learns to[...]
grown up with siblings, [...] [...]er
children pressing their de[...] [...]een
rather free to express hims[...] [...]imself
admonished to be quiet and t[...] [...] an order
that is mysterious and awesome [...] [...]n simple functions such as eating, washing, and going to the toilet have
suddenly become part of this new supersystem, and he feels
the most intimate aspects of his life being swept up into a
rhythm and power beyond his elemental control. It is a
frightening, breathtaking experience!

Some children, faced with the prospect of it all, refuse
to go willingly to school. They do not see why they should be
compelled to leave the safety and routine comfort of life with
mother, and they use the only means they know, crying and
temper tantrums, or sometimes feigned illness, to avoid the
expulsion. When the means do not work, they often feel
betrayed, and do not forget this feeling even years afterward. Unconsciously, perhaps, they feel some connection between the evacuation from the womb and the expulsion from
the home to attend school.

Sometimes the experience of being thrust into this
overwhelming new environment will cause physiological re-
versions in a child, such as a return to thumbsucking or
bedwetting. I remember my first day at nursery school, when
I was five. All morning I was excited and overwhelmed by
the strangeness of everything. At lunch, as I was eating, I
was struck by an overpowering urge to go to the bathroom.
I felt completely helpless. I did not know how to find the
toilet, I did not know the teacher's name. I was embarrassed
to say anything. Suddenly it was too late. I felt my under-
pants filling with warm, almost liquid feces. There was nothing to be done but to send me home; I was too great a mess
for anyone at school to tackle, and besides, I had no spare
clothes there. It was a humiliating experience, and my

mother, apparently sensing this, did not make me return to school until I began first grade.

The experience of teachers is that children suffer most from separation anxiety when first sent to school, at age five or six; that there is a remission at age seven, when the routines have become more familiar to the children; and that then there is another wave of anxiety common to children at about age eight. The reasons for this are varied, but one often suggested by the teachers is the heightened level of expectation, requiring more difficult work of children in the third and fourth grades.

"Difficulties of adjustment," as Herbert says, "are not confined to the opening phases of school life. The school environment is one which, all the time, is evolving toward greater complexity. It therefore continually increases its demands upon the child; demands for greater and wider mastery of intellectual, social and physical skills. Change is a significant factor in the schooling process; long periods of slow, almost imperceptible movement are punctuated by phases of rapid, dramatic change when — as in the transfer from junior to senior school — there may be separation from old friends and familiar teachers, and new subjects have to be assimilated."[16]

Life in the world — in a state of separation from the home and parents — is hard for children. We cannot keep them at home, of course. They must gradually get used to living away from their parents. Sooner or later they must enter society and become integrated into its ways.

What we can do — and must do — is to provide in the crucial early years the gentle care and affection they need for healthy ego development, and to assure them in every possible way of willing support through the remaining years of their youth. But we must also expose them, painful as it is for both them and us, to the societal and environmental realities with which they must cope in the future and to which they must be shaped by the rigors of education and social intercourse. Always to *be there*, with sympathy and understanding, with the listening ear, with well-chosen words of encouragement and explanation — that becomes the important thing.

"My arms are around you," my wife has always assured our children when sending them out into the world, alternately to learn from it and to do battle with it.

And that seems to do the trick.

3

An Agony of Helplessness

One night I dreamed I was a young student. I was taking a course from one of my present colleagues, an occasionally cranky, irritable man who is approaching retirement and plainly does not relish it. Suddenly, in the dream, I realized I had just missed a final examination in the course; I had been completely unaware that it was being offered until I looked at an exam schedule and knew I had missed it. I went to the teacher, explained my problem, and penitently asked if I might make up the exam.

"No!" he replied, shaking his head from side to side in an exaggerated manner I had seen many times. "No way!"

I awoke from the dream in a furious spirit. The professor had been so unreasonably arrogant and unyielding! It meant nothing to him that I had missed the exam and would take a failing grade in the course. Even less than nothing.

The anger diminished as the day wore on, but not without bringing back memories from childhood of adults who behaved with similar heedlessness of my feelings. When I was ten years old we had moved to a new town. I entered the local school in March, when the school year was all but over. I felt a terrible sense of dislocation. Not only the place and the children, but the procedures, were new to me. In the afternoon of my first day, a music teacher came in to give us a lesson. I had never had music before, and did not understand what we were to do with the papers she passed out.

Hesitantly I raised my hand. "Come up here!" the stern voice ordered. "Hold out your hand!" *Whack!* She struck the hand with a ruler. Sorely embarrassed, my heart pounding in my throat, I returned to my seat. I wondered what awful thing I had done, but I dared not ask. Afterward I learned that this particular teacher did not permit students to speak out in class; the week before, to counter an epidemic of handraising, she had made the rule that anyone who raised his or her hand would have it slapped by the ruler. I had fallen afoul of a regulation to which I had not been privy. Surely the teacher knew this; she had never seen me in her class before. Yet she had arbitrarily punished me as if I had been there all the time.

Think about the sense of helplessness and loneliness in all children when they encounter puzzling, unfriendly behavior from adults. What recourse does a child have? Like the invalid in Sartre's *Les Chemins de la liberté* who resents being dominated by the "stand ups," the people who walk around him all day, the child is at the mercy of adults.

Kathryn A. remembers the severe punishment she received in the first grade for "stealing" a pencil box. A mischievous classmate had hidden the box and accused her of taking it. The teacher chided her for stealing and sent a note home informing her mother that she had taken another child's property. Kathryn protested that she had not done it, but her mother, intent on teaching her a lesson she would never forget, whipped her mercilessly. To this day she is hurt and bitter about the episode.

Herman M., 15, received two demerits on the school bus and had to spend Saturday morning sitting in a classroom. He was angry at the teacher-bus driver who had given him the demerits. Another boy had pinched him and he had instinctively thrust his arm out toward the boy. The driver, a martinet for order on his bus, reprimanded both of them and assigned them demerits. No explanations were permitted. Herman was considered as guilty as the lad who had pinched him. When he arrived home that afternoon he was red in the face with anger. As he told the story of what happened, he clenched his fist and drove it into the other hand, declaring he would like to do that to the teacher's face.

It is terrible to be powerless, as children are. "Power is essential for all living things," says Rollo May. If persons have no power, then they will eventually turn to deeds of violence in order to establish their self-esteem, for "violence is the expression of impotence."[1] We know children who have gone this route, who have become demonstrative and even violent because they had no esteem from others and could have none for themselves until they made others notice their erratic kind of power. We can remember in ourselves the passion for committing some awful deed, either to others or to ourselves, to make people sorry for the wrong they had done us or the hurt they had caused us. We have raged against the bars of our impotence, wishing we could produce some act of destructiveness equal to the magnitude of hurt and unhappiness inside us.

I think about my own children, now in their teens. How often have they been hurt in this manner? How many times have I been the unwitting instrument of their alienation, their injured pride, their trampled feelings? I recall a few times when I was aware of it immediately afterwards, clued by some look in their eyes, the shrug of a shoulder, the set of the mouth. It hurt that they said nothing, offered no reproach, for that meant the feeling was not new, that they were accustomed to it, that I had done it before, not once but many times.

Adults, in such cases, usually have an alternative to silence. Even if it means losing a job, we can tell our side of the story. We can write angry letters to the judge who fined us for speeding, tell off the store clerk who was rude, or explode at the person who has injured our pride. But children are often unable to respond to injustice or misunderstanding. They are at the mercy of grownups, who control the purse strings, the car keys, and even the house keys, symbols of ownership and mastery. They must wait until they are older, until they have earned the right to speak and strike back, until their word too carries weight.

It was a young person, I suspect, who invented "giving the bird," the most eloquently disrespectful gesture of our time; it is one of the few ways teen-agers have of sublimating anger at tyranny and repression.

The Credulity Gap

Someone once constructed a house in which everything was oversized. The rooms were gigantic, the furniture was enormous. "I thought it would be good," said the builder, "for adults to be reminded of how the world looks to little children."

Among the world's psychologists, none has done more to remind us of how the child views the world than Jean Piaget. And, of all the important facts Piaget has established in his lifetime of research and publishing, the most basic is probably this, that *children are not born with mature intellectual ways of perceiving the world around them, and they do not acquire these ways quickly and without pain.* Acquiring such ways is a long and arduous process, and we should not expect too much of them too soon.

Children, when they are first born, are almost totally egocentric in their apprehension of reality. Their world is an extension of themselves. They have not learned to differentiate between fantasy and fact, imagination and reality. Dreams are as real to them as anything in their waking hours. Wishes become almost tangible, as though they existed in the three-dimensional world; that is why disappointments are so terrible in childhood, like real bubbles that have burst. The names of things are almost as strong or as magic as the things they signify.

As children grow and become socialized, their minds work through many puzzling ideas. Eventually the world becomes less subjective and begins to assume its perspective "out there," as something external, objective, outside their will and power. They gradually learn that a true estimate of self and world — true at least by society's definition — involves theories and data provided by the experience of many generations of people, and cannot be spun out of their own heads alone. It is a slow and painful process, with many mistakes along the way.

But we forget how slow and painful it was for us, and we expect children to grasp instantly the truths and half-truths for which we had to struggle so long and hard. We expect their view of things to be the right one by our standards, their logic and manner of separating fact and fiction to be like ours. Consequently we are quick to belittle their imaginative statements or to chide them for not reporting the truth as we would have seen and reported it.

Faber and Mazlish cite the following conversations they overheard between children and parents in various meetings. While none of the conversations is in itself of any real magnitude, they indicate, taken as a whole, the failure of parents to take children's words seriously.

> At the zoo:
> CHILD: (*Crying*) My finger! My finger hurts!
> FATHER: It couldn't hurt. It's only a little scratch.

> At the supermarket:
> CHILD: I'm hot.
> MOTHER: How can you feel hot; it's cool in here.

> In a toy store:
> CHILD: Mommy, look at this little duck. Isn't he
> cute?
> MOTHER: Oh, that's for a little baby. You're not
> interested in baby toys any more.

"It was astonishing," say Faber and Mazlish. "These parents seemed unable to hear their children's simplest emotions. Certainly they meant no harm by their responses. Yet, in reality, what they were telling their children, over and over again, was:

'You don't mean what you say.
You don't know what you know.
You don't feel what you feel.' "[2]

Hilary M. says that she was several times "humiliated" during her childhood by the way her mother and her mother's friends would laugh at her perception of how her baby brother came into the world.

I don't know how I ever had the idea, but somehow I had this absolutely convincing picture in my head of how Billy had arrived in our household. I saw the doctor — he was our family doctor, there weren't any specialists in our little town — walking down the sidewalk one evening, pushing a baby carriage. When I ran up to it, he said, "How would you like a baby brother?" I said, "Fine," and he turned in at our sidewalk and brought the baby to us. Actually, mother had Billy in the hospital and I don't even remember where I was at the time. I was only two. Probably a neighbor lady kept me. But I was as certain as I could be of the way it had all happened. I must have dreamed it or something.

When Hilary told this in the family, her mother and father both laughed. She must have been about six or seven at the time, as she recalled. Thereafter, her mother would ask her to repeat the story in front of friends, who invariably tittered.

It infuriated me for them to laugh at me. I *knew* what I had experienced. It was as real as anything to me. I thought, "How dare they laugh! What do they know about it, anyway?" After all, *I* had been there!

Clearly Hilary was wrong in this matter. She may have dreamed that things happened the way she thought, as she said, or it may simply have been a trick of the childish memory. But the hurt was very real.

Because children only slowly learn to discern reality from fantasy — do we ever learn completely? — adults often develop the habit of distrusting their judgments in everything, and *expecting* them to misrepresent the facts. This was perhaps the reason Kathryn A.'s mother did not believe her about the missing pencil box.

Madeleine L'Engle has told in *A Circle of Quiet* about a similar encounter with the credulity gap when she was a child of eight. One day in French class she needed to be excused to go to the toilet. She raised her hand and asked permission; it was denied. Twice more she attempted and was refused. When the bell rang at the end of the period she ran frantically toward the toilet, but was too late. She spent the remainder of the afternoon "sodden and shamed."

> When my mother heard what had happened, she demanded to see the principal. I remember with awful clarity the scene in the principal's office, after the French teacher had been summoned. She said, "But Madeleine never asked to go to the bathroom. If she had only raised her hand, of course I would have excused her."
>
> She was believed. I suppose the principal had to believe the teacher, rather than the child with wet clothes. I was reprimanded gently, told to ask the next time, and not to lie about it afterwards, it really wasn't anything dreadful to make that kind of mistake.
>
> To have an adult lie, and to have another adult not know that it was a lie; to tell the truth myself and not be believed: the earth shook on its foundations.[3]

William E., age 12, was studying Edgar Allan Poe in his seventh-grade English class. When he mentioned this at dinner, his father recalled a few lines of a satirical version of

"Annabel Lee" he had once known. William enjoyed the brief recitation so much that he went to his room and made up his own version of a swinging, fun-styled "Annabel Lee." His parents thought it was well done and encouraged him to show it to the teacher. When William handed it to her the next day, the teacher tucked it into a folder with some English themes, promising to read it. Later, when the themes were returned to the students, William also received his copy of the poem he had written. At the top, the teacher had written, "You should not copy other people's work as your own." Appalled and puzzled, William spoke to the teacher about it, assuring her it was his own composition. She was adamant. "You probably got it out of *Mad* magazine," she said.

"It is hard to say whether William was more hurt or more furious," said his father in reporting the story. "He quit trying to do anything in that class. In fact, it was at a time when he was having some vague problems with school, not able to get his feet under him or something, and that little episode didn't do him any good at all, just sort of shot his hopes down in flames, I suppose."

Sarah B., 16, has a problem with a mother whose fantasy powers work overtime imagining Sarah, who is a pretty, intelligent young woman, in all kinds of amorous entanglements that do not exist. A religiously inclined girl, Sarah spends most of her free time at church, playing the piano for various meetings and helping the secretaries in the church office. Her mother is convinced, however, that Sarah uses her church activities as a front for the various romances she imagines her to be carrying on, and constantly berates her for this. "How can I get her to believe the truth?" pleads Sarah. "She has such a twisted, dirty mind about things — imagines I do all kinds of things I would never do. Sometimes she even follows me, hoping to catch me at something. I really ought to do something sometime, just to see what she would do. She'd probably have a stroke!"

An Unnecessary Order

Sarah's problem is one form of a problem common to many children, in which the adults in their lives seek to impose their own sense of order on the children. To some extent, perhaps, this is necessary, particularly when the children are infants. But it is desirable for the children to grow into reciprocity, able to interact with their social environments, so that they actually contribute to and help to maintain those environments. Sarah is clearly too old, given a reasonably developed moral sense of her own, to be grilled, harassed, and humiliated about romances she claims not to have had.

George Dennison, whose *The Lives of Children: The Story of the First Street School* contains many insights into the interaction between adults and children, says that one of the most damning flaws in most adults' attitudes toward children is their determination that the children shall fit into *their* view of the world, without regard to the children's own feelings and inclinations. Parents and teachers have an absolute mania for stuffing the youngster's interests and preoccupations into preplanned little boxes, whether they fit or not. They do not wish to waste time on the extraneous matters children introduce into the conversation; the only passion they know is order, the only direction, forward. Often, as a result, they fail to lead the children into genuine educational experiences that might have followed if they had pursued the children's interests.

Dennison cites the example of something that happened in a classroom in the First Street School, a small private school in New York's Lower East Side. A Puerto Rican girl, Eléna, age 10, interrupted Susan, the arithmetic teacher, to say that her mother had bought a voodoo charm and it had been stolen. Several other children, both black and Puerto Rican, erupted into animated conversation about voodoo and whether it really works. Susan made no effort to stop it and refocus attention on arithmetic. She listened patiently, and, in about ten minutes, the discussion ended and they all returned happily to arithmetic.

"I would like to quote Rousseau again and again," says Dennison, " '. . . do not save time, but lose it.' If Susan had tried to save time by forbidding the interesting conversation about voodoo, she would first have had a stupid disciplinary problem on her hands, and second (if she succeeded in silencing the children) would have produced that smoldering, fretful resentment with which teachers are so familiar, a resentment that closes the ears and glazes the eyes. How much better it is to meander a bit — or a good bit — letting the free play of minds, adult and child, take its own very lively course! The advantages of this can hardly be overestimated. The children will feel closer to the adults, more secure, more assured of concern and individual care. Too, their own self-interest will lead them into positive relations with the natural authority of adults, and this is much to be desired, for natural authority is a far cry from authority that is merely arbitrary."[4]

Again, it is a matter of remaining sensitive to the fact that children are not *born* with an adult sense of order and truth, but must interact with it until it is appropriated as naturally as possible. When we forget that, we attempt to *force* our world order on them, raping not only their minds but their personal sensibilities. As Dennison suggests, the order will come in good time if we will allow it to do so

I remember an incident in my childhood that brought unnecessary distress both to my parents and to me. It was in the autumn, in football season. I had dressed up in a clean pair of jodhpurs and nicely polished boots, and I wanted to walk up to a friend's house to see if a football game was going on there. My mother said I might go, but that I was to be home in thirty minutes and I was not to venture off the sidewalk, where I might get my boots muddy. When I got to the friend's house, I could see no one anywhere. I considered walking down the driveway and having a look in the

53

back, as the driveway was macadamized, and decided that that would not constitute a real transgression of my mother's instructions. Around back, I heard sounds of a game coming from down in a field. Now my excitement caught me, and I crossed the yard on the grass. I still could see nothing, however, as my friends were off to a corner of the field. A few strands of barbed wire blocked my way, and I thought, "If I could only step over onto the other side, I could watch a few minutes and then return home." My eagerness to see the game now predominated to the extent that I did not notice that the ground on the other side of the fence was soft and muddy. So when I stepped gingerly through the strands of barbed wire and put my foot on the other side, it slipped sideways in the mud, causing me to lose my balance and tear my jodhpurs. By the time I had rescued myself, I was in the pasture with muddy boots and a torn pair of pants. I felt guilty for having disobeyed but decided, as long as I was there, that I might as well watch the game a few minutes. After a few exciting plays, my adrenalin was flowing so freely that, when asked to enter the game, I immediately joined in. An hour or so later, I returned home. "You're late for dinner!" my mother scolded as she heard me approaching. Then she saw me. I must have looked like a poor ragamuffin. Following a tongue lashing, I was made to wash up and eat dinner; then I received my corporal punishment, which came as something of a relief after the moral harassment.

As I reflect on this occasion, I do not think I learned anything of significance through being disciplined. I was sorry *before* I returned home that I had disobeyed. The harshness from my mother only made me resentful, as it seemed unnecessary, superfluous, after the fact. She did not realize, I am sure, how much vaguer and more slippery my world was than hers, how natural it was for me to ease into the backyard via that macadamized driveway, and thence to the fence, and from the fence to the pasture, and from there to the football game. Her world had all kinds of lines and safeguards built into it; she and others had been working at them for thirty-odd years. But I was only learning. My world was still fluid, and I floated about in it rather freely, swept this way and that by the currents.

I try to remember this when my own children come in covered with grass stains and dirt and blood. They too are shadow-boxing with the world, trying to find out where the lines of interaction are. And my wife, fortunately, is good at shrugging her shoulders and saying, "They'll wash!"

The Injustice of It All

Occasionally, of course, a modicum of punishment is not only deserved but necessary, especially when children are small and cannot be reasoned with. Otherwise no boundaries are established and the children themselves become frantic. I visited in a home recently where this was true. The young parents were so permissive toward their three-year-old that he was literally terrorizing their home. It was plain to me, as an outsider, that he was wildly applying himself at every possible boundary, trying to find one that would not give with his onslaught; he craved regulation but the parents were not providing it; they were fearful of producing a complex by punishing. As a result, the poor little fellow was worn out. He kept no regular hours, he refused to eat except when and what he wanted, he watched television as much as he liked and whenever he liked, he interrupted his parents continually when they tried to talk — in short, he was on at all hours, and the pace was killing him. To him, moderate punishment for misbehavior would have been merciful.

As children grow older, however, they need less and less external pressure to conform.

Piaget has made a convincing case for this in his book *The Moral Judgment of the Child*. In their early years, says Piaget, children hold a very objective sense of moral duty: they are to conform to the laws, rules, commands of adults, and they expect constraints to be applied if they do not. But as they grow older, at ages 11 and 12, they begin to understand moral law as a participatory process in which *intention* counts as much as fulfillment. For example, in the earlier years children regard a lie as a lie, without extenuating circumstances; later, when they are eleven or older, they realize that there are degrees of untruth, and that people's motivation for bending the truth is important in determining the wrong they have done. The same applies to stealing. To very young children, there is no excuse for theft. Later, they realize there are occasions when other considerations (for example, to feed a starving child) may take precedence over honesty. Now children also develop from one stage to another in their attitudes toward behavior and punishment. In the earlier years, they see punishment for wrongdoing as necessary; Piaget says they view it as expiatory, and as restoring the wrongdoer to his or her social unit. In other words, the small child, as much as he or she personally dislikes to receive punishment, would not feel reunited to the parents until the fine for wrongdoing had been paid. After age ten, however, the same child begins to understand punishment in a more sophisticated way, and realizes that it may not be necessary if its aim, the restoration of the social bond, can be achieved another way.

Here is a portion of a conversation with a child, as cited in Piaget's book:

> Do you think it fair that you should be punished?
> *No, not fair.*
> Why?
> *Because I can understand much better when people explain things to me.*[5]

But what happens when the child passes out of the stage when he understands punishment as a necessary retaliation into the stage when he feels that explanations are better, and the parent continues to punish as if he were a small child? Then the child begins to feel, as the conversation above indicates, that the adult is being unfair in exerting superior force instead of reason. It is at this time that the child really begins to experience for himself the meaning of justice and injustice. Before, he may have had a rather vague notion of it while watching exaggerated plots in movies and TV shows or while reading certain children's stories; now it becomes more sharply defined and personally focused.

Take the case of Delores M., age 12. Delores's friends were beginning to wear lipstick and fingernail polish. She too wanted very badly to try these symbols of adult femininity, but was afraid to ask her parents for them. Her mother used lipstick, but Delores was fearful of using it lest her mother become angry with her. So one day, unable to think of another way of acquiring some lipstick and polish for herself, Delores took five dollars from her mother's billfold and used it to buy the desired articles. Her mother subsequently found the items in Delores's bedroom, questioned her, and learned the truth. As punishment for the theft and secret purchases, she ordered Delores to remain in her room for the entire weekend, emerging only for meals. Delores was furious.

"It was completely unfair," she says. "Mother should have understood. It's not as if I were a petty thief. I only took the money because I didn't have any of my own. Another mother would have seen that her daughter needed those things and bought them for her. I only did what she should have done. Oh, I knew it was wrong, that I shouldn't have sneaked and taken the money like that. But she didn't help matters any by acting the way she did. I know I'll never be that way with a child of mine."

Another controversial aspect of punishment at the age when children are coming into a strong sense of what is just or unjust is the practice of corporate or group punishment — making two or more children pay for what one has done. Both parents and teachers are guilty of this, usually in hopes that the other children will deter the mischievous or rambunctious one from misbehaving. It is also a tactic often used in penal institutions, where peer pressure is expected to enforce good behavior. Younger children (under ten) do not seem to object to the practice, as a rule, while older children see it as another example of adult tyranny.

Paul K. was in a science class under a man engaged in his first years of teaching. It was a large class composed of boys who had just come into the seventh grade from several other schools about town, and discipline was not easy, even for the school's more experienced teachers. Finally, in desperation, the teacher began trying to keep order by making all the boys remain after school if one of them interrupted the proceedings by talking or creating a stir. For several weeks he kept the entire class in at least one or two times a week. Here is Paul's reaction:

> He really shouldn't have done it. It is really only one or two boys who make noise or interrupt all the time. He knows who they are. He should punish them, not the rest of us. It isn't fair to make the rest of us pay for what they do. They can't help it, really. Jim is just so active, he can't sit still. And Tom gets tickled and laughs at him. But the rest of us don't do anything. Mr. Brown just doesn't know how to handle kids. Now the fellows are getting worse and worse, because they don't like what he is doing to them.

An interesting crossover takes place at about age nine or ten. Before then, classmates very readily hand over guilty parties from their midst when the teacher asks who did something, yet accept solidarity of punishment without qualms. After those ages, they begin to practice solidarity to protect a guilty person in their midst, refusing to "snitch" on him, but become resentful about enduring solidarity in punishment.

Again, it is the arbitrariness of adults that most incenses children when they begin to understand the difference between justice and injustice — an arbitrariness that acts to punish unilaterally, without consulting the children involved or attempting to explain how the punishment is really aimed at preserving or restoring social unity. More indignation is caused by arbitrariness than by any other character fault in adults.

During classroom recitations prior to selection of a student to represent the class in the all-school recitation contest, John E., an eighth grader, recited a humorous narrative his father had written. Called "The Day I Joined the Girl Scouts," it was a frolicsome piece about a boy's having stood in for a little girl who was sick the day she was to be inducted into the Girl Scouts, and ended with the girl's recuperating and deciding she didn't want to be in the Scouts anyway. The last line of the narrative was "I could have bopped her right on her Girl Scout cookie!" The class was delighted with the recitation and voted for John as their representative. The teacher took him aside after class, however, and told him he must change the last word of the narrative. He did not understand why, but understood from her tone that he should not question her. He said he must ask his father whether it would be acceptable to him. When he asked his father, his father realized that the teacher probably thought the word suggestive. But the father could think of no acceptable substitute for the line, and, feeling that the punchline of the story was too good to jettison, told the boy to stand his ground. When the boy told the teacher his father did not want to change the word, the teacher said John could not be in the contest. At this peremptoriness, the boy became incensed for the first time. His father told him he could go ahead and change the line if he wanted to, but he refused. "She has no right to be that way," he insisted. "Maybe she thinks there's something wrong with the word, but that's just her dirty mind! I would rather not be in the contest than give in now, because it isn't right."

Ann J., a musician, still resents the arbitrary way her father made her take a pair of shoes she did not want when she was a girl of twelve:

All the other girls were wearing loafers, and I was dying to have a pair too. But my daddy went with me to buy my shoes — he wouldn't trust me to go by myself — and he insisted I needed a good sturdy pair of shoes with shoelaces. The clerk showed me some loafers too but Daddy was unyielding. "Those would come apart in a month," he said. I lost. I never wore the shoes he bought. I showed them to mother and cried when I got home. They were horrible — real clodhoppers! I'm sure he thought he was doing the best thing, but he didn't understand how important having the right shoes was to me. I hated him for it at the time. I don't hate him any more, but I still resent his dictatorialness. I was old enough to make a decision about my own shoes.

Much has been said and written about the problems parents have with teen-agers. Many of these problems stem from a failure of communication during these sensitive years when children have a more fully developed notion of the nature of authority and wish to be permitted to participate in it. The parents still think of them as little children and continue to direct them as though they were. The children, on the other hand, begin to see their parents as belonging to the same scheme of moral responsibility that embraces them, yet falling short of the same laws and regulations and escaping punishment. Resentment builds, and often flashes out when there is a contest of wills. If the parents are immature and incapable of accepting criticism, they react in punitive fashion, widening the breach between themselves and their children. Often, at this time in the family saga, children overtake their parents in terms of sensibility and true moral responsibility, and it is the adults who act like children while the children behave like adults.

"Pick On Somebody Your Own Size"

There is frequently a great deal of unfairness in the battle of the generations, when you think about it, primarily because the parents have so much weight and leverage. They are physically larger (I did meet one boy, now in a correctional institution, who at thirteen was larger than his father and one day, by his own admission, "lit into him and beat the livin' stuffin' out of him"). They are more experienced. And their years of undisputed authority and superiority give them a psychological advantage over the children, many of whom are incurably sentimental about their relationships to parents.

The unfairness is visible in as simple a matter as teasing. The basic or original meaning of the word "tease" had to do with a pleasant or agreeable manner of paying attention to someone, and much teasing of infants begins that way, as affectionate laughing at them for losing their front teeth, or having freckles, or tripping over their own feet. But teasing can also mean baiting or mocking, in which case a kind of unpleasantness or even a venom enters into the picture and it is not taken kindly. What began in fun when the child was small is often continued with malice when the child is older and there are intergenerational tensions involved. Then the child is made to suffer for all his or her inadequacies, often in the name of good sport — for having an ugly face, for getting an unbecoming haircut, for being fat or thin or ungainly, for having big feet, for failing in school, for fumbling in an athletic contest, for forgetting a line in a school play, for having an unrequited love. Often, without realizing it, the adult takes out his or her own frustrations on the child through an ambiguous form that can be defended as affectionate if challenged as vicious. The child may take recourse to teasing as well — giving in kind — and focus attention on mother's gray hair, father's receding hairline and nonreceding waistline, or other sensitive subjects. But it is invariably the parent who has the right to call a halt to teasing when it is cutting too close. Never the child. Children are often reduced to tears by adult provocation, especially during the teen years when personal uncertainties are so strong and numerous. But the parent, when the barrage is becoming too heavy, simply declares an end to the teasing.

The major abuse in the unevenly matched contest, however, is probably in terms of actual physical domination — parents beating or otherwise physically enforcing their will on children. Physical abuse is hardly limited to the dramatic cases that come to the attention of authorities.

Margaret B., for example, came from a respectable, middle-class home. Her father was a school principal. One day when she was nine or ten years old, she and her father had a conflict about the food on her plate. Her father insisted she eat everything, though she said she was full and could not eat another bite. He became irate and forced her to eat it.

> I was bursting when I finished, and I was mad. If *he* hadn't wanted to eat what was on *his* plate, nobody would have made *him*. I got up from the table as soon as I was through, and went outside. On the way out, I slammed the back door. It was the only expression of protest I could make, as he would have slapped me for talking back to him. He got up and tore after me, when he heard the door, and ordered me back onto the back porch. Then he got a big switch off the tree outside and whipped me with it until my back was bloody. It made great big cuts and welts all over my back, right through my dress. He was like a mad man. I'll never forget it. I have seen him beat the dog like that, as though he wanted to kill it.

Now, as a grown woman, Margaret says she no longer hates her father for what he did then, but she recognizes that something happened to her relationship to him when he beat her so hard. "It was as though I didn't belong to him anymore," she says. "Morally, he was no longer my father."

There is obviously a great deal of repressed aggressiveness in many adults that manifests itself in such maltreatment. Charles Dickens's savage schoolmaster in *Dombey and Son*, "for whose cruel cane all chubby little boys had a perfect fascination," was unfortunately not unique. Teachers frequently have a "whipping child" on whom they vent their frustrations. And many parents are little better than street bullies, reacting to their children by cuffing, poking, shoving, or beating them as though they were recalcitrant animals.

Silverstein and Krate, in their study of low-income families in Harlem, found that physical force is there the primary method of gaining compliance from children. Parents freely beat children with whatever is handy — ironing cords, belts, ropes, fan belts, coat hangers, shoes, boards, brooms — anything. There are seldom any attempts to reason with children, even when the children reach their teen years. The habit of smacking or beating the children, begun when they were mere infants, simply continues until the children are old enough to leave home or large enough to threaten retaliatory action.[6]

In some states there are CBA societies — Child Beaters Anonymous — that try to help adults who cannot curb their outrageous tempers when dealing with children. These organizations recognize that childbeating, like alcoholism, is a sickness. But they reach only an estimated ten or fifteen percent of the people who need them, and they don't begin to touch the millions of insensitive adults who only occasionally maltreat a child physically. For many children it is a hard world.

Second-Class Citizens

"I'm afraid we're only second-class citizens," said one bright 14-year-old girl named Peggy. "It may not cost any more to go first class, but it's impossible to get a ticket unless you already have one."

In a way, she's right. Many adults do regard children as second-class citizens. Not only do they withhold the rights to drive a car and to vote until the children are physically grown, they withhold a lot of other rights as well — the right to decide what they shall wear, the right to watch the TV program *they* want to watch (when the adults want to watch something else), the right to choose the menu, the right to vote on family finances, the right to select a vacation spot, the right to pick the family car — even the right to have the best medical or dental treatment.

Graham Greene recalls in his autobiography *A Sort of Life* that his parents sent him to a dreadful old dentist in their little village of Berkhamsted, while they themselves traveled all the way to London to a very good modern dentist. He resented this, he says, and thought of the old dentist's chair as a "chair of torture"; he felt sure that Mr. Crick, the London dentist, "was as painless as he was expensive."

Leona M., now a grown woman, still resents the fact that while she was a teen-ager becoming very conscious of nice clothes, her mother allowed her only the meagerest of expenses for dresses, though she paid extravagantly for her own.

Once, when I was to be in a recital, Mama refused to buy me a dress at all. "I can make something that will do for only one night," she said. And she did! Out of an old piece of curtain material! I was mortified, but there was nothing I could do. It wouldn't have mattered so much if we had been poor and couldn't afford better. Mama was just too stingy to put it on *my* back. She much preferred to put it on *hers!*

The crowning blow came when I got married. Mother and Sister took me shopping for a wedding dress and trousseau. I should have known better! They found an old floor sample of a gown that was soiled and yellowed. It was on sale for a pitiful amount — ten or fifteen dollars, I think — and they insisted that I take it. Imagine, at your one and only wedding! Even the veil was broken all over. It wasn't ripped, it was just so old that the netting was falling apart. I was so ashamed. We sent the dress to the cleaner's, hoping it would get rid of the yellow, dingy look, but it didn't. "Nobody will notice," Mama said. "Besides, it's only for fifteen minutes!" That was her attitude — only for fifteen minutes. Yet she spent sixty dollars on a dress for herself. Of course she reminded me that she could wear it all season, not just the once.

My trousseau was a disaster too. I had always dreamed of having a whole suitcase full of beautiful new things — nightgowns and dresses and slippers and panties and things. But Mama and Sister insisted we go to Lerner's, where the dresses then sold for like three for eleven dollars. My whole wardrobe, I think, cost under fifty dollars — less than Mama's one dress. I don't know why I stood for it, except that I was very young and didn't know how to stand up for myself.

But I've never forgiven her.

Parents are unfortunately not the only offenders. Many adults other than parents do not take children seriously because they are young and powerless. Children are often overridden in conversation and overpowered in arguments. They are made to wait at ice-cream counters and fast-food windows while adults push past them to get their orders. They are shown high-powered ads for toys on television, then dismissed by clerks in the stores when the toys are faulty and they attempt to return them. They are rudely treated by operators when they try to place telephone calls. They are talked down to by Sunday-school teachers and told by neighbors to stay out of their yards.

Maybe it is characteristic that, of all the liberation movements spawned by this freedom-conscious age — Third World, Black, Women's, Gay, and Gray — the one group not yet represented is the children.

When we remember what Rollo May said about power and resentment — that people who are abject and powerless dream of a time when they will have power and will exert it to be somebody — we don't wonder any longer why the world today seethes with radicalism, terrorism, and a counterculture mentality. It is because the traditional system, the Establishment, has resulted in unhappiness for a lot of children, and they were determined to take things into their own hands when they grew up. We can only hope there have been a lot of kids who had a good experience in childhood, and that their maturity and love will save society from becoming an absolute shambles.

If there is an active antidote to the kind of disintegration produced by tyrannical adults and powerless children, I think it is in people like Maria and Martin, the unselfish parents in Michael Deakin's book *The Children on the Hill.* Maria and Martin took their responsibilities of child-rearing so seriously that they withdrew from their occupations as social workers and settled for ten years in a remote village in Wales, where they could devote themselves to the children and create a controlled environment during the most formative years of the children's lives. There they turned an old house into a children's dream house, where everything was designed with the children in mind — low-built tables, shelves and shelves of books, cabinets with paints and tools and chemicals, reconditioned musical instruments, aquaria for fish, turtles, and reptiles, and cages for animals — though the animals were also permitted to roam through the house.

But the children weren't given only a house. They were given love, patience, understanding. Maria especially, as the teacher, dedicated herself to listening to everything the children were saying, tuning in to everything they were feeling and thinking, and to putting new ideas and concepts just a little in advance of where they were, far enough so they had to stretch to reach them but not so far as to discourage them. She invented new toys, told new stories, developed new teaching aids. Together, she and Michael provided an atmosphere of serenity, joy, and excitement in which the children could grow with the constant assurance of love and self-worth. And when the time came for the children to attend the village school, the parents were there to assist them in the transition between home and world, cloister and marketplace, listening, interpreting, encouraging, loving — always loving.

"Maria's main motive," says Deakin, "is simply this: she believes that she is educating a new type of person, that her children aren't simply precocious, or even, as is often suggested, geniuses. She sees them as 'free' — in the eighteenth-century sense of *homme libre*. As the result of the 'process' they have no violence in them, no irrational guilt — quite simply are free of the feeling that stirs in all our bones in the darker watches of the night that we are some-how obscurely guilty of an original sin. What most of us see as a faintly embarrassing abstract concept of the total power of love, has been for Maria the basis of ten years cut off from the social life and patterns she wishes and hopes one day to indulge in again — music, painting and a dialogue with like-minded people." [7]

Think what parents like that are doing for the world — they are sending into it our only hope for tomorrow!

4

The Damage Done by Schools

Several years ago, we lived in Paris. Our oldest son, Eric, was six years old at the time, and attended a British-American school called Pershing Hall. It was a very free, open kind of school centered on the children's abilities and the richness of the environment. Eric had had two years of preschool training and was already reading, writing, and doing simple math, so after two weeks he was advanced from first to second grade. He had a marvelous year. The class made numerous excursions around the city, and took a two-week skiing holiday in Switzerland. History lessons were often given at the Louvre, as the children stood around famous paintings or pieces of sculpture.

When we returned to the States the next year, we sent Eric to the public school nearest our home. He was admitted into the third grade, and seemed to have no difficulty with the work. Yet something happened to his spirit that fall. In September we watched him rush off to school in the mornings full of excitement and enthusiasm for the day; but by December he was dragging off reluctantly and seemed on the verge of school refusal. My wife phoned the principal and arranged a conference with his teacher. The teacher, one of the prized older women of the school, admitted there was a problem.

"I'll come straight to the point," she said. "Your son has been to too many places and seen too much for his age.

He's too inquisitive. It's disruptive to the rest of the class. He's always raising his hand to ask a question or to add something to what I've said. I have too many children in my classroom for that. The only way I can control it is by cuing the other children to laugh whenever he raises his hand."

My wife barely resisted reaching across the desk and strangling the woman. This time *I* called the principal and asked if the teacher had ever been analyzed. I was told that she was a fine teacher with an irreproachable record. I received, in short, the old runaround. The principal had to stand behind her teacher — or thought she had to, which amounted to the same thing. Nothing would be done.

Equidistant from our house in the opposite direction from the public school was a fine old private school. We had hoped, partly because we could not afford private schooling for our children, not to have to go that route. But we were desperate. We telephoned the headmaster for an appointment. It was midyear, and a vacancy had occurred in the second grade. The headmaster did not think it would matter that Eric had already been through the second grade, as the work in his school was quite advanced. Would we consider putting him back? Actually we were delighted, as we had never favored the idea of his being physically behind the others in his class.

In January, Eric began work at the new school. Within a week he was going off in the mornings with the same old bounce of enthusiasm and eagerness as before. And this time there was no let-down.

We have often, in the years since, given thanks for the decision we made in that crisis. What if he had remained in the school where the teacher thought he was too inquisitive? What if there had been no alternative, and he had had to remain there?

The Silence of the Children

Our son would not have said anything to us about the school. At that age, he was too young to realize there was something wrong with the teacher's behavior; he thought there was something wrong with him. Consequently he kept silent, as children do.

Madeleine L'Engle did not tell her parents that she was miserable at the school she attended in New York:

> I spent three years when I was very young in a school which was, as far as I was concerned, a foretaste of hell. It was a private school with a fine reputation, academically and socially. It was one of the "proper" schools for a New York child to attend. It did not occur to me that I could tell my parents that I was unhappy. I assumed that it was something to be gone through, and that if I was unhappy I had no one but myself to blame.[1]

Even when children do occasionally speak out, the parents are usually in a quandary about what to do. Are the child's sensibilities to be relied on in such matters? Usually, if enough fuss is made, the parents do eventually go to school for a conference, but nine times out of ten the burden of blame falls back on the child's shoulders. "Billy doesn't apply himself." "Suzi hasn't learned to be aggressive enough in class." "Johnny will be all right in a year or two; give him time." Rarely, if ever, does a parent hear: "I think Dottie is right; I have been misjudging her abilities, and I'm sorry; she will have a new hearing from now on."

Robert Graves, the English poet, records in his autobiography that he hated Charterwell, the grammar school he was sent to — absolutely loathed it. The children there, he said, were bestial, and the teachers not much better. The place was a den of homosexuality. He complained of it to his parents, but they only wrote a letter to the master, saying that he was unhappy. The father apparently did not wish to upset the master by agreeing with his son; the son might be wrong.

Nor does it often help much for students themselves to go to teachers and principals about their problems. I know a boy of thirteen who was having trouble with two of his teachers in the eighth grade. One was a male history teacher and the other a female language teacher. The boy came home one night and told his parents he was going to talk with the teachers about the way he perceived their classes and they perceived him. Perhaps they would help him adjust to their methods and he would be happier. When he approached the teachers, each in a scheduled appointment, they were not receptive to his overtures; each as much as told him that he or she was the authority in the class and that he would have to get "with it" or get out.

A week later, feeling that the teachers had moved from an oblique dislike for him to active antipathy — the male teacher, he felt, was especially hostile — the boy announced to his parents that he was going to make an appointment with the principal and talk to him about the problem. The parents were proud of the businesslike attitude the boy had adopted; it was one of the first signs of latent aggressiveness in him. But the principal was not helpful. "They are both good teachers," said the principal; "you will just have to adapt to their ways." The boy felt helpless. He had made his first awkward step toward negotiating as a mature young man, and was effectually knocked back off his feet. For the next two years, said his parents, he seemed noticeably lacking in self-confidence. They offered to go and talk to the teachers for him, but he shrugged the offer away. "It wouldn't do any good," he said; "their minds are closed."

Here is the situation: When children come to school for the first time, they are still in the earliest stage of their moral development, as Piaget has shown, and do not question authority. An adult's word is law, above suspicion. Therefore if there is any problem, the children must suspect themselves, not the teacher. Later, when the children are nine or ten, they begin to realize that the teacher could be wrong, that there are varying points of view, that personal considerations can color interpretations of the facts. If the children are very aggressive and feel very secure in themselves, they may begin voicing this realization; if not, they nourish it slyly, and probably, for the next two or three years, only occasionally. When they are twelve or thirteen, they have learned that teachers' views are challengeable, and openly talk of this matter among themselves. Whether they raise their individual voices against the teacher again depends on how aggressive and secure they are, as well as on what they guess to be the receptivity of the teacher.

The teacher's receptivity depends on (1) the teacher's own degree of inner security, (2) the teacher's care for the students, and (3) the teacher's *image* of teacher and whether that image permits student challenges. I include Number 3 because some teachers, especially younger and less experienced ones, while having achieved a certain amount of personal maturity and being willing to engage with students on an open basis, are blinded by the mystique that attaches to their profession. Instead of asking, "What is good for the student?" they ask, "What does the profession say is good for the student?" If the answer to this question comes back, "It is important to maintain an authoritative distance between the teacher and the pupil," then the teacher, though normally an open, communicative person, will probably opt for a smokescreen and disappear behind it.

Dinkmeyer and McKay conclude that most teachers, as products of an autocratic system, are more concerned about their images than anything else. "A child I can't make learn or behave well," said one teacher, "makes me look like a bad teacher." [2]

On the question of the teacher's inner security, many critics of the school system feel that the majority of teachers help support an authoritative system because they themselves are in need of authority and wish to exert control over other people's lives. Theodore N. Clark, a therapist, bluntly says that American schools are agents of oppression for molding young people into a grossly commercial network owned by the people who presently make the most profit out of America, and that teachers and principals are co-opted by the funding process to be the hirelings of that network.

> Schools are *first and foremost* institutions designed to defend against change, in other words, to control students and to instill in them patterns that are intended to prepare them to desire power while accepting passive-dependent attitudes of submission to those in power and to prepare them to desire to profit while instilling in them a need to consume. The rhetoric of "education" is a mystification of this process, designed to create and sustain the illusion that schools are for the benefit of students and are there to educate them. It distracts people from what schools *really* do and persuades them to cooperate with the schools, even when their *experience* of schooling (either in terms of its effects on students from the viewpoint of concerned parents or in terms of its effects on the students themselves) is negative and contrary to their desires and feelings.[3]

Schools achieve their desired end of oppression, says Clark, by the emphasis on order, efficiency, and control. Students are notoriously unfree. Their time is not their own, with the result that they look forward to their days off and their vacation time. Their movements are strictly controlled; they must be in certain rooms at certain times, in their chairs or at their desks, and cannot take too much time even to go to the bathroom. They are assigned classes, grades, and even roles (class wit, butt of jokes, underachiever, overachiever, A student, perennial failure, etc.).

The teacher too has a role, says Clark. "Schoolteachers are very powerful. They can grade students, embarrass them, humiliate them, and create anxiety at will. They are, because of their importance to the quality of the students' performance (teachers grade students in terms of performance and behavior), always an object of fear and anxiety."[4] Some students become absolutely phobic about teachers. Others, despairing of pleasing them, become chronic delinquents. "Once we realize that the role of teacher is invested with terror-creating capacities — *at all times teachers create anxiety* — it is easy to see why people would want to be teachers or to reach the equivalent junior executive level in any other bureaucracy."[5]

The Teacher and the System

Not all teachers, fortunately, are as malevolent as Clark tends to paint them. Teaching is not an easy profession. Most teachers' colleges are themselves notoriously poor; their curricula are like froth, all bubbles and film, whipped up from the bureaucratic system they serve. Professors are often inexperienced with children, with *real* children, and seek to impress their classes with boring résumés of irrelevant statistics or with personal prejudices masked as the latest psychological "findings." One woman of my acquaintance, who was in her thirties and decided to complete her requirements for a teaching certificate because her children were in school and did not need her during the day, quit in disgust at the end of a single semester because the work was an affront to her intelligence. In some classes, she said, her presence was a threat to the professors, because she had had more experience with children than they and was not willing to sit in open-mouthed reverence as many of the young unmarried students did. And, when a teacher has completed this demeaning route to certification, there is the often humiliating period of induction at some poorly rated school, with frequent lunchroom, playground, and parking-lot duties that were not bargained for when the profession was anticipated.

Working conditions in many schools are substandard; rooms are overcrowded, laboratories underequipped, libraries spotty and ill chosen, and personal amenities, such as a place for privacy, nonexistent. Add to this the frightening behavior of many students today, particularly in the inner-city schools, but also in suburban areas, where genteel teachers must often cope with products of ghetto barbarism who have been imported into their provinces by busing. It is sometimes difficult to understand why anyone who has spent four years in college to earn a degree is willing to work at all under these conditions, much less do it for a third the annual salaries of long-distance truck drivers or plumbers or electrical workers who have not, in some cases, completed a high school education!

Still, Clark's criticism, that teachers are more interested in programing than in educating, is not entirely unrealistic. Most teachers *are* unwitting tools of a system that intimidates students. Even teachers who personally care about children are inevitably torn between caring and serving the system. Most TV programs about teachers gravitate monotonously toward this theme, for it is the built-in drama of the teacher's existence. If, as the TV hero or heroine does, the teacher defies the system and saves the child, it only serves to underline the abnormality of this choice; in real life things rarely turn out that way.

The system, bent on its own "success," cannot but foster a sense of alienation in most students, even the ones it appears to be rewarding. The very rhetoric of education, with such phrases as "child-centered" and "development-based," is often used falsely, for it seems to be focused on the children while in fact it is oriented toward the system, which is filled with hypothetical students, never with real live, wriggling, squealing kids. Within the system, individual children often sense that they do not count for much except as they exhibit model behavior and "progress," or, on the other hand, when they get out of line, frustrating the system and calling attention to themselves. Little wonder, in such a setup, that so many youngsters become delinquents and drop-outs!

One of the most eloquent and striking condemnations of the American school system I have seen comes not from an "expert" but from a 16-year-old girl who brandished a cap-pistol as she addressed a congress on runaway youths at Ohio State University. She said:

> Young people in our society are oppressed, which may be difficult to understand for adults who believe that today's youth have a higher standard of living than any other generation. But our oppression takes many forms. In childhood we are forced to an educational system which does nothing to meet our real needs, but rather imprisons us or tries to mold us to a standard of society. Politicians who were not elected by us and that do not represent us pass laws regulating much of our lives. We are seen as the property of our parents who can exercise whatever control they want over our lives even to the point of signing away to institutions. If arrested, we are legally entitled to only some of the rights that adults have and, in practice, we are not even certain of receiving those rights. These problems are all interrelated.
>
> The schools condition us to unquestioningly accept the unjust laws. These laws in turn force us to be dependent on our parents and to attend schools. Laws such as the child labor laws and compulsory school force young people to be dependent on adults. This dependence in turn allows adults to get down on us and treat us condescendingly. Thus the problems facing youth today will not be solved just by changing a few laws. Rather, they are a symptom of a society which is based on oppression and discrimination. And so, the liberation of youth depends on radically changing the entire society. Public schools and most private schools are not democratic. They aren't intended to be; nor do the schools exist to help the students and the majority of the people. Rather, they are designed to allow the upper class of North American society to keep their power and prestige while training the majority of the people to be good, obedient workers for the upper class. In other words, the schools of the U.S. do not teach students to look objec-

tively at their society, to criticize and question it; instead we are taught to blindly follow orders, to be docile and unquestioning in the face of authority.[6]

This sounds very much like Clark's analysis — or like one by Ivan Illich or Paulo Freire.[7] The girl obviously believes, as they do, that the present school system serves as an instrument to facilitate the integration of the younger generation into the larger social pattern dominated by the upper classes. Teachers, in such a scheme, are the unwitting dupes of the system. And students are the real victims, helpless pawns who must spend years of their lives in virtual imprisonment, mastering material in which they are not interested but that society says they must learn.

The Boredom of the Classroom

In December 1967, the British newspaper *The Observer* invited secondary-school children all over Great Britain to enter a contest by writing a description of "The School That I'd Like." Thousands of entries poured in. Edward Blishen, who read them all and later published a book that included many of the responses, said, "I have never read so much that was so full of complaints and criticisms, of schemes for imaginative innovation, and yet that was, as a whole, so very sober." There was striking unanimity in the criticism, Blishen found; it all centered around learning as "being told what to do" and how to do it.

> The picture they build up of learning as it now most often is in the schools is one in which they, the pupils, are passive, sometimes very reluctant, recipients; the teachers are the providers — aided, if that is the word, by textbooks that also, oppressively if not dully, *provide*. It is this pattern of passively receiving, magisterially providing, that the children worry away at. Some do so at the naivest level. School is boring; it is always a matter of listening to the teacher,

never saying or doing anything of your own. Others put it more sophisticatedly. They too say that school is boring — it is the word that united all the essays that allow themselves to be freely critical — but are subtler in their analysis of the cause. "Everything learnt is second-hand if it comes from the teachers, and very often out-of-date and misleading if it comes from the books." "Children do not want to be taught at, but want to find out things for themselves." "The people who write textbooks do not make mistakes — and the best way to learn is by your own mistakes." "Instead of stuffing children into a classroom, within four boundaries, let them get out and see, feel, smell, hear and taste the subject." [8]

School is boring. That is the consensus of opinion among our children. That is why they feel imprisoned in the classroom.

Consider this page from the diary of a 14-year-old girl:

> Every day, first I go to school and listen to Mrs. A. try to quiet the class, maybe give out a few detentions. Then to Mr. B's class to hear him talk for 49 minutes. Then wonderful ten minute break and a few cigarettes. Ph.Ed. with Mr. C. and basketball. Science with Mr. D's stuffy room. Then lunch with leftovers. Then math with Mr. E. I could and never will [sic] be able to do math. Spanish with Mr. F. I can't do Spanish either. Finally speech. Quite a boring class. Poor Mr. F. can never get the class's attention. Then home on the bouncy bus. Throw my books and coat on the bed. Then to take my frustrations out on the poor piano. That is a very boring day in my opinion. [9]

David R., a 15-year-old boy in a private school, feels similarly about much of his school experience:

> It's really a drag most of the time. I have a couple of teachers who are not so bad. Mr. R., my English teacher, tries real hard, but he isn't too experienced and has trouble making the guys be quiet so he can get on with the lesson.

I guess he doesn't know how to go about it, though; we're reading *The Scarlet Letter* line by line for the symbolism, and most people are bored out of their trees by that. I like Mr. P. in biology too. He's older and seems to know a lot about his subject. He's also very human, and keeps us entertained with all sorts of stories and observations. But the others are for the birds. I really hate Latin. Mrs. O. is too serious about it. She ding-dongs at you until you want to tell her to take it and stuff it. And Mr. D. in geometry is — well, he bullies you all the time. He's a showoff, and likes to trick you out and things. He's all the time giving us proofs to do without showing us how, and then fussing because we haven't done them.

The relationship of all this to children's loneliness should be readily apparent. To the extent that school drives a wedge between their energy and the desire to learn, and drugs their natural curiosity by requiring of them ritualized responses to printed material, it divorces them from the world of excitement that would counterbalance their sense of being alone. Instead of fostering an agreeable unity between them and their environment, in which they are aggressive and outgoing, always making and enjoying new relationships, it actually distances them from the environment, demanding that their apprehension of it come through secondary sources, the screens and grids of books, maps, charts, formulas, and data provided by the so-called "experts."

Little children come to school filled with excitement for discovering the world around them. It is still magical to them. Colors are still primary, splashy, brilliant. Rain is still fun, and so is mud. So are bushes and creeks and crayfish and all sorts of animals and snow and stars and mechanical things. But school has a program to push. Math, reading, writing, history, geography, and many other things, all part of the system. Little Susie and Johnny must fit in. All the students must make progress together. There is little time for individuals. The system not only dictates what Susie and

Johnny must learn, but the schedule on which they should do it. Their lives are given over to tests and measurements. Soon the colors are less splashy. Rain becomes a bother. Curiosity is left behind. Dullness settles over everything.

The children are taught to distrust themselves and their own senses, and to believe instead in whatever is printed in black and white, in whatever the teacher says, in whatever is recommended by the system. In short, they are alienated from their own world and bored in the process, and alienation lies at the very core of what it means to feel lonely. The sense of disparity that many students feel between themselves and the world of knowledge will never go away. It will haunt them all their lives.

The Word from Mr. Holt

A few years ago, a bombshell of a book exploded on the American educational scene. Its author was not a philosopher or a social scientist or a professor of education. He was a teacher. The book was a distillation of what he had seen and felt and wanted to say through several years of being in the classroom, observing children, and dealing with school administrators and other teachers.

The teacher was John Holt. His book was *How Children Fail.*

What Holt had to say was startling, particularly because he was saying it from inside the system. Now, in retrospect, it is easy to see that what he said had less effect on the system than many people thought it would. But what he said was important. It was honest, articulate, and to the point. It still needs to be heard.

Holt did not believe, like Theodore Clark, that there is within the system a serious intention to dominate students and turn them into workers for a society controlled by the upper classes. Instead, he saw the system as a kind of mindless development no one had planned or organized, but which had simply grown on its own into an impersonal, bureaucratic way of doing things.

The heart of the problem, he was convinced, lies not so much in the aims of our educational institutions but in our methodologies, in the ways we teach. Our methodologies, he said, ignore the way children really learn and favor instead a kind of rote memorization that is almost unexceptionally tedious and deadly to the spirit of inquiry.

"To a very great degree," he declared,

> school is a place where children learn to be stupid. A dismal thought, but hard to escape. Infants are not stupid. Children of one, two, or even three throw the whole of themselves into everything they do. They embrace life, and devour it; it is why they learn so fast, and are such good company. Listlessness, boredom, apathy — these all come later. Children come to school *curious;* within a few years most of that curiosity is dead, or at least silent. Open a first or third grade to questions, and you will be deluged; fifth graders say nothing. They either have no questions or will not ask them. They think, "What's this leading up to? What's the catch?"[10]

Soon, Holt continued, children develop the habit of resisting education. Bored by the tasks they are given, they unconsciously withhold effort, and work with only a small part of their attention, energy, and intelligence. In a word, they do their assignments stupidly — even if correctly. This soon becomes a habit. They get used to working at low power and develop strategies to enable them to get by this way. In time they even start to think of themselves as being stupid, and to think that their low-power way of coping with school is the only possible way.

Education began in the child's early years as a process of discovery. That is why it was exciting. In school it becomes only a matter of coming up with the right answers. The personal side of the process is ignored. How learning makes children *feel* is overlooked. The answers become everything.

Wrong answers, in the present educational system, receive no credit at all. Children are not taught that an incorrect answer can be as rewarding and important in the search for truth as a correct answer, or that the process of seeking answers is of more significance to them than coming up with any answers at all. In the educational game they are divorced from themselves, from their inner beings, because they come to understand that it is the answers, not their relationship to the world, that are primary.

Holt described a visit to a fourth-grade arithmetic class where the teacher was regarded as one of the real gems of her school system. The children were reading out answers from their marked papers. Everything went smoothly until, after one child had read an answer, another raised his hand. "What is it, Jimmy?" asked the teacher, with a slight hint in her voice that the question might not be important. "Well, I didn't get that answer," said Jimmy, "I got . . ." But before Jimmy could say any more, the teacher said, "Now, Jimmy, I'm sure we don't want to hear any *wrong* answers." And that was that!

> This woman is far ahead of most teachers in intelligence, education, and experience. She is articulate, cultivated, has had a good schooling, and is married to a college professor. And in the twenty years or more that she has been teaching it has apparently never occurred to her that it might be worth taking a moment now and then to hear these unsuccessful Jimmies talk about their wrong answers, on the chance that from their talk she might learn something about their thinking and what was making the answers come out wrong. What makes everyone call her such a good teacher? I suppose it is the ability to manage children effortlessly, which she does. And for all I know, even the Jimmies may think she is a good teacher; it would never

occur to them that it was this nice lady's fault that they couldn't understand arithmetic; no, it must be their own fault, for being so stupid.[11]

For being so stupid — that is of course the way many children are taught to feel. Worth, in the world where they spend most of their time, is measured in terms of answers.

The Rating Game

If there is a single linchpin in the whole educational system, something that keeps students in their places and teachers in power, it is the system of assigning marks or grades. If, by some miraculous feat of surgery, this system were to be removed, the educational situation would be transformed overnight. But it will not be removed, for it is an outgrowth of the situation itself; to remove it would require such major adaptations from the administrators and faculties of our schools that they would simply not know how to function without it.

Grading is the primary hold the teacher has over the student, and therefore the main tool for producing the kind of anxiety most teachers arouse, either consciously or unconsciously, to get their students to perform. Without grading, the leverage would be gone, and teachers would have to resort to gaining the students' interest, to showing them the real relevance of what they are doing, to engaging them at the raw edges of their own lines of growth and excitement. Not only that, parents would have lost their simple index to what the kids are doing in school, so that they would be compelled to examine the matter more thoroughly and personally, and anxiety-ridden students would themselves be thrown upon previously untouched inner resources for knowing how they were doing in their classes. Even the administrators would be plunged into chaos, having lost their readiest guide to the teachers' performances ("Mrs. Brown produces more A students than anyone else in the fifth grade") and their index for qualifying students for college and recommending them for jobs.

There is absolutely no assurance that grades are in any true sense related to the acquisition of knowledge. They may *seem* to be, especially if the question of relationship is never raised, but there is no essential connection.

As most students admit, there are tricks to getting grades. Clever students can pick up clues very adroitly — sometimes almost out of the air — that tell them how to answer questions the way the teacher wants. They learn to spot questions that will be given on tests and exams. They "psych" the teacher early in their relationship, then feed him or her the things he or she is interested in. They learn to stare right between the teacher's eyes, so that they can be daydreaming about a thousand things, yet convince the teacher that he or she has their undivided attention. In the end, they get the grades, but not an education. Or, if it is an education, it is like Oliver Twist's — lessons in picking Fagin's pocket!

Here is what one girl told me:

> It's easy to get a top mark in Miss Smith's class if you're willing to put out a little effort. I nod my head whenever she says anything sort of emphatically, and I can tell she's pleased. I always sit in the first three rows. I try to get all the daily assignments, even if I don't understand them. I don't think she reads them anyway most of the time; just checks to see if you've done them. On most tests, I study with two girl friends. We can usually spot the questions. Then we memorize the answers. Sometimes, when we miss one, I mean fail to spot it in advance, I get real panicky on the test. But usually it pays off. Teachers will usually give you the benefit of the doubt if they think you're interested in their classes.

The system is not only educationally without promise, it produces anxiety in the students by seeming to relate them to the world without actually doing so; on the contrary, because it teaches them to be afraid of wrong answers and mistakes, it relates them to a false view of life and divorces them from the real world and a proper estimate of their place in it.

This goes for good students as well as poor ones. If anything, the ones who consistently earn top marks are more anxious than the ones who make low marks. They become actually phobic about C's and D's. They get so nervous over exams that many of them develop ulcers, migraine headaches, and other psychosomatic symptoms. Then they go through life — or many of them do — with the same anxieties about measuring up.

Holt believes that many children fail because it is the easy way out. That is, it is finally easier to be known as a failure, or at least as a poor student, than to maintain the image of a good student.

Notice sometime the difference between good students and poor ones as they approach a test. The good ones become very tense. Their adrenalin has to be made to flow. They have to store up a lot of information. They have to get it down right on the paper. It is all tension-producing. The average or poor students, on the other hand, are relatively relaxed. They may have a few anxious minutes at the time of the test, but those are nothing in comparison with the tension the good students have gone through for hours or even days.

Which students are smarter, the good ones or the poor ones? In life, we often think the people who know how to avoid tension-producing situations are basically smarter than others. Why do we assume, because students make good marks, that they are necessarily smart?

We might call what happens to poor students "negative success." That is, they succeed in breaking out of the system on the lower edge. By refusing to let their tension escalate over tests and requirements, they exert more personal independence than the good students.

Take Woody, for example. Woody is 15 and still in the seventh grade. He has been kept back two years in the school he attends. He is not a stupid boy. In fact, the teachers admit he is very clever; he is articulate, imaginative, and fun. But they cannot get him to work. He fails more courses than he passes. He is a charming boy, with an infectious smile and dimples, and a shock of red hair that falls almost to his eyes. He laughs softly as he talks about not having any brains. Several times in our conversation he used colorful metaphors that led me to believe he has a strong aptitude for language, an ear for the telling word or the singing phrase. But this facility has never been encouraged. Woody fell afoul of the system almost from the first. He came from a poor section of town and both his parents were uneducated. When he did not make proper grades in his first two years, he was kept back in the second grade. From then on, everybody knew he was a failure. The teachers knew it, the other children knew it, and, worst of all, Woody knew it. The right teacher may still convince Woody that he has some real sense and does not have to be a failure in life, but I doubt if it will happen; the system is against it. Woody has "succeeded" in it on the bottom side.

Labeling students as poor, retarded, or uneducable does lasting injury to them. As Nicholas Hobbs has shown in his book *The Futures of Children* [12], there is primary correlation between teachers' expectations of students and their ability to teach the students; if students enter their classes with a reputation for being slow or stupid, the teachers expect and require less of them. The same stigma follows these children into life beyond school. In fact, it has been transferred to the students' own minds, so that they perceive themselves as others have perceived them.

Most parents, unfortunately, accept the judgment of the schools on their children and reinforce the characterizations placed upon them. If children bring home report cards with C's, D's, and F's, the parents immediately conclude they are either dull or not applying themselves. There is rarely a question about whether the teachers know what they are doing. Some parents threaten to discipline their children if the children bring home low marks, adding new pressure and fear as the children approach their work.

Many middle-class parents who had poor educations themselves are doubly bent upon their children's having good ones. Knowing little about the learning process and assuming it has to do primarily with studying hard and making good grades, they not only drive the children to do better and better but pester the teachers to give them more and more homework and to require more of them in class. They are so phobic about failure that it bothers them to see their children playing and behaving like normal children when they are home from school; they want the children to be working, working, working.

"It's almost a sickness with many of our parents," the headmaster of a private school told me. "They want us to work their children beyond all reason. The kids do great work. Our teachers are very demanding. I wouldn't have the stamina to do what the kids do here and then go home and have two, three hours of homework. But the parents don't think we give them enough. They call me and say, 'I wish you'd speak to Miss So-and-so about giving my Cindy more to do at home. She's been finishing her homework by seven-thirty every night!' God, I want to say, 'How would you like to work a twelve-hour day the way your daughter does?' "

When children are not doing well by the teachers' standards, these parents can be overpowering in their demands. One of the few ways children have of combating such pressure is simply to cop out, to fail and fail big. Then, they hope, they will be left alone.

It is the old game of feeling loved for what we do instead of for who we are. Children who are unduly pushed to make grades, or the ones who fail and cannot be pushed, get the unequivocal message from their parents: "I will not care for you if you do not succeed." Either way, it is a losing game. Even if they care whether their parents love them, and put on the extra effort to make good marks, they are left with the hollow consolation that now their parents will love them because of the marks, not because they are their parents' children and are lovable in their own right.

Missing the Excitement

From the perspective of the children's lives, it is a shame that more teachers do not realize the great excitement that could be theirs if they had the inner security to defy the system of tests and grades and merely try to get in touch with each child's inner potential for growth and creativity. Standardization is for machines, assembly lines, fast-food chains, not human beings. The richness of living is evoked from the variety of gifts and strategies, not an interminable sameness. Why should children be weighed and found wanting like eggs or milk or sacks of flour? Why should they be judged for not fitting the same mold or being able to memorize the same facts and mathematical tables? What is important in education is the children's progress along their own lines of development, not their false progress along the lines of someone else's program. Getting in touch with where the children are, making contact with them there, and enticing them from there to another point or points identifiable with their own interest — that is true education.

As Holt says, "We must recognize that children who are dealing with a problem on a very primitive, experimental, and inefficient level, are making discoveries that are just as good, just as exciting, just as worthy of interest and encouragement, as the more sophisticated discoveries made by more advanced students. When Dorothy discovers, after long painful effort, that every other number can be divided into 2 equal rows, that every third number can be divided into 3 equal rows, she has made just as great an intellectual leap as those children who, without being told, discovered for themselves some of the laws of exponents."[13]

Dennison concurs: "There is no such thing as learning except (as Dewey tells us) in the continuum of experience. But this continuum cannot survive in the classroom unless there is reality of encounter between the adults and the children. The teachers must be themselves, and not play roles. They must teach the children, and not teach 'subjects.' "[14]

Our family recently spent a sabbatical year in Oxford, England, and the children attended the state-supported school in our neighborhood. Toward the end of the year, I asked them for a thoughtful comparison of that particular school system and the ones with which they had been familiar at home. Their experiences in American schools had been essentially good ones, with highly competent teachers in largely protected environments. But they were surprisingly quick to praise the British system over the American one, and said their year abroad was the finest they had experienced. "Why?" I asked. "Because," they said, "over here [in England] you work to learn, not to make grades. At home your marks are everything, testing is everything. You memorize, you stuff your mind until it's ready to burst, and you go in and pour it all out on a test; then you forget it. Here, you have an adventure. You try different things. You find out what works and what doesn't, and why. You *really* learn."

"This is the first school I have been in," said our oldest son, "where it is all right to make mistakes. The teachers don't mind if you make mistakes. They say you can learn from mistakes. At home, mistakes are fatal. You are only permitted to have correct answers. No mistakes. You get so uptight that you don't learn anything. Everything is geared to the tests — to being able to reproduce what the teachers want. They spout out all this material and you are supposed to absorb it all instantly and be able to repeat it at will. Over here, it's different. You explore. You feel your way. Then what you learn is really yours."

Holt would endorse our sons' experience, I think. "When kids are in a situation where they are not under pressure to come up with a right answer, far less do it quickly," he says, "they can do amazing things. Last fall, about November, I gave the afternoon section some problems. I said, 'You have never seen problems like these, you don't know how to do them, and I don't care whether you get them right or not. I just want to see how you go about trying to do them.' The problems were basically simple algebra problems, like the one about Anne and Mary, or a certain number of nickels and dimes adding up to 85 cents — the kind of problem that many first-year algebra students find so difficult. These fifth graders tore into them with imagination, resourcefulness, and common sense — in a word, intelligently. They solved them in many ways, including some I hadn't thought of. But it was about that time that the school began to worry about my going too slowly. Soon I was told to speed up the pace, which I am ashamed to say I did, and the children lapsed right back into their old strategies. Probably for keeps."[15]

What an insight Holt got into children's abilities — and what a sad word his last one was. Imagine a revamping of the entire educational system that permitted students to use their minds to solve problems and did not penalize them for the mistakes they made while doing so! Maybe they would go through all twelve grades (would that terminology have to go?) without losing the starry-eyed looks they bring to school the first day they come.

And maybe the educational process would not be driven like a wedge between their inner feelings and the work they are doing, so that they become cosmically lonely and ill at ease in the world they will have to live in for the next sixty or seventy years!

5

The Cruelty of Peers

"The world of my clientele," says social worker Neal Silver, "is a vicious, cruel world. These youngsters have been hurt, spat upon, cursed, hit."[1]

What is Silver talking about — a center for battered children? A reformatory? No. He is talking about ordinary school children who come to him at Children's Village in Dobbs Ferry, New York. The hurts and indignities they have suffered occurred in the classroom, on the playground, on school buses, and on the streets leading to and from school. And these hurts and indignities were inflicted not by adults, as one might have expected, but by other children.

The experience of pain, both mental and physical, at the hands of one's fellow children is not exactly a new phenomenon. Edward Bulwer-Lytton, the famous novelist and historian, was so bullied at school that it broke both his health and spirit, and left him with a lifelong loathing of meanness and tyranny. Anthony Trollope said that the indignities he received at the hands of other students were too awful to be described, even with his great talent for fiction. William Cowper, the poet, was so abused by a fellow student that he was afraid to look at the boy above the knees, and said he knew him "by his shoe buckles better than any other part of his dress." Chevalier Jackson, the nineteenth-century surgeon, wrote of the perpetual torment he suffered from older students in his school, who would waylay him, swing him around by the feet until his head felt as if it would explode, and even choke him around the neck until he experienced the approach of unconsciousness. They filled his lunch pail with sand or rotten eggs, removed his boots and threw him into snow-covered fields, dipped him in a watering trough, and suspended him bodily over a deserted quarry, threatening to drop him. The happiest day of his life, he proclaimed, was when he left school at seventeen to enter the University of Pittsburgh and study medicine.

Even lonely, harassed students may themselves join in the hazing or taunting of other students, says sociologist Silver, who has made a study of the way students behave in groups. Some do it because they hope to deflect attention or punishment away from themselves to other victims. Others do it because they too have latent streaks of cruelty in their make-up and enjoy being on the upper side of the tormenting relationship for a change.

After all, children are hardly paragons of virtue. They bring to their schools all the prejudices, resentments, aggressiveness, and pent-up hostilities they have been taught at home. They act out in schoolroom and play yard the ideas and emotions that have been imposed upon them by parents, television, and older siblings.

For many of them, school is an unpleasant experience of confinement with hundreds of other children whom they fear, suspect, and dislike. Some are literally afraid of physical proximity, especially in situations where disorder prevails and there is no protective adult present. A large percentage of school refusals are a result of children's revulsion toward arbitrary groupings, which rarely take into account the individual child's sensibilities or likes and dislikes.

To the general uneasiness some children naturally experience at school, add the teasing or bullying of classmates, and the result is almost overwhelming. "Some days," writes a teen-ager about his experience in the lower grades, "I was so scared and unhappy that I thought I would vomit. I couldn't concentrate on my studies for worrying about what the other students would do to me. I was afraid to go to the toilet or the water fountain. Recess was the worst, that and after school. Anytime the teacher was not around. That was when they tried to get me."

Cynthia M. says that being a girl, she believes, is even harder than being a boy:

> The boys all think they can pick on you because you're a girl and don't know how to fight back. If you do try to defend yourself, the teacher picks on you, because little girls are supposed to be "nice" and not fight like boys. Then, when you get a little older, it's the girls you really have trouble with. Some are really meaner than boys. And jealous?! Man, are they jealous of you if you happen to have pretty hair or a new dress or something. I used to cry almost every day, until I learned to give as good as I got. Then they started leaving me alone. But some girls never learn. They let the others make their lives a misery.

Norma R., a teacher, says that she was shocked, when she first began teaching, at the viciousness of some children:

> I mean, it wasn't just defense mechanisms at work. Some of them seemed to take an absolute delight in bedeviling others. I have a little fellow in my second grade class now who makes life hell for the other children. He gets this glint in his eye and takes after one of them. Several times I've rescued someone as he was about to baptize the poor thing in the fishtank, headfirst, or stick someone's hand on the hotplate, or cut off somebody's pigtail with the scissors. He's a terror. Some of the children probably have to cope with worse at home, and they aren't bothered too much. But two or three of them have nightmares from it. I know. Their parents have told me.

Psychologist John Gottman of the University of Illinois, who has studied the problem of students' fears and loneliness, thinks that one of the major reasons for their unhappiness is simple shyness. Coming from homes where they have been able to retreat from difficulties instead of facing them, they are ill at ease in social situations involving confrontation, especially with large numbers of other children. Many of them therefore tend to "hover" on the edge of the crowd, or to withdraw from active participation with other students. These hoverers are easily spotted by the more aggressive students, the bullies, who naturally pick on them.

Gottman is trying to train such diffident children to be more outgoing, to look other students in the eye, to stand up to their pressures, if necessary, and affirm their own worth to the group. It is not an easy task. Many students feel helpless before their peers. They buckle under indications of their peers' disapproval or rejection, especially if they come from homes where they have been uncertain of love and acceptance. Patterns that were set at home are simply fulfilled by the social grouping. Unhappiness and rejection become a way of life.

Teasing and Name-Calling

Children with physical handicaps, speech problems, or obvious physical or behavioral peculiarities are ready targets for teasing by other children. Nicknames such as Skinny, Fatty, Four Eyes, and Peewee are common in almost every school grouping. Adults who have long grown out of the awkward stages of childhood can often still remember the pain of rejection they knew when their classmates greeted them with such epithets.

"As a child," one young man told me, "I was overweight and the nicknames I was called — Jellyroll, Blubber, Whaletail — caused me a lot of pain. I felt terribly rejected and did not like myself. Even though I am no longer fat, I still cannot shake the feeling of rejection that was drilled into me during those awful years."

Thoughtful parents often try to shield their children from the unpleasantness associated with physical differences, but peers are very blunt about them. In one sense, this is not a display of cruelty but of directness; children have simply not learned to dissemble as adults have, and they call a spade a spade.

The hurts that result from such stigmatizing are often deep and lasting.

Carol W., now a pleasant-looking secretary, is noticeably shy and withdrawn. She believes her sense of insecurity stems from the fact that she was often teased as a girl for having protruding teeth.

> They were pretty bad, before the doctor gave me braces and straightened them. Some of the girls teased me about it a lot. They said no boy would ever want to kiss me — that it would wound anyone who did. I used to lie in bed and cry at night. I wanted to have them all pulled out and have false teeth, but mother wouldn't hear of it. I guess that's why they finally got the braces. I kept my hand over my mouth a lot of the time when I talked.

Jimmy B., an insurance salesman, recalls the unhappiness he suffered because of an unusual voice:

> About the time I was twelve or thirteen, when your voice begins to change, mine got real low. Not just deep. It was funny-sounding. Sort of spooky, if you know what I mean. The other kids began to call me Froggy. I hated the name. I used to tear into boys who called me that — even some that were bigger than me. That only egged them on. My voice improved after I got in high school, but the name stuck. I was back at a class reunion ten years after graduation, and that was what everybody remembered me by. I still hate it.

As Erving Goffman has pointed out in his book *Stigma*, children often suffer from association with a stigmatized person, whether the stigma is physical or nonphysical. He cites the following letter written to columnist Ann Landers:

Dear Ann Landers:

I'm a girl 12 years old who is left out of all social activities because my father is an ex-convict. I try to be nice and friendly to everyone but it's no use. The girls at school have told me that their mothers don't want them to associate with me because it will be bad for their reputations. My father had some bad publicity in the papers and even though he has served his time nobody will forget it.

Is there anything I can do? I am very lonesome because it's no fun to be alone all the time. My mother tries to take me places with her but I want to be with people my own age. Please give me some advice.

An Outcast[2]

Because of this "stigma by association," children often seem antihumanitarian in the swiftness with which they desert the stigmatized child in their midst. They do not wish to be known as "the girl who plays with blind Sammy" or "the boy who runs around with crazy Tommy." Therefore, as soon as they notice that other children avoid the person with a stigma, they too begin to keep a safe distance from the person. Only the occasional brave or rebellious child, or the one with another stigma of his or her own, is willing to pay the price of friendship with the desocialized individual.

It is hard to say where the norms come from by which very young children judge their peers, but the evidence increasingly points to the possibility that some of them are almost instinctive. This is not true of racial distinctions, but it is true of distinctions regarding physical attractiveness. A University of Minnesota study has shown that nursery age children are already using degrees of attractiveness and unattractiveness to establish the popularity spectrum in their group. In some cases, they show actual fear of children who are ugly, and associate these children with bad dreams. And, on the other hand, they show a natural propensity for following good-looking children as their leaders. Whether the concept that beautiful people are good and ugly people are bad is innate or learned, it is very hard on young children whose genes did not bless them with pleasant faces and physiques.

I recently observed a group of school children boarding a bus for an outing. One boy about twelve or thirteen years old stood apart from the group, waiting for everyone else to board before he attempted to do so. The unfortunate child had been born with a huge birthmark covering three-quarters of his face. He looked as if he were wearing a stocking mask over the upper part of his visage. What kind of social life could that lad possibly have, I pondered. He was clearly demarcated from the rest of his class. No other child associated with him.

But there are hundreds of children in every school, thousands in every city, who suffer nearly as much as he, even though with lesser afflictions. If they perceive that they are not accepted by their peers, they are hurt. And peers are quick to discern the vulnerable spots in their classmates. To discern them and attack them. Often they are like a flock of chickens when one of the chickens discovers a fleck of blood on another; the flock will not give up until they have pecked the poor chicken to death.

An Intolerance for Failure

Tender, sensitive children are targets of their peers especially if their sensitivity involves weakness of any kind. There is an unwritten code among youngsters about the level of physical and mental performance they should be able to reach, and woe to those who for any reason are unable consistently to attain it.

Among boys, the code most often shows up on the playground or in physical education classes. Boys who can't perform as well as others become "sissies," especially if they are not overtly masculine.

John A., now a physicist working for the federal government, recalls the hell of his childhood gym experience:

I was an only child, and didn't have much association with other children before going to school. Consequently I was not prepared for the rough-and-tumble of P.E. and playground sports. I couldn't hit a baseball, I couldn't shoot baskets or dribble a basketball, and I was deathly afraid of football. I wore glasses, and that didn't help. Somebody was always knocking them off, and I felt helpless without them. The other boys razzed me constantly, calling me a sissy and a mama's boy. I didn't help any by crying, which I did often in the first few grades. It was sheer misery. I hated P.E. And it didn't end there. Everybody knew I was a pushover, so I got the treatment on a regular basis — at lunchtime, recess, after school. I was the scapegoat, I guess you'd say; I got the knocks from everybody, no matter what their gripe.

We often think of a lack of machismo as a male problem. But girls encounter similar treatment when they are inept. Joyce A. recalls:

I was never any good at sports, and the kids made me live hard as a result. Whenever we had relay races of any kind, or anything involving team sports, I made my side lose. Once there was this rope-climbing deal — two ropes, you know, and each team had to go up in relays — and I couldn't make it. That was all there was to it, I simply couldn't make it. Everybody was yelling at me to go on to the top, but I couldn't. I was frozen. I couldn't go up or down. The girls were disgusted with me.

Students are usually more tolerant of classmates' failures in mental or intellectual feats if the failure does not affect the group. But when team efforts are involved, it is often another story. Jerry S. was a poor student, generally unprepared. He recalls how he was treated after a spelling bee or a math turndown:

I was no better than dirt to the rest of them [the other students]. They really got mad. Sometimes I got roughed up on the playground for it. I hated to always be the weak link in the chain, but I couldn't help it. I didn't have my act together. Boy, there was no understanding in that crowd.

Another student remembers that the teacher in one of her classes had a way of inciting the other students against her when she failed them in a team project: "He would say, 'Are you going to let her make you lose?' " The teacher seemed to take a pleasure, she felt, in provoking the animosity of the other students.

The Role of Jealousy

It isn't only the poor student, physically and mentally, who is punished and abused by other children; sometimes it is the exceptionally good one as well, the one who is noticed and rewarded by the teachers for being bright or dedicated.

Robert S. consistently attracted the attention of various teachers for the neatness of his homework and his high scores on tests. In one of his fourth-grade classes, the teacher had all the students make clocks with movable hands that they could use in learning to tell time. Robert made his of wood instead of cardboard, which all the other students used, and employed a wood-burning set to stencil the numbers and a decorative motif on the face; then he shellacked it and added wooden hands that were painted gold. The teacher was so proud of his work that she complimented it endlessly, not only in that particular class but in other classes throughout the day. By the time school was out, everyone in the school had heard about Robert's wonderful clock. The next week, when the clocks were returned to the students to take home, several boys clustered around Robert as he left the school ground and snatched the clock away from him. Mockingly praising it, they ripped the hands off, defaced it, and finally stomped on it and broke it. When Robert cried, they pushed him around a few times and left him lying on the ground by the smashed clock.

Emma G. is a sixth-grade student. Her class staged a special play at Christmastime for the school assembly. The best part in the play for a girl was that of the announcer. The announcer was to be an angel and to speak lines intermittently throughout the play. Three girls wanted the part and were good enough to hope they might get it. When the teacher assigned it to Emma, the other girls became very snippish and unfriendly toward her. One said she was having a birthday party during the holidays but was not going to invite Emma. During several rehearsals, two of the girls made faces at her while she was reading her part, and talked in an undertone, but loud enough for her to hear, about how poorly she was doing.

"I don't know why they acted that way," said Emma. "I wouldn't have if one of them had got the part. It took all the fun out of it. I wished I hadn't got it, I was so miserable. But mother said to go ahead with it and not pay any attention to them. I tried."

For some reason, students are harder on other students who achieve intellectually than on those who excel physically. Perhaps they tend to be afraid of those who are athletically superior and simply don't pick on them. It is also possible that it is human nature to distrust those who are cleverer and more intelligent than we are. Some historians think Adlai Stevenson was denied the presidency of the United States because he had the image of an egghead.

At any rate, people who are intellectual failures are often more popular with classmates than those who are intellectual successes. The children who work hard to succeed at their studies have a hard time understanding this. Their parents praise them for their achievements, and so do their teachers; it baffles them when their peers are unhappy with them for the same reason.

Ernest S. recalls the trouble he had as a good student,

usually from boys who were academically inferior but athletically superior to him:

> I was constantly accosted by bullying types who were getting even for my modest academic success. If I got a better score on a test than they did, they would take it out on me on the football field by running into me, tripping me, or pommeling me when I got the ball — which they saw that I did. Once, in the sixth grade, we had just received our report cards before school was dismissed for the day. One of the tough guys in the class came up to me and wanted to see my card. I didn't want to show it to him, but he insisted. When he saw it, he belted me hard in the stomach and ran on down the stairs. I folded up in pain, it hurt so bad.

Bullying

Brutalization of this sort is one of the most painful memories many children have of their grade-school lives. Children who are physically smaller than others, or who are keenly afraid of being hurt, seem naturally to attract trouble from their larger or more demonstrative peers.

"I lived in mortal fear," confesses an adult who is now an English teacher in a junior high school. "I couldn't stand combat, and the other kids seemed to be able to smell it on me or something. They picked on me constantly. I think I cried at least once every day until I was in the fifth or sixth grade. They pushed me, shoved me, knocked me down, stepped on me, ran into me, slugged me, threw rocks at me, everything. Now, when I see a child being mistreated, all those old feelings flood back in on me, and I almost feel nauseated all over again. It's a terrible experience!"

An abhorrence of violence, which is pronounced in some children, becomes intensified when they must cope with larger and older schoolmates. The teacher cited above elaborated on this:

> The worst problems I had were with the fallbacks — the perennial failures who were not passed on from grade to grade at the normal pace. By the time I was in fifth grade, there were three or four boys in the class who were two or three years older than I was. When I was in the eighth grade, there were three who were sixteen and ready to quit school at the end of the year. They were grown men compared to me — tall, muscular, and tough. I saw one of them in a fight with a male teacher once — a big, tough teacher — and he picked the teacher up bodily and slammed him on the floor. I didn't see this, but one of them, one day, backed a teacher into the corner of the laboratory in a science class and pulled out a penknife and, holding the teacher's necktie up high so it almost choked the teacher, cut the tie off just past the knot. I tell you, it was pure hell going to school with kids like that. They terrorized me and a few of the other kids. I was relieved when I finally got to high school and most of them dropped out of school. They didn't care what they did to you. They were rough!

In many students' minds, busing to produce racial integration is associated with violence. Ghetto children have often been raised differently from those in more fortunate environments. With both parents working, they have grown up with many children competing in a highly charged atmosphere. They are physically more self-confident and aggressive than most other children. This in itself poses a considerable threat to the other students, especially the males, whose machismo is at stake. The racial situation further complicates the busing problem. Black or Spanish children often band together against the whites, or vice versa. White children usually suffer the greater fear from such racial encounters. Of twenty white sixth-graders I interviewed in an integrated school, only two said they were ever bullied by other white children, while sixteen admitted being afraid of specific black children who had threatened, jostled, or otherwise had personal conflict with them. Of twenty black children in the same grade of the same school, twelve admitted being afraid of other blacks but none said he was afraid of a white child.

White children unaccustomed to the rough-and-tumble of life are often at a loss in coping with the more aggressive blacks. For example, Andy R. is a quiet, sensitive white student 13 years old. He enjoys poetry and music, and often spends his allowance to purchase records. When he carried a record to school one day to share it with a favorite teacher, a black student grabbed it away from him. Andy protested and tried to recover the record. The boy held it away with one hand while grasping Andy by the neck with the other hand and slamming him against a locker. Frightened, but determined to recover his record, Andy went to the principal. The principal called the black youth in and confronted him with Andy's charge. The black student promised to return the record, and the principal released him to go with Andy to get it. Once they were out of sight of the principal, the black student pulled a knife from his pocket and told Andy he would slit his throat if another word was said about the record, either to him or anyone else. Horrified, Andy abandoned his attempt to recover his property. A few months later, haunted by nightmares and anxieties, the child had to be given psychiatric treatment. His background had simply not prepared him for dealing with physical violence the way the black youth's had.

Parents and teachers seldom realize how much emotional energy may be required of children in a hostile, unpleasant environment. Silverstein and Krate, in their study of ghetto youngsters, cite a distinction developed by Jerome Bruner between "coping" and "defending." "Coping" has to do with finding a solution to a problem; "defending" refers to the invention of strategies for avoiding stressful situations that involve personal danger or humiliation. Children who have had distressing experiences with other children usually deploy the energies needed for exploration and problem-solving (coping) into defensive postures, constantly scanning the environment for potential threats and attacks. For many Harlem children, accustomed to continuous ridicule and physical punishment, say Silverstein and Krate, the constant perceptual alertness required to defend themselves makes coping with schoolwork almost impossible.[3] It does not take much imagination to transfer the insights of this conclusion to situations in every neighborhood school, or to guess at the loneliness and terror many children experience in unfriendly environments.

Nor do children soon forget their experiences with threatening behavior.

I talked recently with a man who had just come from seeing a one-act play that focused on irrational violence. He did not remember the name of the play or the author, but described the action in great detail. It was about a timid young university student who had gone upstairs to ask the tenants there to please hold down the noise in their apartment because he was studying for exams. The two men in the apartment behaved at first rudely and then violently toward him, refusing to let him leave their apartment. The man who had seen the play said he was very upset by it, and, had he not been with friends, would have gotten up and left in the course of it.

> You see, it brought back all these horrible memories I have of the violence I constantly perceived around me in grammar school. I relived my childhood terror in that theater — all the pushing and poking, the malevolent teasing, the barely restrained violence. It was awful! I saw in those two characters who were torturing that boy all the brutes that had tortured me during my early years — the mindless, persistent needling and discomfiting that went on. I hadn't forgotten any of it. It was all present to me right there in the theater. I didn't think I could last to the end.

I have heard other adults say they have similar experiences when they see violent scenes in plays or movies. One person told me he felt twinges of an old nausea when he saw Edward Albee's *Zoo Story,* which features a fight between a mild-mannered man and an irrational, aggressive man who intrudes upon his lunchbreak on a park bench. Another says he gets playbacks of childhood ruffians in his nightmares, even though he is now a successful businessman in his late forties. Still another confessed he had to switch off a TV movie about a family on a camping trip that was menaced by a gang of motorcycle thugs carrying knives. "It was too close to where I once lived," he said.

Children seldom report their school terrors to their parents, for fear the parents will think them cowardly or chide them for not standing up to the bullies. One eighth-grade boy told me he did not dare tell his parents he had troubles with other boys; once his father had demanded that he stand up to the toughest boy and hit him in the face, but he did not have the nerve to do it, so his father had whipped him and told him he must choose between the lesser of two evils.

Language and Sexual Initiation

Many children are repelled by abusive or obscene language, and find themselves isolated from other children by their refusal to talk "dirty." Some object to it on moral grounds, having been taught that it is either impolite or wrong to speak crassly. For others it is a matter of sensitivity, as it was for Alyosha Karamazov, of whom Dostoevsky wrote that he could not bear to hear "certain words and certain conversation about women" and would stop his ears whenever anyone around him began to use vile or vituperative speech.

Mark S., a twelve-year-old, says he does not like to go to the toilet in his school because it is there that the boys use foul language. "Sometimes," he says, "they write the words on the wall, and draw terrible pictures, and they make me ashamed." Mark will not repeat the words he has heard or seen, but he will spell them if prevailed upon to do so. He blushes even to do that.

Girls apparently use profanity and obscenities as freely as boys. Shelley P., a college student, recalls: "We thought it was the 'in' thing to do, I suppose. It didn't seem especially wrong — just a way of talking. Some of the girls didn't like it. That made us worse, I suppose. We really blasted them with some shockers then." Did they talk the same way around the boys? "Yes," says Shelley, "a lot of the time. It gave you a sort of intimacy feeling, you know. As if you belonged."

Jane D., a housewife, was unhappy with such language. "It made you feel dirty just to hear it," she says. "I didn't like to be around it. A lot of girls talked that way, but they weren't usually so bad if they knew you didn't like it. Some of them, anyway. Some were actually worse, I think, because they resented you."

Phillip M., a high school sophomore, says he deplores such talk especially when there are girls around. Asked if he has old-fashioned ideals of feminine purity, he replied: "Maybe, I don't know. I just don't like it. It doesn't seem right for girls to hear such things. It embarrasses me for them to have to listen to it."

The baiting of children with an aversion to dirty talk often takes the form of sexual allusions, producing in them an acute sense of embarrassment and humiliation. A junior high teacher told me that she had had problems with a small group of girls in her class who enjoyed teasing two or three sensitive boys in this manner. They would get a boy off by himself, say in the hall or the lunchroom, surround him, and begin using highly suggestive language, causing him to blush or to break away and seek refuge in the boys' restroom or elsewhere. Once the teacher had had a long talk with one of the girls and had learned that some of the language was not only suggestive but scurrilous. The girls merely laughed about it, apparently enjoying the tormented reactions of the boys.

A psychologist said he had spent several counseling sessions with an eighth-grade boy, during which the topic of other students' sexual knowledge and language had come up. The boy confessed he was always embarrassed by the words used by some of his peers. They knew this, he said, and often employed the words merely to see his response. One episode had bothered the boy more than others. Another boy in his class, sitting by him in study hall, had begun teasing him about how little he knew about sexual relations. He had pretended not to pay attention, but the boy had persisted in talking about it. "Have you ever seen a girl's thing?" the boy asked. The boy had placed a pencil in the bend of his arm, clamping his arm over it so that the point showed in the lip of the flesh. "That's what it looks like," he said. "It's like a slit with this little red thing that keeps darting out." At this, the boy made the pencil point move in and out. The boy being counseled was disturbed by this image, said the psychologist. He didn't know very much about sexual matters, and it bothered him to hear this inaccurate report from an apparently knowledgable classmate.

As in the cases of children who do not do well in athletics, peers tend to pick on children who are sexually less experienced than they. They often delight in the embarrassment they are able to produce.

Thomas Kochman, Roger Abrahams, William Labov, and other students of the black experience have written about the verbal phenomenon known as "sounding" or "playing the dozens" among black children, primarily boys, in schools and on the streets.[4] It consists of the hurling of obscene insults, often in an exchange of mounting fury, and normally centering on the opponents' mothers. One boy may begin by saying he has had intercourse with the other boy's mother; the second may speak of the dozen men he has seen going into the first boy's house when the father was away;

the first may reply that he saw the second's mother being mounted by an elephant; and so on. The more scandalous and shocking the accusation, the more likely the insulter is to provoke his opponent into overt physical reaction or into an exclamation of defeat.

Sensitive children become highly distraught in the presence of "dozens" players, and are frequently reduced to tears when the attack is aimed at them.

A Curriculum of Caring

Must children behave so cruelly to other children? Not always. Some children really befriend others, and help them to make it through difficult times of adjustment.

In Bruno Bettelheim's story of kibbutz life, *Children of the Dream,* he notes the unusual harmony with which children work and play together in Israeli farm communities. Removed from their parents' care while they are still infants, they think of their peers as their family, their ordained social matrix, and treat their peers as brothers and sisters. Bettelheim says he did not see a single case of bullying in the kibbutzim. When the children are small, weaker ones occasionally get knocked over by the larger ones, but never intentionally; and, when they are, larger ones always go to their aid, helping them up and steadying them. By the time they are toddlers, says Bettelheim, the children are comrades, not competitors.

> If one is stronger, he will use and occasionally misuse his strength, but not for long. Very soon the group spirit asserts itself, and he feels the disapproval and desists. The spirit of helpfulness among them is much more evident than the desire for dominance. Since there are no parents around for whom to vie, and since the competitive spirit is frowned on, the push is towards acting like brothers and sisters, where the stronger one exerts some controlling influence, but also feels called on to use it in the interests of his brothers and sisters.[5]

What the children learn at an early age, in the absence of parents, is the act of caring for one another in a thoughtful, responsible manner. This is precisely what is missing in most American education, whose stiff emphasis on tests, grades, and achievement individuates children instead of incorporating them, makes rivals of them instead of interresponsive citizens.

Perhaps what is needed in our schools is an additional kind of emphasis — what Urie Bronfenbrenner calls a "curriculum of caring" — in which children are taught the importance and benefits of being tender and kind to one another. It is surely a matter as important as any they have to learn. They could be shown through textbooks, film strips, and role playing how much more productive and harmonious life is when people are sensitive to the feelings of others. The example of the kibbutzim shows that children are capable of genuine caring. Maybe all they need is some guidance in that direction. The result could be startling. They might even transform the entire educational system, with its impersonal emphasis on individual mastery of basic data, into a matrix of loving relationships. At the very least, they would discover that caring is a significant antidote to loneliness and fear.

6

The Kingdom of the Jocks

I knew that sports is big business in America, but I did not realize how fully it had pervaded the lower schools of the nation until the night I attended a junior high athletic banquet with my son. My son was in a private school with an excellent reputation for academic studies. I suppose I knew it had a rather tough physical education program, requiring fourth-graders and up to suit out for football, but I had digested that as part of the "sound mind in a sound body" approach of the school and had not reflected at all on the real place sports occupied in the hierarchy of values.

Suddenly, at the banquet, I saw that despite what the brochures said about scholastic emphasis, the school was really consumed by a locker-room mentality. Every male teacher doubled as a coach in at least one sport. Some handled two or three. As they made speeches and presented awards throughout the evening, it became abundantly clear that they all viewed the students in terms of athletic performance. Not just that evening, but all the time. They obviously *liked* the outstanding athletes better than they liked the other students. My son, who was great at singles sports like tennis and swimming but had an optical problem and had never liked contact sports, was *nowhere* in their eyes. Worse, I feared as I sat through the evening, he was nowhere in his own eyes. How teachers think about students, after all, usually becomes how students think about themselves.

When the headmaster stood to make a speech, I expected some sobering remarks about how important it was that the night's winners were more than mere athletes, they were intelligent young citizens with a maturing grasp of philosophy, art, and history. But these remarks never came. Instead, it was all gridiron, arena, and "How-we-socked-it-to-them" talk.

I looked around the big hall at the other fathers and their sons and daughters. Bankers, insurance executives, brokers, lawyers, corporation men — they were all beaming like a bunch of college sophomores, basking cheerily in the afterglow of their own athletic careers, dreaming of second glory through their children. When the headmaster talked about the character-building aspect of hard athletic contests, they looked positively reverent and spiritual.

As we walked home that night, I felt sad for my son. He had never complained about the emphasis on athletics in his school. He probably didn't realize he had the right to complain. It was just the way things were. But I knew how he felt about organized sports. He had spent the first year of required football scrimmage in quiet agony, trying to keep his breakfast down.

I determined to keep an eye on the way things worked at the school. It was too late to pull my son out; he would be leaving for another school the next year anyway; and our second son was a natural competitor who loved contact sports; he would be all right. I watched the teachers' selections of students to be prize-winners at the annual commencement services; they were invariably outstanding athletes. I watched the way students related to one another at school fairs, at evening events like plays and musicals, and on the school ground after hours; it was the athletes who were most popular. I listened to the teachers and administrators talking about the school and students; they always smiled when they mentioned the successful athletes.

I talked to the athletes. Most of them were nice kids

— modest, happy, and self-confident. I talked to non-athletes. They were nice kids too, often with better personalities and quicker minds than many of the athletes. But something happened to them when the athletes were mentioned. It was as if a blush of uncertainty clouded their faces for a moment. Then they would smile and say something nice about the athletes. I could tell they were conditioned to think the athletes were the most important people in their school.

God, I thought. If it's this bad in a private school that brags about being an educational institution, what must it be like in the public schools, where there is academically less to be proud of?

I had to readjust my thinking, to refocus, to remember what a jock nation ours is. Muhammed Ali fights drew purses of $5,000,000, more than ten times the amount the average schoolteacher earns in a lifetime. Dallas Cowboy games outpoll serious dramatic and musical programs on TV by at least six to one. The average city newspaper spends five times as much on sports reporting as it spends on cultural coverage, including book reviewing. Universities lay out more money for sports arenas and athletic budgeting than they do on arts, humanities, and, in some cases, even the sciences. The typical person attending the Indianapolis 500 will drive more than 250 miles one way to get there, then camp outside the speedway in order to be sure of getting in. Jack Nicklaus will draw a bigger crowd any day of the week than the Secretary-General of the U.N., the Chief Justice of the Supreme Court, and the top executive of the Boy Scouts of America combined, and probably even more than the President of the United States. Joe Namath was paid more for plugging Pantyhose than most U.S. mayors, congressmen, and university presidents earn in a year. Our culture is unabashedly pro-athletic.

What chance is there for a kid who isn't athletically inclined?

The Fact of the Non-Athletic Child

I sat at a football game recently and watched a paraplegic child. He appeared to be about 15 years old. His father and mother wheeled him along the sideline to the bleacher aisle on the 40-yard line. Then the father picked him up and took him into the stands while the mother carried the chair. The chair was re-erected on an aisle platform about three-fourths of the way up, and the child set back in it.

As I watched, the boy's face was alternately sunny and gloomy. Whenever there was excitement in the stadium, it lit up with animation. He cheered when others cheered, and was happy when the home team was galloping downfield with the ball. He had a small cowbell, and rang it whenever there was any great outburst from the crowd. Bless his heart, he was participating as fully as he possibly could in the winning of that ball game.

But I wondered about the gloomy times, when his face would go slack and dead, and a great sorrow seemed to sit upon him. Was it simply his "at rest" pose, the mask of mortality we all wear when there isn't anything happening to animate us? I feared it was far more than that. I imagined the boy was dreaming, in those slack times, about himself as an athlete, taking the ball from center and crashing through the line, or, intercepting some long pass, running back with it through a field full of hostile players until he finally crossed the goal line, holding the prized ball high in the air. And the gloom, the sadness, was for the realization that he could never do anything like that because he was an invalid.

The paraplegic boy was an extreme case, of course. But there are millions of children with sound limbs who will never be able to race triumphantly down a gridiron gauntlet any more than he could, for they are not superbly coordinated and gifted with speed and athletic prowess. They are

113

simple, ordinary children who manage to walk and skip and ride bicycles and stand up on roller skates and ice skates but who lack that *extra* ability required to become real athletes, that added adrenalin it takes to be winners in the arena. They too daydream about winning games and snatching sudden victory from the jaws of defeat and being applauded and carried on teammates' shoulders but they will never do it because they are earthbound and that heaven is too far away from their talents and abilities.

There are children with one leg shorter than the other, children with twisted hips, children with weight problems, children with weak eyes, children with bad muscles, children with trick knees, children who are too short, children who don't weigh enough, children who get pains in their sides when they run — in short, there are simply a lot of non-athletic children.

Imagine what they feel like in a world where the athlete is exalted as the ideal person and society is structured around that idealization.

It may be an exaggeration to say that society is structured around an athletic motif — not all physical education teachers are frustrated coaches who want to turn the daily P.E. period into a training time for future gladiators, and not even all coaches are fanatically committed to producing winning teams. I know two or three high school coaches who still insist on playing as many youngsters as possible in every game, despite the effect on the scoreboard, and one or two P.E. teachers who work as hard with the non-athletically inclined students as with the class stars.

But by and large the athletic emphasis in American schools *is* on the high-visibility performance sports, and little consideration is given to the real physical fitness of the students who are less-than-average performers. Instead of accepting these weak performers where they are and trying to engage them in a form of sports activity that will appeal to them and lead to a permanent body-building program, there is a tendency to shame them and punish them, causing them to despise physical activity and turn away from it for the rest of their lives.

Richard Y. is an example. Richard is a seventh-grader. He is a quiet, introverted boy who has been raised with a younger sister in a suburban neighborhood where he has had no male friends and has had little real sports experience. He is pale, slightly overweight, and an awkward runner. He tries to participate in the athletic games at school, but is almost invariably one of the poorest players. When the boys choose up sides, he is one of the last chosen. If he ever gets the ball in football, he is immediately tackled and usually fumbles. If he gets it in basketball, he stands glued to the spot, afraid to dribble, pass, or shoot; usually someone knocks the ball out of his hands and the other team gets possession. In baseball, he is easily struck out, and batters try to knock the ball in his direction, confident that he will miss it.

Instead of accepting Richard's ineptness and working with him to improve his ability, the coach becomes angry and scolds him. Often, during football season, Richard can be seen wearily chuffing around the perimeter of the field, doing laps assigned because he missed a ball or failed to tackle a player. He hates football, his mother says, and can hardly wait for the season to end. Little wonder. For him it is a time of humiliation and punishment, as if he had done something reprehensible, like cheating or stealing.

Girls are not exempt from expectations either. Mildred G. is a high school student. Her phys ed instructor is a tough, masculine-looking woman who expects skilled performance from all her students. But Mildred is not well coordinated and there are certain things she is plainly afraid of on the field and in the gym. One is turning a flip. In the winter, when the class was learning gymnastics, Mildred could not find the confidence necessary to leap off the springboard. The instructor became irate:

> She said if I didn't turn a flip and do it right then she would give me an F in the course. That scared me, and I

tried. I ran up to the springboard but I couldn't do it. I couldn't make myself. It didn't matter what she did to me, I couldn't do it. I told my mother and she said to go to the principal about it, which I did, and he said he would see that she didn't flunk me. But I did get a D.

Allan R. is a freshman in high school. An only child, he has been overprotected by an anxious mother. His father, a railroad engineer, is away from home for days at a time. Consequently he has not grown up as a robust young man, but is tender, sensitive, and, according to other boys in his age group, a bit of a sissy. On a rainy day when the gym classes could not go outdoors, the instructor, who is also the head football coach of the school, decided to have the boys engage in a boxing tournament. Pairing them off, he put the heavy gloves on them, one couple at a time, had the other boys form a ring around them, and instructed them to "slug it out" for three minutes. Allan was frightened. He had to leave his thick glasses off, and could not see clearly. He was matched against a boy smaller than he, but one who was every inch a boy. Stoically, when his turn came, he put his gloves up. "Go to it," said the coach. Allan tried to cover his face with the gloves and his stomach and chest with his arms. His opponent waded in ferociously, slugging hard. The boys laughed and cheered. "Get 'im!" they shouted as Allan crouched and turned, trying to avoid the blows. "Stand up and fight!" the coach yelled at him. In less than a minute, Allan collapsed to the floor, feigning injury. He felt scared, humiliated, overwhelmed, deserted. The other boys were whooping and laughing. Allan saw the coach laughing too. The next day he had his mother write a note excusing him from P.E. because of a sprained wrist. Actually, he was too embarrassed to go back. It was Friday, and he wanted the weekend to elapse before facing his classmates and the coach again.

Is it possible for us to extol sports and games as an

important part of children's educational experience without expecting all students to do well in them?

The Lingering Effects of Failure

James S. Coleman, author of *The Adolescent Society*,[1] asked hundreds of high school boys and girls to name the students in their schools they would most like to be friends with. Top athletes clearly led the polls, with other students trailing far behind. Athletes received nearly twice as many nominations as scholars, and seven times as many nominations as ordinary students. Athletes were also perceived as being seven and a half times as popular with girls as ordinary males!

Growing up in this kind of ethos, young people who cannot achieve success in athletic contests often come to think of themselves as perennial failures. This is particularly true of boys, to whom gladiatorial images continue to cling despite the movement in recent years to open more strenuous sports events to women and sanction gentler, traditionally feminine qualities in men.

"During my freshman year in high school," writes a college boy who came from a small town, "all the guys in my class tried out for the basketball team. There were six boys in the class and all of them except me made the squad. This was a crushing moment in my life. I remember feeling that if there was any way possible, I would never go back to school again. The peer pressure to be a jock was tremendous. I was the ninety-seven-pound weakling among all the superstars. I developed a deep-rooted inferiority complex that I have never been able to overcome."

"The most traumatic, life-changing event in my life," says another student, "was my failure to make the junior high football team. We had just moved to Florida from a small town in New York where my older brother was the captain and star of the team. My family bragged to everybody that I was even better than he was. I went to opening practice a bit concerned about whether I could pull down a permanent slot on the first team. Ironically, I did not make the first team *or* the last. The first week of practice, I and four other guys were cut from the team. I cried all the way home. I remember waking up in the night, crying. I have never gotten over that experience. It haunts me today. I live in mortal fear that I will fail at whatever I undertake."

The "six-million-dollar man" and the "bionic woman," says Neil Isaacs in his book *Jock Culture, U.S.A.*, are the appropriate symbols of our sports-conscious society. They are appreciated not for what they are but for what they do. In every episode, they manage to demonstrate that they can run faster, jump higher, throw farther, and lift or bend or push or break more grandly than any other human beings. With an unerring grasp of the American pulse, says Isaacs, the authors of these programs have created the ideal heroes for a sports-minded society. They have given us a true measure of our dreams and values, statistical champions who embody the qualities of brawn and force we respect above everything else.[2]

It is no wonder that the ninety-seven-pound weaklings go through life with an abiding sense of failure and disappointment, willing to trade everything they have, if a Faustian bargain could be struck, for some minor glory in the arena or on the athletic field.

The Pressures on the Athletes

Sometimes it is the athletically gifted children who are driven and punished. Coaches who find themselves with potential stars on their teams often push the children relentlessly, fearful that they will not extract all they can from them. A junior-high school coach told me this:

> I don't like to run a kid for more than he's worth, but neither do I like to let him off for less than he's worth.

It reflects on me if I do. I work under the high school coach. If I have a boy who's good and I don't get the stuff out of him and he goes under the head coach, the head coach will know it, and it's my shirt he's after. He wants these kids ready when they get into their freshman year. It's my job to see they're ready.

Parents are often harder on the children than the coaches are. Billy R., for example, is a promising young ball handler in almost every sport he plays. He is small, however, and now, in the eighth grade, many of the boys outweigh him by several important pounds. Billy's father and mother are both sports fanatics, and are anxious for him to succeed in team sports. From the time he was in fourth grade they pushed him in football, but now that he is lagging behind in size they have begun to concentrate on basketball and baseball. The father often comes to school with Billy late in the afternoon and on Saturdays to drill him in layups on the basketball court or to let him practice pitching and hitting on the baseball diamond. He shouts constantly and sometimes curses if he is displeased with the way Billy responds. Billy doggedly tries to obey. He is a capable player, and often performs extremely well. But he seldom looks happy. I suspect that he will give up sports altogether when he is old enough to declare his independence.

At ball games, Billy's father and mother are always conspicuous rooters. They yell and shout instructions through every game, and are off the sidelines at the slightest hint of an unjust decision from the referee. Billy never says anything. His teammates grin about it, and one suspects that Billy suffers a great deal of embarrassment, but he doesn't let on. Once, at a basketball game, the referee refused to let the game go on until the father left the gymnasium.

James Michener, in his delightful book *Sports in America,* has described a similar case of parental devotion. Someone had taken him to see the midget car races at a track near his home in Doylestown, Pennsylvania. He watched a daredevil young driver known as the Red Baron whipping his car in and out like a professional on the way to winning a silver trophy. A woman sitting next to Michener was hollering, "Look at him go! Keep hittin' 'em, Roger!" Michener turned to her and asked, "How old is that child?" The woman was the boy's mother. She said he was five. Michener watched in amazement as the boy coolly guided his speedy little car through the maze of other cars toward the final triumph.

Investigation revealed that several of the woman's children were in racing. Besides Roger, there was an older brother and an older sister. The father had a special trailer in which he pulled their cars to races all over the eastern United States. It had a sign on it that said "The Fighting Rigsbys." "Where there's cups to be won, we go," said the mother.

Each car was specially tuned for its individual driver.

Michener asked how much they cost.

"We use a special Japanese quarter-horsepower engine," said the mother. "Our cars cost about eighteen hundred dollars each, but with 'em we win."

She said they were buying a fourth car the next week. Michener asked who for. She pointed to a blond-headed little girl sitting nearby. "Fleurette." Fleurette was barely four. She was a quiet, dreamy-faced little girl who hardly spoke in sentences. Yet she was going to be piloting a race car.

"You gotta start 'em young," said the mother.

It was no wonder Roger was winning his race, Michener thought, and driving all the other little boys into the bales of hay that marked the track. He was already a professional. At five years old, his mother and father had disciplined him to be a hardened little track eater. The other kids were only amateurs. They didn't stand a chance against such parental devotion.[3]

I have a friend who is an ardent basketball player. He also plays tennis, but basketball is the game he loves and lives — has lived, in fact, since his own days as a high school star. He has four children — three daughters and a son. He could hardly wait for the son to become old enough to dribble a ball and shoot baskets. But when his son was ten years old he fell off a shed roof and had a concussion. The brain damage was slight, but it did impair the boy's coordination. When he was able to play basketball again, it was evident that there was a split-second's hesitation between his receiving the ball and his decision about what to do with it. The split-second was too much. He had lost his edge as a ball player. The father was heartbroken. His dreams of a great ball-player had been smashed. Then he noted that his youngest daughter was becoming a natural athlete. He began taking her to the school court with him in the evenings and on Saturday, and working out faithfully. As she showed more and more promise, he spent more and more time with her. He left the son behind. After all, the boy would only slow them down. He brags of the daughter constantly. The son is never mentioned. The fulfillment is in the daughter.

I have watched the two of them on the court. The father is relentless, even merciless. Sometimes, in a game, he seems to be enjoying himself. But he is still all business. If the daughter makes a bad move, a mistake, he corrects her and lectures her at once. He says he is helping her. It sounds like nagging. Nagging all the time.

Stories are legion now about the interference of parents in Little League baseball games and Pop Warner football contests. They run out on a playing area, shout at the umpires, curse the opponents, and slap their own children when the children make mistakes. The poor youngsters are bewildered. Instead of playing games like normal, healthy children, they are fighting for their lives, for the honor of their parents, for peace with the adults who tyrannize them. They are at the mercy of the Golden Dream.

The Golden Dream

The Golden Dream is of the superathlete, the decathlon winner, the indomitable gladiator, the gridiron hero, the young Ty Cobb or Don Meredith or Wilt Chamberlain. That is who the parents hope they are raising, who the coach hopes he is training. It is the idealization of the athlete as consummate humanity that haunts little children barely able to hold a Louisville Slugger or hoist a basketball up to the rim. It is a dream afflicting — and skewing — the entire society.

Michener was a basketball player when he was young, and his high school team won a championship. He recalls the great moment at the end of one game when he hooked an impossibly long ball just as the final buzzer sounded and it went through the net, winning the game. That Saturday he spent the day going around town explaining how he made the unbelievable shot and hearing men say that the whole town was proud of him. He needed the experience of acceptance, he says, and found it wonderfully heady.

But he adds this somber note:

> It was remarkable, I now realize, that during those years of athletic achievement in high school I was also earning straight A's in my classwork but I cannot recall a single instance in which any member of my community gave me any accolades for such accomplishment. In Doylestown, in those days, all that mattered was sports, and even today across America things are not much different.[4]

The same might be said about kindness, caring, citizenship, artistry, or a dozen other qualities and achievements of young people. It is athletics that takes the spotlight.

"I don't know why we don't have a better hall to practice in," I overheard a young girl with an oboe saying one Saturday afternoon when the Junior Symphony in our city was meeting for practice. She was referring to the abandoned church building that had been partially renovated as a practice hall. It was furnished with a few folding chairs and nothing else.

As the girl made the remark, she was looking disgustedly across the parking lot toward the university stadium, where the first preliminary noises of a football game were beginning to be heard. From where she was standing, she could just make out the top of the McGugin Athletic Center, a new facility ostensibly erected for the university community but, as everyone knew — certainly the students and faculty — put up as an added inducement to ballplayers the university was trying to recruit. It had all the latest equipment, including expensive whirlpool baths, ultrasonic therapy machines, and a Nautilus shoulder exerciser, besides a number of handball courts, squash courts, and the usual gymnasium and sauna facilities.

I remember Barney Adams, the sharpest all-round athlete in our high school when I was there. He had a falling-away hook shot in basketball that was the nemesis of every team we played. It was a great shot because nobody could block it, and he hit more than fifty percent of his attempts during his best season, a phenomenal record. In both his junior and senior years, Barney was on the all-district, all-region, and all-state teams, and the town, not to say the school, idolized him.

The thing about Barney was how dumb he was. He couldn't learn anything. The English literature teacher used to ask him questions just for a laugh. He was the only student I know who ever graduated from our high school unable to name even five of the eight parts of speech. He simply could not learn them. But he graduated. A lot of brighter people didn't, but Barney did. The teachers saw that he did. He was never detained for want of grades. He was a hero, and heroes have to be made respectable.

Barney went on to the state university, where the word was he had a full scholarship to play basketball. But apparently not even the excellent array of tutors the university maintained for its jocks could get Barney to pass his courses, and he flunked out at the end of one year without ever getting his name in the papers. I heard that he went to Florida to play for some junior college there that was hot to build a big team, but then there was never any more news from him. He just faded away.

I'm glad Barney had what he had while he was in our school. If he hadn't had that, he wouldn't have had anything in life. But the point is that there were a lot of kids much better rounded than Barney, more intelligent and certainly more wholesome members of the community, who didn't have as much as Barney had because the cultural perspective of the school and the community dictated that non-athletic youngsters receive practically no attention at all. One young man who was a whiz at mathematics never once got his name in the papers for anything, as far as I can recall. A girl whose mother died when she was twelve took over the management of the household for her father and three brothers, cooking and cleaning like a grownup, and still made A's and B's in her schoolwork, but never got an ounce of public recognition until she was a sophomore in high school and became, in addition to everything else, the liveliest cheerleader on the school pep squad — and then the recognition was only for her activities as a cheerleader. Another girl who was a superlative musician and played for clubs and churches all over town, selflessly accompanying choirs and soloists and playing at school functions for years, never received public honor for it, and used to grieve that she was not either a majorette or a cheerleader so that she would share a little of the girls' spotlight.

There is the crux of the matter. The child or young person who is not athletic or connected to athletics in at least an ancillary way (team managers, waterboys, cheerleaders, band sponsors) feels overlooked and neglected in our society, and undervalues himself as a person because the community sets an unrealistically high value on the athlete. Practically every adult who has not been an athlete has fantasized about being one, about being the center of attention, about sinking that final dramatic basket or kicking that victory-making field goal. Everyone who has had the chance to play team sports publicly can find consolation in memories of a few good plays or maneuvers, even if he or she was not a big-hero type. But the nonathletic person who never made a team has no golden memories to rekindle, and is prone to recall only the emptiness of going unnoticed, the loneliness of not having public value.

The Message Gets Through

We may say to youngsters that it isn't whether they win or lose but how they play the game, yet nonverbally, in every way possible, from the media glorification of sports heroes to the kind of money spent on successful teams, we are drilling into them the advice of Vince Lombardi that winning is everything.

This philosophy infects every form of sport from Soap Box derbies to the World Series. People are rabid about winners. They quickly desert losers. Coaches with poor seasons are forced to resign. When Bill Battle, the genial basketball mentor of the Tennessee Volunteers, didn't resign after building a great team and then falling on some low seasons, fans burned crosses on his yard and sent threatening notes to his family. The message is effective. It descends to high school coaches and P.E. teachers and eventually to the kids themselves. You're nobody if you're not a winner.

Research has shown that the older they get, the more value children assign to winning in sports and the less value they give to the importance of fairness and honesty.[5] This change is known in the jargon of sports sociologists as "professionalization." That is, as kids grow older, they think more and more like the hustlers who manage big-time sports in this country.

Sports, as Robert Lipsyte says in *SportsWorld,* becomes

inextricably meshed with politics, ethics, child-rearing, war, business, everything they are ever going to do. Young people carry over from the playing field into later life the ideals of being tough, competitive, and shrewd; of gaining revenge for losses; and of subjugating everything else to team effort and the desire to win, win, win![6]

They lose their perspective on play. It is no longer recreation, adding grace and pleasure to life. It becomes a business. To the loneliness of the kids who are not adept at sports, who yearn for the limelight given to others, we must add a kind of moral loneliness that occurs whenever persons are divorced from the centers of their own beings and activities are not engaged in for their own sake.

Perhaps it is all summed up in the words of the thirteen-year-old boy who said: "I think school sports could be great if they would just let us play. I used to enjoy a good softball game when we chose up sides and played for an hour or two. It didn't matter who won. Sometimes you even cheered for somebody on the other team if he got a good hit or caught a hard fly. But it isn't much fun when the coaches organize everything and chew you out for your mistakes. Everything gets too serious, and a lot of kids get nervous and don't do their best. But I guess it's just like everything else. That's the way of the world, as they say, and you have to learn to live in it."

What sad words they are!

7

The Unattractive Child

It is not merely gratuitous that such stories as "The Ugly Duckling" and "The Frog and the Princess" exist in our repertory of fairy tales. They fulfill an urgent fantasy need for people who are less than normally attractive or who at least perceive themselves to be less than good-looking. To dream of becoming a beautiful swan and causing everyone to gasp in admiration, or of being kissed by a delicate princess and turning into a handsome prince, as striking on the outside as wholesome on the inside, is natural for both children and adults who think other people have never found them exciting to behold.

Few people ever have the equanimity about their unfortunate features that was ascribed to Alexander Woollcott, the clever writer who was grossly overweight all his life. During Woollcott's college days, his fraternity was eagerly seeking new pledges and he was anxious to help. His fraternity brothers, fearing that the sight of their portly friend with the uncomely features would have only the opposite effect on prospective plebes, begged him to stay out of sight until rush week was over. Eager to be of service, Woollcott had a bright idea. He put on his dowdiest corduroy suit, went down the street, and perched on the front porch of a rival fraternity house, waving and leering at students as they passed.

For most people, the lack of good looks is one of the most painful facts of life, one they learn early and rarely elude for the remainder of their lives. Eleanor Roosevelt said that she was told by an aunt when she was a very young girl that she was the ugly duckling of the family, and that the hurt of this left her ever after filled with shame for her appearance.

In their naive way, children with plain features often think that if they were only beautiful they would have everything they wanted in life. "If only I looked like Robert Redford," the pimple-faced boy thinks, "then I could make a million dollars." "If I looked like Farrah," says a teen-age girl, "I could have any fellow I want." Looks seem to be the *open sesame* of life, guaranteeing fame, fortune, friendship — everything.

Unfortunately, therefore, children who cannot view themselves as attractive have difficulty conceiving of themselves as being truly successful in life. Even if they are high achievers in school and have significant extracurricular accomplishments, they feel that something is lacking.

Yolanda R., for example, is a talented young cellist. She is always well-groomed and beautifully dressed. Her voice is gentle and well modulated, and carries an interesting hint of the accent she learned from her parents, who were born in Europe. She speaks three languages, is a good conversationalist, and likes people. She has a reasonably nice figure and moves gracefully. Her one physical deficiency is her mouth and chin, which are not quite symmetrical, making her appear to speak slightly out of the side of her mouth, twisting her labial muscles as she does. It is not a pronounced feature, but to Yolanda it is devastating.

"I would give anything to be pretty," she says. "My mouth is so ugly. Why couldn't I have been born dumb and pretty like Erica [her sister]? I would give anything — anything — to have a beautiful face!"

Robert M.'s problem is hair — stiff, wiry, unruly hair that covers his head thickly like a wig of twisted wool. He is so embarrassed by it, his mother says, that he doesn't want to go to school. He has tried every way he knows to make it lie flat against his head — one day he even plastered it down with hair oil — but despairs of finding a solution. At 15, he is interested in girls, but is too ashamed of his appearance to ask one for a date; he knows he will be turned down.

It is easy for adults to be flippant or unthoughtful about children's anxieties over their appearance, but the anxieties are nonetheless real and painful. Some children torment themselves about the unpleasantness of their features until they are completely lacking in self-confidence. Each day is an agony of self-doubt and self-criticism.

"My problem was fat," reminisces Gerald W., a tall, decidedly overweight lawyer. "I can talk about it now, but there was a time when I couldn't mention it. I couldn't stand it when somebody else alluded to it either. We didn't have a mirror in the house I could see all of me in. I used to take my clothes off in the bathroom and try to get back far enough to see myself, but of course I couldn't, and I would be so disgusted that I would slap myself hard on the stomach or the thighs. I remember whimpering like a little puppy, I was so unhappy. I tried to diet, but it was no use. It was part glandular, I've since learned.

"The worst part was my love life. Or, I should say, the lack of it. I never had a date. Once in a while I would screw up my courage to ask somebody, but the response was always so humiliating that I didn't do it often. I used to think, 'God, if I were only skinny! I would give anything in the world to be skinny.' I'd hear this thin person complaining, you know, that he couldn't put on weight, and I'd think, 'You don't know how damned lucky you are.' Miriam is the only girl I ever dated. Seriously, I mean. I really sweated out my proposal to her. I didn't think she'd accept. I mean, being married to a fat slob all her life, and all that."

Another young man, James R., grew out of his overweight problem only to encounter something worse — his face became marred by acne.

"Some people call it acne," he said, "but mine was more like leprosy. My face was a solid sheet of white bursting sores when I was in the tenth grade. Plagued by the fear of rejection, I seldom asked a girl for a date. I thought, why would anybody want to go out with me the way I look? One girl I dated had a younger brother. He was anxious to meet me because of my football reputation. Then he saw me. He screwed up his face and said, 'What's wrong with him?' I tried all kinds of cures, even radium therapy. It was awful."

Few children — perhaps only one-tenth of them — are exempt from doubts and misgivings about their appearance. As one psychologist told me, "Children's deploring how they look is almost universal. Nine out of ten kids I talk to wish they looked like somebody else. It's an epidemic!"

Children with Stigmas

The most unfortunate children of all, of course, are the ones who have physical handicaps associated with unattractiveness, such as skin diseases, prominent birthmarks, crippled or amputated limbs, and proneness to epileptic seizures. These afflictions are burdens to all who have them, but especially to children, who are still trying to measure their acceptance or nonacceptance in their families and in society.

Occasionally we meet handicapped persons whose cheerfulness convinces us that they feel secure in the affections of others despite their handicaps. Once when I was lecturing at a university in Texas I rode to the airport with a student who was a double amputee. I wouldn't have known this if I had not crossed my legs in the car and accidentally struck one of his legs and asked his pardon. "Didn't feel a thing," he said, and tapped on the hollow-sounding leg. In the conversation that followed, he told me the other leg was artificial as well. The student driving the car was his roommate, and they laughed and described how they treated the boy's handicap. "We race across the campus," said the driver; "I spot him fifty yards and then if I catch him I trip him." "He's telling the truth," said the boy; "and when we're coming down the staircase from our room, I have to be careful he doesn't do the same there!" Their relationship was extremely open and wholesome.

"People ask me if I don't grieve about not having two good legs like everybody else," said the student. "I tell them no, because not having my legs has taught me something I probably wouldn't have learned any other way. When I was twelve years old and had to have the legs removed, I found out how deeply my parents loved me. A lot of boys never know that. I also found out how much I could trust other people, how much they cared about me. That has been a rich experience, and I'm still enjoying it."

One only wishes that this marvelous attitude were more widespread. Afflictions often affect people differently, unfortunately, and cause them to become withdrawn and unhappy.

I think about Gail L., 16, whose face was slashed along one cheek by an accident with a wire clothesline, leaving the face slightly disfigured. When she talks to anyone, she turns her face at an angle, trying to hide the injured side. She never smiles or laughs. It is as though her face were plastic and she were afraid it would break if she became animated. The disfigurement has become a veil between her and the world, and she cannot interact freely with her environment.

Or I think about 14-year-old Gary D. who was badly burned in a car wreck. Even the miracle of transplanted skin could not erase all the telltale signs from his ear and neck and shoulders. Once lively and ebullient in conversation, he has become hesitant and fearful, as though terribly uncertain about how other persons are thinking about him and responding to him. The only time he seems to be his old self is when he gets into a game of touch football or basketball and in the heat of playing forgets about himself. But the instant the game is over he withdraws into his cocoon.

Even a temporary condition can be very destructive for a child. A friend told me about his son's going into the hospital for a brain operation. The boy, who was 13, was happy and outgoing, and was able to laugh at himself when they gave him a mirror to see himself after his head had been shaved. But there was another boy on the ward who was undergoing a similar operation and had also had his head shaved, and the boy was so unnerved by his appearance that he lay day and night with his face to the wall, unwilling to look at anyone. Eventually the friend's son was able to cheer him up and get him to laughing by making fun of his own baldness, and the boy became sociable again with the nurses and doctors and his family.

The problem is that we ourselves make value judgments about people's appearances, and therefore know they are making such judgments about us. When something happens to change our appearance we become suddenly confused about things; we do not know any longer how we must be taken by the persons viewing us and talking with us. In the insecurity of our confused emotions, we may flee from all relationships, even those with the people of whom we had been most sure. The whole world has not changed, but we feel that our situation in it has, and that therefore everything is altered for us.

Besides the physical stigmas we have been discussing, there are also certain "stigma symbols" (the phrase is Erving Goffman's) such as eyeglasses, hearing aids, crutches, canes, and dental braces that are deeply embarrassing to some individuals, especially sensitive children.

Beth C. was very farsighted, and feared that her glasses greatly distorted her facial appearance. Although she had worn glasses since she was six, she began, when she was about thirteen, to remove them as she left the house and to try to get through the entire day at school without wearing them. "They made me look hideous," she said, "and I couldn't bear that. It was foolish, I know, but how I looked was very important to me." Later, as more and more of the children began to wear glasses, she became less self-conscious about hers and resumed wearing them, though she said she was never really comfortable with them in the presence of boys.

Parents who dismiss such feelings in their children as mere vanity do not appreciate the magnitude of the personal insecurity they represent. "Now, you wear those glasses and don't pay any attention to what people think of you" can seem the epitome of heartlessness or stupidity to a child still struggling to find his or her identity in the world.

I talked recently with parents whose 14-year-old son had just gone into orthodontist's braces, the kind that involve a trapeze framework out in front of the face, as if the child were all set to do a harmonica act. The boy was naturally shy about having so much hardware in his mouth and around his head, but the parents were wonderfully reassuring. "We know it's hard on Robbie to wear his apparatus," they said in his presence, "but we have told him what it is going to do for him. It's tough now, but he'll be happy with the results in a few months. When the wires come off, he'll be a new person. He'll have to carry a ball bat to beat the girls off!"

The parents understood the boy's concern with his appearance, but appealed to his ability to put up with a present discomfort for a future benefit. They knew the issue precisely — he wanted to look good to the girls — and that was what they were promising.

The important thing to remember is that it is not how children actually look to others that is important, but how they *think* they look. Liv Ullman, the glamorous Scandinavian actress, has said that she felt very ugly when she was a girl growing up, and that it made it very difficult for her to establish relationships with other people. It is almost impossible for us to imagine that she was ever less than magnetically attractive, and her photographs as a girl reveal her to have been very pretty. But the point is that she did not *feel* pretty, and her inner uncertainty inhibited relationships as much as if she had actually been ugly.

Adults should be patient with their children, therefore, when the children express doubts about their appearances. The doubts are real, and will not be brushed away by an "Oh, you are so pretty, you're just fishing for a compliment." Fishing for a compliment, yes. Children often do that. But they do it because they are not certain, and because it matters immensely to them that they appear attractive to others.

The Testimony of Research

Psychological research has in recent years validated the concerns we all feel about the importance of looking good to others. People *do* respond more positively to attractive persons, it shows. Dr. Ellen Berscheid, a professor at the University of Minnesota who has investigated the relationship of personal attractiveness to human behavior, says, "Attractive people are assumed to be kinder, more genuine, sincere, warm, sexually responsive, poised, modest, sociable, sensitive, interesting, strong, more exciting and of better character" than less attractive people.

Dr. Harold Sigall of the University of Maryland has produced evidence to show that good-looking people are usually evaluated as doing better work than people who are less good-looking, even though the accomplishments of both groups are the same. His research has also demonstrated that good-looking adults appearing before judges and magistrates for criminal offenses receive lighter sentences than their less good-looking counterparts.

Professor Thomas Cash of Old Dominion University finds that good-looking people are almost always given preference over unattractive people in hiring practices. The girl who complains that she lost out in the competition for a typing job to a gorgeous blond who could not type ten words a minute is probably right.

Researchers at the University of Wisconsin have shown that teachers favor good-looking students and believe them to be more intelligent than less good-looking students.

And Professor George Allen of the University of Connecticut, in a similar vein, found that mentally retarded children who were physically attractive received more attention from their teachers than children who were not attractive, and were perceived by both teachers and supervisors as being less retarded.

"I understand that," said a teacher with whom I shared these reports. "Last winter I left the class treasury box on my desk while I was out of the room, and two or three dollars in change disappeared from it. Only two girls had been near the desk while I was gone, and I questioned both of them. One is a beautiful little girl named Sandra and the other, whose name is Gina, is only so-so. Both denied taking the money, but I insisted to Gina that she must have taken it. She cried and protested that she had not. Later, Sandra confessed that it was she who took it, and I was astounded. I just couldn't believe that that pretty little thing would have touched something that didn't belong to her."

Studies in adult behavior indicate that people even think more highly of other persons who are in some way *connected* to a beautiful person, even if they themselves are not attractive. Thus, a man who is married to a lovely wife is judged to be smarter than one married to an unattractive woman, and a woman who is seen with a handsome man is thought to be somehow superior to one whose friend is not handsome.

The importance children attach to being pretty or handsome, then, is not entirely misguided. At least in the more superficial relationships that constitute their arena for living, they are correct in thinking that to be good-looking is tantamount to success.

Those Awkward Years

Most children, unfortunately, are entering their least attractive period of life just as they become deeply concerned about appearances. It is in their teen years, when their bodies are growing at an accelerated rate and many of them seem to be all elbows and feet or all teeth and freckles, that the biological urge becomes powerful and they want to look their best for persons of the opposite sex. Nature seems to have played a dirty trick on them, combining these two trends moving in opposite directions.

Arnie M., 15, is an example. Only recently, at a time when he has become concerned about girls, his face has begun to break out in pimples and sores. He has tried everything to conquer them — frequent scrubbing, infrequent scrubbing, pastes, tonics, bromides, squeezers, extractors, buffing paper, prayer — and nothing works. They only get worse as he worries about them. One of the several doctors he has been to told him that this is probably the trouble, his anxiety level is too high, and that they will go away in a few years. Meanwhile, there is nothing to be done about Arnie's anxiety level — the thicker the pimples, the higher it goes, and so on in a vicious circle.

Children often develop, during their adolescent years when this concern for appearances is so great, a new period of shyness reminiscent of and not unconnected to the one they went through when they were babies first becoming acquainted with persons outside the family circle. Shyness can be, after all, a form of defense. As Martin Herbert says, "The shy person fears being attacked in some way, so he tries to defend himself by submissive behavior. His obvious diffidence and tentativeness, his attempts to be almost invisible or to take up as little room or as little of the limelight as possible, communicate the idea that he is not worthy of attack because he is not aggressive, but, rather, helpless and timid. It is difficult to be aggressive towards someone who is shy." [1]

Translated in terms of personal appearance, the shy child feels very insecure about his or her looks, and so submits timidly to the social judgments of others. He or she says, in effect, "You may not like the way I look, therefore I am coming on slowly and gently, subject to your approval. If you do not like me, please be easy on me. I am not very confident of myself."

Social confidence, in such a case, must be relearned. It *will* be relearned if the child's belief in his or her looks is bolstered by confirmation from without. If the confirmation is lacking, however, the child, once bold and aggressive, may now remain shy and withdrawn throughout adulthood.

Henry P. is a sad example. He had a happy, normally aggressive childhood until he was in junior high school. At that time he began to grow at an incredible rate, achieving the physique of a full-grown man before he left the eighth grade. He even developed a very full dark beard, so that, even though he shaved twice a day, his face was always masked in black stubble. The older children teased him about his gigantism, especially when he tried to sit in the small desks in the classrooms of the school. He became very stoop-shouldered, probably in an attempt to look shorter than he was, but he still loomed over his classmates and, in several cases, his teachers as well.

By the time he entered high school, Henry had become extremely shy and withdrawn. He spoke in a very soft voice and seemed to retreat from every social contact he could avoid. Sometime during high school, he met a serious-minded young woman who had quit school after her sixteenth birthday and gone to work in a local department store to help support her widowed mother. The two of them apparently fell in love, or discovered some common need each fulfilled in the other, and Henry married her on the day after he graduated from high school. He was a brilliant student and was particularly keen at electronics, and his teachers supposed he would go on to the university and have a successful future. But marriage made that impossible, as neither he nor his new wife had any money with which to go to school. Henry took a job with the local utilities company and immediately settled down, at the age of seventeen and a half, to the serious responsibilities of married life. His shyness, extreme to a fault, had led to an early avoidance of larger society and the sacrifice of a more promising future.

Other children retreat from normal encounters in other ways. Susan T., a reasonably attractive little girl, developed acne when she was a teen-ager, and was so ashamed of her appearance that she let her hair grow long and drift over her face most of the time. She became withdrawn and acted as if she were not interested in boys. She wore sloppy, ill-fitting clothes, always of male appearance, and took up motor-biking. In her helmet and men's clothing, she could not be detected from the boys as they all gunned their bikes up across open terrain into the hills.

Later, when the acne had finally healed, Susan began to emerge in female clothing, had her hair cut in a page-boy style, and developed a laughing, happy personality again. Her parents were amazed at the change in her, but a psychologist friend explained it very simply: "She doesn't need to hide anymore, does she?"

One young woman, Karla M., joined an order of nuns shortly after graduating from high school. She was a beautiful girl, and people constantly remarked that they could not understand such a lovely person's aspiring to "hide herself away in a nunnery" like that. Her hair was sunny blond, and the hardest thing for people to accept was that she would cut most of it off and install the rest under a nun's bonnet. When Karla left the convent a few years later, a friend asked why she had left. Was she unhappy there? Karla explained that it was really because of all the nice things people had said to her when she joined the convent. "You see, I didn't have any confidence at all in my appearance. I never had had. Then, when everybody seemed so amazed that I would put on a nun's habit and cover myself up, so to speak, I realized for the first time that I didn't have to be ashamed of how I looked. That kept working on me, I think, and finally I had to get out. I felt confident about facing life on my own."

The feedback that came belatedly to Karla was all she

needed to blossom as a person. Children and young people hunger for such feedback. They need to know they look okay. Otherwise, they may slip into cocoons of loneliness for the rest of their lives.

The Real Meaning of Conformity

One way shy, uncertain children manage to hide is by carefully adopting the modes of dress and manners of other children. It is the game of "You Can't See Me, Because I'm Like Everyone Else." Thus Wilma must have a dress just like Sallie's and Mary's and Janie's, and Tom feels a compulsion to wear his hair cut like Jim's and Bill's and Bob's.

Again, it is in the teen years, when youngsters are most insecure about their appearances and how they relate to other persons, that conformity to the styles and behavior of the group becomes *de rigueur.*

The children to pity are the ones who for certain reasons are unable to play the game as everyone else is playing it. They are entitled to feelings of desperation, for not only are they insecure for the usual reasons, they are also insecure because they are left out of the group, exposed in no man's land, as it were — public spectacles with no place to hide.

Take Jamie O. Jamie is not especially good-looking and is painfully aware of this. But unlike some of his classmates who are not good-looking and attempt to deflect attention from this by wearing flashy clothes and mod hair styles, Jamie comes from a poor family and cannot afford either the nice clothes or having his hair styled. He wears suntans and a pair of brogans handed down from an older brother who was in the army. His mother cuts his hair at home and he does not have a blow-dryer to fluff up what is left of it when she has recently given him a cut. In other words, Jamie cannot hide in the look-alike anonymity of his friends; his lack of good looks is, at least in his own mind, more apparent than theirs.

Margaret S. admired her friends' chic raincoats and asked her mother for one. Her old coat was much shorter than the new ones, and was both soiled and frayed. Her mother told her the coat was perfectly all right for the time being and that she could not have another.

"I was so embarrassed by the old coat," she said. "All the other girls' coats were pretty and bright-colored. Mine was tan and dirty. Sometimes I would wear mine almost to school and then I would take it off and roll it up and carry it under my arm with my books so nobody would see it. I'm not that particular now, but then it meant everything to be able to dress like the other kids."

For some identity-conscious teen-agers, a car is an important means of concealing unattractiveness and appearing flashy and debonair. Boys with no means for owning one are often embarrassed by their lack of one, especially around boys who do possess cars. They watch other boys asking girls for dates in their cars, and feel resentful that they cannot do the same. A car is a masculine adornment, a phallic extension, and to be without one is to be deprived of machismo, especially in a mobile culture and a large city where getting around is difficult.

Girls often feel the need for cars too, but not so universally as boys. Many girls, especially the more popular ones, never want for someone to take them where they wish to go — ball games, drive-ins, parties, dances. But some, who do not get asked very often to accompany boys to these places, stress the need for their own transportation, just like the boys.

Alice R. says: "If I hadn't had a car in high school I would have been lost. It was the one thing that made up for not having a steady boy friend. I could swing by Jill's and Rona's house and pick them up and we'd go down to Burger Chef by ourselves and sit there and talk to the boys who drove up in the next alley. We would have been left out if it hadn't been for that."

How Can We Help?

Erik Erikson says that the formation of identity is the chief work of children in the adolescent period. And identity formation depends largely on how adolescents perceive that they are being seen by the world around them. That is, identity is not something arrived at in a vacuum; one does not go off into the wilderness to decide who he or she is. Identity is what emerges from a person's readings of other people's responses to his or her way of looking and behaving and speaking in their midst. It involves feedback and monitoring of the feedback.

There are certain givens in a child's makeup — some inherent and some learned in the family. But personality emerges from the meeting of those givens with other people's personalities and the decision by the child that "That is what I am like, I can see it now." In other words, a confirmation process is occurring all the time the youngster is negotiating with the environment; he is finding out who he is as he goes along, and is accepting or rejecting bits of information that will in the end establish his identity.

In many children the process is a very delicate one. If their early rearing in the family has not already socialized them and given them a fairly strong indication of who they are, they are placing great weight on the feedback they get from persons outside the family, especially their peers and teachers. Naturally eager to be approved by others, they are made unhappy by information that says people are less than enthusiastic about them. If they do not get the kind of care and attention they desire by normal social means, they may even resort to anti-social behavior, on the unspoken theory that the wrong kind of attention is better than none at all. Ideally, what all children seek is confirmation that they are beautiful, good, and intelligent in the eyes of others.

Adults should always remember this and realize what

an important part they can play in helping children shape their self-images along satisfactory lines. It is easy, when they forget, to be destructive to the child, even when destructiveness is not what is intended. For instance, one woman told me that her mother once said to her, "Well, you won't win any beauty contests, but you're a good girl, and I hope some fellow comes along and finds that out. He'll be glad he did. Pretty girls aren't anything but trouble anyway." The mother meant well; she was trying to teach a value lesson to the girl that she believed would compensate for the girl's lack of attractiveness. But the way she phrased her advice was both unkind and unnecessary; she not only gave good advice, she informed her daughter that she was not pretty.

It is not good to lie to children about their appearance. They soon learn if the information from a well-meaning parent is the opposite of what they are learning from other sources, and when they do they will reject that particular piece of information and may even resent its source. But it is important to encourage them within all the boundaries of truthfulness, to set their real qualities in the best light possible, so that they themselves are constantly in touch with the best that is in them. Self-image is often the only guide a child has to his future, and if the self-image he perceives is negative, the future may well be one of rejection, bitterness, and even crime. Teachers are frequently not sensitive enough to this fact, and implant in children they do not like or admire the "encouragement" that sets their feet in the wrong direction. It is a basic rule of humanity that we must feel good about ourselves in order to be good and act wholesomely. Therefore utmost care should be taken by all adults to help children perceive themselves in the best light honestly possible.

Some teachers, notably in California, have been impressed with the encounter movement as a strategy for helping children to deal openly with problems of self-image and projection. A few have reported what they consider to be real success in the use of Thomas Harris's "I'm OK — You're

OK" techniques, where the children are taught Harris's basic rubrics ("I'm OK — You're Not OK"; "I'm Not OK — You're Not OK"; "I'm Not OK — You're OK"; "I'm OK — You're OK") and are helped, in groups, to move from the third position ("I'm Not OK — You're OK"), where many of them are, to the fourth ("I'm OK — You're OK"). Although this method has been assailed by critics who think it is superficial ("It doesn't deal with the deep underlying problems"), I cannot help believing it commendable if for no other reason than that it gets children to verbalize among their peers how they really feel about themselves — their fears, anxieties, desperation, and desires — and permits them to learn that these are not abnormal at all, but are part of every child's mental baggage. Once a child realizes that he or she is not alone in experiencing life as he or she does, but that it is a process whose ways are chartable and explainable with reference to other persons, a lot of the trauma is removed and the child can deal with personal emotions in a more equitable and intelligent manner.

It is incredible that so much research should be done on the psychology of childhood, and so many rich, important books should be written about it (think of Piaget, Erikson, and Bowlby, to name only three outstanding authors), without there being established in the public schools from the third or fourth grades onward seminars and courses in the psychological factors shaping students' lives. Of course knowing how a house is built does not make every person a carpenter, and there is no shortcut to turning every child into a psychologist capable of analyzing his or her own situation. But it does relieve children's inner pressures to understand something of the developmental process by which they respond to their environment and form personalities. Having the language with which to think and speak about the process would enable them to cope with it much more effectively than they can when it is going on as mere subliminal pain and pressure in their existence.

Child care is still evolving from a deplorable kind of

medievalism that persisted strongly in most areas of the world until this century. We are only on the threshold of becoming truly sensitive to the inner needs of children, and to the importance of gentle guidance as they reflect on who they are and how they are related to the world. We have much to learn before we can be more helpful. One place to begin our education is with the child's feelings about the way he or she is perceived by others. These feelings lie close to the heart of personality.

8

Childhood and Mobility

It was 9:30 P.M. and I was sitting in the Dallas-Fort Worth air terminal, waiting for a plane to Nashville. The waiting area was full of milling people. Cigarette smoke hung heavy in the air. Some passengers calmly read books. A few were talking. Two or three were sleeping. I watched a young family of five. The three children were all under six. The youngest was a baby of perhaps six or seven months. The mother laid the baby out on her lap and proceeded to change a disposable diaper. The father, his business suit crumpled from several hours of travel, looked harassed and fatigued as he tried to soothe the oldest child in his arms. The middle child leaned wistfully against the father, sucking her thumb. The boy in the father's arms refused to settle down. He twisted restlessly this way and that.

"I want to go home," he said plaintively but firmly.

"Hush, dear," said the mother, buttoning the sleepsuit on the baby; "we don't live there anymore."

She said it calmly, evenly, without a show of emotion. She was probably accustomed to moving. Her husband, I guessed, was an engineer, a salesman, or possibly a corporate executive. He had been offered a better job at a higher salary with more perks, and all moving expenses thrown in. He had agreed to take it, and here they were, halfway from Los Angeles to Darien or Bakersfield to Albany, making the move in the middle of the night. They got up in one house and would go to bed in another, all the way across the country. Many things would look the same the next morning as they had the morning before — the same three-bedroom split level, same gleaming appliances in the kitchen, same color TV in the den. Yet everything would be different — different people, different stores, different playmates for the children, a different school for the oldest.

They were part of a constant flow of people in the world today. In an average year, between thirty-five and forty *million* people in the United States change their residences. This family was only one ten-millionth of the human cargo movement in our country (children under one year of age are not counted in the totals). It isn't any wonder that demographers — people who keep track of population shifts and relocations — are among the busiest professionals in the nation. Every year since 1948, one out of every five Americans has picked up, moved into a new house or apartment, and started life again.

In 1972, the popular sociologist Vance Packard assembled an impressive array of data about mobility in our country. The average American moves 14 times during his or her life. The annual "disconnect" rate for telephone service in Los Angeles is more than 40 percent. A survey by the National Foundry Association of 141 foundries across America revealed an annual turnover rate among employees of 75 percent. Besides the enormous number of migrant farm workers who move with the crops, there are thousands and thousands of professional athletes, actors, truck drivers, pilots, salespersons, and people in other professions constantly on the move. Even the retirees constitute a major migration force.

Packard called his book *A Nation of Strangers.*[1]

The effects on our lives and culture are enormous. It means we are a nation of nuclear families without extended membership, because only nuclear families can bounce around so freely. Michael Young and Peter Willmott have given an example of what this means in their study of Bethnal Green, an East London tenement project. A small boy in the project came home from school one day and said, "The teacher asked us to draw pictures of our family. I did one of you and Mummy and Mickey and me, but isn't it funny, the others were putting in their nanas and aunties and uncles and all sorts of people like that."[2]

Our high rate of mobility also means that *place* is no longer what it was in our vocabulary, the solid locus of being where we were born, reared, and expected to die. Of 110 high school seniors Packard questioned in Montvale, New Jersey, only two were living in the houses in which they were born.[3] We no longer think the way the Bengalese do, who, according to a doctor who worked in a clinic among them, proudly recite the names of their tiny villages as if everyone in the world knows where they are; for, as the doctor said, to them they are the important hubs of the world. We smile at such naiveté; we have moved so often that it strikes us as medieval or childish. "Never," says Alvin Toffler, commenting on our modern nomadism, "have men's relationships with place been more numerous, fragile and temporary."[4]

The average family in America moves so many times that the very conception of the nature of a home has changed. It is no longer important that a home be good for fifty years, or in many cases even ten years. It does not pay to plant trees that will take years to mature, unless some altruistic homeowner wants to do it for the third or fourth family that will succeed his own. Whole suburbs spring up, blossom, wither, and virtually die in as little as twenty years. There is no human commitment to place, to property, to the land, such as there was for centuries preceding our own. Uniqueness in homes is seldom treasured, because, frankly, it makes them harder to sell. Now a dreary sameness characterizes most houses; people can leave home, move half a continent away, and think they haven't left home at all. Holiday Inns and Howard Johnsons' are part of the whole scheme of self-delusion; every one looks like every other one, so that you can drive six hundred miles a day and stay in a room that looks just like the one you vacated at seven in the morning. All property is expendable and interchangeable. Only the people are different, and the sociologists tell us that living in a world of sameness will eventually affect this as well.

At one level, living in an interchangeable world has made people more open to each other. We settle more quickly into the new apartment buildings and neighborhoods than we once did. In three days' time we have learned the major streets, tried the major department and grocery stores, located a church and the children's schools, and had a quick drink with the neighbors on one side of the house. The Welcome Wagon lady is the Peter Pan of the new society, descending with her wand to make all our contacts swift and to answer all our questions from her notebook of quotable gossip and raving recommendations. Corporate wives are even expected to hold open house no later than the second weekend in their new homes, to prove with fixed smiles and quick-frozen hors d' oeuvre that they are one hundred percent behind their husbands and are ready to go anywhere but the Sahara Desert and the North Pole for the sake of the company and the Dow Jones averages.

But at a deeper level it is a hopelessly superficial way of life, for it does not afford the kind of time — *years and years* of time — that are necessary to become rooted in a place, to really know the neighbors, to truly belong to the community, to celebrate the great milestones of life that can be celebrated in a home church or synagogue, to feel, deeply and responsibly, that there is a bond between ourselves and the land, ourselves and the house, ourselves and the neighborhood, that nourishes and replenishes our beings. Packard was right to call us "a nation of strangers." We do not become friends by shaking hands, having a highball together, and comparing golf scores or travelogues. Any human relationship takes time for seasoning, for testing, for the kind of slow, casual knitting that will not break apart under the first signs of stress or strain. In the old days, one belonged to the place where he lived because his roots grew "thick as hair and entwined as a mat" with the roots of his neighbors and acquaintances; now most of us belong to no place because we are like hothouse vegetables that are fed by injection tubes instead of roots.

What does it do to the children? In a hopeful mood, we say they are becoming a new breed, adapted to living in the atmosphere of a changing society without putting their roots down in any one place. We boast that our offspring have traveled more widely by the time they are six years old than we had by the time we were thirty, and it is true. They speak as casually of taking a summer trip to Antibes or Katmandu as we did of going into the county seat to do the weekly shopping, and they can be found, during any vacation time, lolling by a fountain in Copenhagen, taking photos of the Acropolis, and water-skiing on the Klong of Thailand.

But how does it really affect them as individuals? What does it do to their tender psyches to be moved around as often as many of them are, leaving homes and playmates and schools behind?

One psychiatrist of whom I asked this question took me to a door and told me to look through the glass panel. Inside, a colleague of his was patiently sitting with a boy who appeared to be twelve or thirteen years old. Occasionally the psychologist would say something to the boy. I could not observe the boy responding. "Autistic," said the psychiatrist outside. "Won't talk. Complete withdrawal. Fourteen schools in five years."

The boy's father, I subsequently learned, is an executive with a national baking company. Eager to climb the corporate ladder, he has moved to a new city whenever there has been an opening for which he was suited. For two years he was an overseas trouble shooter; eight of the fourteen moves were during those two years.

For a while, the boy adapted. Then, a year and two schools ago, they noticed that he was tending to withdraw a great deal. He spent a lot of time in his room, and wouldn't sleep without an old toy dog he had had since he was an infant. Three months ago he had drawn the curtain completely, and wouldn't talk. A company psychiatrist had arranged for his treatment in the medical school of the local university. That was where I saw him.

I thought about the little girl in Robert Coles's story of migrant workers' children, whose mother said they were riding along one day and the girl began crying in the back seat. She was crying because they didn't have a house to live in, the way other people did, and because their lives seemed hard.[5]

I had felt sorry for the girl at the time I read about her, but I had thought as little as possible about the plight of the migrants' children because they were a special group, caught in an unfortunate socioeconomic situation. When I looked through the glass panel and saw the son of the baking company executive, I realized that the girl, poor as she was, was really a symbol of millions of children in our time, most of whom are not poor in this world's goods at all, but who, like her, are riding up and down the nation's highways wishing they had a home to go to. A *real* home, with roots and memories. If that boy had had one, he wouldn't have needed a psychiatrist.

There is, in fact, in Coles's subsequent volume about the children of the wealthy, a parallel story about an 8-year-old girl named Susan. Susan's father was a corporate executive on his way to being president of a company. Here is the way Susan described her migratory existence: "We have moved a lot. We have never lived in the same place more than two years. Daddy is going to be the boss in a business one day, but it takes time. He has to go where there's a good job. Each time we move, he gets a better job."[6] Susan was born en route to a new job. Her father stopped off long enough to get her mother entered in the local hospital, then hurried on to Chicago where his job was waiting. He sent a grandmother to stay with the mother and Susan. When the grandmother became ill and had to return home, he hired a maid and sent her.

Mobility doesn't necessarily know any class structure.

Moving and Bereavement

It is easy to overdraw the picture, of course. Most children do adapt to changes in environment more readily than their parents, if their parents are loving adults and provide a sense of security in the midst of the relocations. One 12-year-old told me, "We've moved four times since I was five, and lived in three different states. I kinda like it. You get to start over again every time. If you goofed in one school, you get another chance."

But not all children move as blithely as this one apparently did, and none moves without some damage to his emotional system. When a person moves, he leaves his entire context behind, with the exception of a few personal belongings and the members of his family. His nervous system must accommodate itself to new patterns of response, a new house and neighborhood grid, new personalities in teachers and classmates, even to subtle emotional changes in his parents, who are simultaneously undergoing stress. Part consciously and part unconsciously, he actually grieves for things that have passed out of his life. It is as though part of his life had died and all the things in it had died too.

For small children, who are still in the animistic stage of life, normally inanimate objects like benches, swings, steps, and outbuildings are endowed with feelings and personalities as though they were playmates or brothers and sisters. The child who is uprooted and taken away from them may well miss them in the same way an adult would miss a friend or neighbor. Billy R., age 4, cried several times for Sam and Bam (his names), two rocks in the city park he visited daily before moving to another city; his mother said he wondered aloud many times over a three- or four-week period how they were, and expressed the desire to see them. Rachel, age 5, grieved for the brick wall, about two feet high, that ran around her family's patio in the home they left in Mobile; her mother said she played on it nearly every day, converting it into a tea table, a train, a dolly bed, or whatever she wanted it to be. Once, in their new home in Atlanta, she attempted to construct her own wall with some loose bricks and planks lying at the base of the house, but abandoned the project when the planks kept falling off the bricks.

Leaving toys behind can have a similar effect on children. Johnny E., age 8, sold a riding toy, a large orange tractor, when his family moved to another town. His parents told him he could keep it and take it with him, but they were selling several items to a used-furniture dealer and he caught the fever of selling. When the dealer offered him three dollars for the tractor, he took it. Several years later he recalled:

"I longed for that old tractor the way people long for their sweethearts. I would be out riding on my scooter and think, 'Gee, wouldn't it be nice to be on my tractor!' Or I would see some other kid riding his tricycle, and I'd think, 'Boy, if I only had my old tractor, wouldn't it be great!' You know, I can still work up a case of homesickness for that thing if I think about it! I never should have sold it."

Often children are forced to leave animals behind when the family makes a move. Martha K.'s family moved into an apartment when she was seven. No pets were allowed in the complex. Her mother and father decided to have Major, her old black dog, put to sleep, as he was nearly blind and they had no one to take him. They told Martha they had found a nice home for him. After she moved, she wrote several letters to Major. Each time, her father would take them to the office with him, promising to mail them, and then discard them. Robin S.'s parents moved to Australia when she was eleven, but she was not permitted to take her beloved poodle Nadia with her because of the six months quarantine law for pets entering the country; she agreed that

Nadia was too sensitive to live through the quarantine, and reluctantly consented to let a friend have the dog. She cried wretchedly for the next few days, and even after a year in Australia, would weep at the mention of the dog's name.

Many children are of course heartbroken at the necessity of parting with best friends when their families move. On the very day I was writing this chapter, a letter arrived from a former student informing me of an upcoming move. It contained this paragraph:

> We are in the process of buying a house, which has proved a very overwhelming experience. I have long ago ceased understanding what it is that I am signing away when I put down my name. But, in the long run, I know it will be wonderful to have our own home. Shawn is not so sure, however. He has declared numerous times that he is not moving, but will instead live with our next door neighbors here. Sometimes I feel the same way. I think we have stayed a year too long to be able to leave without the move hurting a great deal.

Shawn is three years old, and the home they will be leaving is the only one he has ever known.

Adults usually make new friends wherever they go. They possess at least rudimentary skills at this sort of thing. But children, contrary to a popular myth, often do not. Friends to them are gifts. When a good friend is lost, he or she is very hard to replace.

William M., who is 12, is a shy, sensitive boy who does not get along easily with classmates. For three years he has delighted in the companionship of William S., also 12. Besides sharing the same first name, they have played together on weekends, done homework together, gone to movies and summer camps together, and been nearly inseparable. But William S.'s father was recently transferred to another job two hundred miles away. The effect on William M. has been devastating. He now seems more marginal than ever in classroom or playground situations, and has lost interest in nearly everything. He and William S. exchange letters with decreasing frequency, and speak of visiting each other in the summers. But the impact on their lives is immeasurable. William M.'s parents are quite distraught by the change in him. They even considered the possibility of asking William S.'s parents if their William could move in with them and attend school in their city, but decided that this was too much to ask.

Difficulties of Adjustment

It isn't just missing friends and possessions that makes moving to another home so difficult for children. There is also the problem of adjusting to new patterns of existence on the other end of the move. Even children who seem relatively placid about leaving a former home can encounter a great deal of anxiety while learning to live in a new one.

Philip S., age 7, awakened his parents by crying in the middle of the night a week after they had moved into a new house. His father ran to his room, switched on the light, and found him lying on the floor. Rising in the darkness to go to the bathroom, Philip had forgotten he was in a new house and had tried to negotiate his way as he had in the old one. He crashed into a bookcase where he thought the door should be, and simply crumpled up in pain and shock. "I thought we were *home*," he whimpered.

A fourth-grade girl, Bettina L., wrote: "I have hardly any friends in Royal [her new school]. The teacher is very nice, but not as nice as Mrs. Marshall, my old teacher. Susan and Mary Jo have been nice to me too, and that helps a lot. It is not easy being in a new school like this. At first you feel very confused."

Robert M. was in the fifth grade when his parents moved to a new city. As he recalled the move several years later, it was an exceedingly difficult time for him:

> I was either becoming very nearsighted or had been that way for years, I don't know which. Anyway, I had managed to offset that in my old school by always sitting in

the front of the class where I could see the board well. The new school had already been in session two weeks when we moved, and I had to take a seat in the back of the room. The math teacher soon noticed that I copied many of the problems wrong, and told my parents. They were amazed to learn how blind I was when they took me to an optometrist. There were other problems associated with my near-sightedness. In the old school, I had been with the kids for four years, and had gotten to know them. In the new school, it was very hard to remember people, especially as I could not see them very well unless I got up in their faces. And walking to school! That was the real panic. In our old town, we lived just three blocks from the school on the same street. In the new town, or city, I guess it was big enough to be called a city, we lived more than a mile away, and you had to go through the main part of town and wind around a funny way to get there. I lived in terror every morning for two or three weeks that I would take the wrong street and become lost. I don't know why I thought that was so bad, but I did at the time.

Robert's father was not happy in his new job, and remained in it only six months, when he moved the family yet again. This time Robert could see much better, having obtained eyeglasses, and was less terrified of his walk to school, though he felt a bit shaky the first two or three days. But in this school he ran into another problem: bullying. Every class has its pecking order, among girls as well as among boys, and new children must face up to that and suffer accordingly until the other children have satisfactorily determined their location in the order. In Robert's new school, he encountered overt hostility from two directions, one physical and the other academic:

> I had never seen so many bullies in one class. There were four or five older boys, who had failed a grade or two, and they were very competitive with each other all the time. When I came in, I guess I was a diversion for them. Any-

way, they all started picking on me, mainly on the playground, to see whether I would fight and, if I did, how well I could handle them. I was never much of a ruffian, and I supposed I caved in disappointingly early for them. But not before they had spent several days roughing me up. The strange thing was, though, I was getting similar treatment from the other end of the line, from the boys who were academically at the head of the class. I don't know why they were so jealous, but they immediately perceived that I was no slouch in that department and set to work to try to intimidate me. They never came right out and threatened me if I made good marks, but they questioned me, fed me a lot of malarkey about the work in the school, and seemed irritated with me whenever I got answers right in class. They seemed menacing, even if they didn't do anything overtly to me.

Girls are more inclined to be hostile to new girls in their classes who stand out for some personal reason (well-dressed, poorly dressed, attractive, unattractive, witty, dull) than to girls who are either bright or slow in their academic work. New girls who are average, and do not tend to the extreme in personal qualities, normally get on and are accepted more easily than those who are characterized by the extremes. Wilma R. recalls the day her friend Rowena came into her class in the eighth grade:

> Her family had just moved to town from the country, and it was written all over poor Rowena. She was wearing an obviously homemade dress — you could tell it was at first glance — one of those starchy little pastel things that girls used to wear to Sunday school — and she had a big ribbon to match in her hair. She was very awkward, and stood off at the edge of the group looking silly and moon-eyed, the way Baby Snooks would look in a cartoon, I suppose. I felt sorry for her because all the other girls ignored her, and I went up to her and asked her where she lived and then showed her around the school and tried to introduce her in the group. Most of the girls just cut her dead,

though, and she acted almost too stupid to know they were doing it. It became a kind of game. You know, Get Rowena the New Girl. They played it for two or three days and then lost interest, and gradually she was accepted as part of the scenery.

Dwight G., a graduate student, recalls what it felt like to go into a new school when he was a child:

> There was always a lot of jockeying for position — you know, hierarchy, the mob, that sort of thing. They all looked you over, girls sizing you up as a potential boy friend, boys appraising your strength, cleverness, etc. After a few moves — my dad worked for the government and we moved quite a few times — you kind of learned how to take advantage of new situations because you knew you had several things going for you. It was easier for you to feel them out than it was for them to do the same to you, because they would tell you things about each other and you didn't have to tell any more than you wanted to. I made up a lot of bull when I went into a new place — about all the places I'd been, the girls I'd dated, things like that. They usually fell for it.

Many children who move into a new situation never quite get over the feeling that they are not at home there like the other children. One high school student said he had come into the small town where he was in school as a fourth-grader but still had moments of wistfulness when he remembered that he was a "newcomer" to his class and wished that he truly belonged the way the "oldtimers" did. A young adult, recalling her move to a new school when she was in the second grade and again to another school in the seventh grade, said, "It doesn't matter how long you've been a member of your group, you always think, 'These kids go back together further than I do; they have a prehistory that I wasn't part of.'"

This is one problem that children of military personnel do not face when they are enrolled in private military schools on service bases in various parts of the world, though they must face it when living in areas in which the military uses local school systems. The schools specially operated by the military are full of transient students; there are usually no other students there, unless they are the children of school personnel.

It has been said that these children are well adjusted because they have always been accustomed to making moves and can "land on their feet, like a cat." Most of their teachers and parents tell a different story, however; they can see the pressures and strains imposed on the children by being always on the move, with never more than three or four years in a single location, and often much less than that. "We have three counselors for two hundred kids," one counseling officer in a U.S. high school abroad said, "and it isn't enough. There's something missing in these kids' lives — stability. They shuffle along and make the moves, all right, and they don't complain much about it. But you can tell when you're in the business, you can tell."

"Imagine," said a teacher, "having a class of twenty-five kids who have had most of their training in eighteen or twenty other schools. Suddenly you've got them all together, working at eighteen or twenty different levels. It's madness!"

"It's hard on the kids," said the wife of an Air Force officer. "They just get attached somewhere and the orders come to go. After a while they sort of quit trying, become lackadaisical. Our daughter graduated two years ago and is in college now. She's doing all right, but she doesn't seem happy. Our son is only twelve. He worries me most, because he seems listless most of the time. Doesn't like to go outside and play the way we did when we were kids. Just mopes around the house, looking at a magazine or watching TV. It isn't an easy kind of life."

Jo Ann Wendt, an Air Force wife with a master's degree in guidance, has written a helpful article for service

families, entitled "Helping Your Teen Cope with a Move." [7]
She focuses on teen-agers because they are more likely than
other children to be working through identity problems that
are complicated by moving. As she says, "A move, to a teen,
is a little like being shot by the town sheriff!" Every move is
a loss, a "little death." Friends, possessions, even pets, get left
behind. Children often develop illness symptoms because of
relocation — stomach cramps, headaches, vomiting. It is important, says Wendt, for parents to understand the trauma a
move can occasion for a child, and to help the child cope
with it.

School Busing as a Form of Moving

Our day has seen a new form of moving in which
home base stays where it is. For adults it is known as com-
muting. For children it takes the form of school busing.

There have been numerous studies by educationists
of the effects of busing school children to achieve racial balance, and some of the more recent ones indicate that the
daily removal of children from their neighborhood environments has a negative effect on their ability to concentrate
and learn during school hours. It is impossible to measure
adequately the anxiety of children who are moved about in
this manner. Knowing what we do about the impact of separation from home and parents on children at the younger
end of the spectrum, it is easy to imagine the augmented
effect when the same children are put onto buses carrying
four dozen other children in a state of more or less organized
bedlam and driven as far as twenty miles away from their
own neighborhoods, past slums, billboards, business complexes, and various residential areas. Children are terrified
by the episode in "Hansel and Gretel" in which the brother
and sister are abandoned by their parents and stuffed into
an oven by a wicked old witch, because they can so easily
identify with the storybook children; and the part of the

story about the trail of crumbs is most delightful to them because it suggests that children can somehow find their way home again after being lost in the deep, dark woods. But no child who is bused a dozen miles away on highways that run one way and then another, carrying thousands of dangerous vehicles, can dare to hope he can make his way home in an emergency. He may as well be in a concentration compound during school hours.

"Lisa is terrified," said the mother of one 6-year-old. "We have a problem every morning getting her onto the bus. Someone has to stand at the road with her or she will hide and not go. She won't say what it is that bothers her so, and that makes it difficult to deal with. She just clings to me and begs me not to send her."

"It's all right, I guess," said George, a handsome black lad of nine years, as we chatted on the school ground. "But I liked it better when I was at Scoby. I could walk there with Bill. He's my brother. Seemed like the kids were nicer too. I dunno. It seems funny, being here."

One articulate fifth-grade teacher said she was getting out. The teachers had become babysitters since the busing was imposed, she thought.

"Make that 'policemen'! I mean, that's all we have time and energy to do, is to try and keep order in the classroom. When the kids come off of those buses they hit the door like a tornado! Half of them are hyped up and ready to attack anything that moves, and the other half are scared to death, crying, withdrawing into a shell for the rest of the day. It's no way to earn a living. I'd rather work in a shoe store or count change in a grocery. I'm not a teacher any more, I know that. Not since this business started."

This is a new kind of mobility; it is not the usual mobility, which involved families' moving from one town to another. But its effects on the children are similar to those produced by interurban moving, and it affects millions of children in present-day America.

Missing the Earth

One of the most unfortunate aspects of the whole contemporary mobility picture is the increasingly urban nature of the existence that promotes and grows out of mobility. In 1900, nearly three out of every four Americans lived in rural areas of the country. By 1970, only one of every four still lived in those areas. Three-fourths of the U.S. population were crowded into a mere little more than one percent of the total land area of the entire country.

The sociological effects of urbanization have been noted so often that they now seem trite to us, important as they are. Living in a state of dependence in a technological culture, people become suspicious, nervous, and less friendly. John Calhoun, a psychologist in Washington, D.C., has demonstrated that even rats become anti-social when overcrowded. Experimenting with a rectangular box or pen about nine feet by nine feet, Calhoun kept food and water supplies stable for the rats, so that they were able to multiply as quickly as possible in the box. At first they were quite content to live there, eating, drinking, playing, and sleeping. But as the box became crowded, the rats became increasingly restive and anti-social. By the time there were several hundred in the box, they were tense, vicious, and cannibalistic, devouring their own young. Mother rats deserted their offspring immediately, and homosexualism became rampant. Perhaps it is easier to see in the rats, but people respond in a similar fashion to life in large cities, apartment houses, and tenement buildings.

Yet it is into urban areas that most children are taken when their families move. Corporate migration seldom sends them into rural areas. This is an important fact, for, if they were to move to the country, there would be compensations in nature for the privations of moving. Nature heals. Rural landscapes, creeks, meadows, woods, ponds — the very words have a capacity to invoke serenity and healing. Cities, streets, heavy traffic, warehouses, department stores, elevators — these words do the opposite.

Robert Coles has noted that one of the few advantages possessed by migrant workers' children is that they get to live outdoors in open country. Although there is little softness, richness, excitement, or humor in the children's lives, he says,

> . . . the children find that excitement or humor, if not the softness and richness; to the surprise of their parents they make do, they improvise, they make the best of a bad lot and do things — with sticks and stones, with cattails, with leaves, with a few of the vegetables their parents pick, with mud and sand and wild flowers. They build the only world they can, not with blocks and wagons and cars and balloons and railroad tracks, but with the earth, the earth whose products their parents harvest, the earth whose products become, for those particular children, toys, weapons, things of a moment's joy.[8]

I was on a lecture program once at Auburn University in southern Alabama, and was sitting on the platform listening to an exchange between another lecturer, a priest from Washington, D.C., and the students in the large auditorium. The priest was a sixties activist, and he had been describing his horror at the shanties and sharecropper houses he had seen on the road across Georgia into Alabama. They were unforgivable, he said. To his surprise, several students stood up and announced that they had grown up in such shanties by the southern roadsides. "You come from the city, don't you?" they said. "Do you have tenement buildings in your cities?" The priest responded that there were tenements in most large cities. "We will take where we grew up over your tenements any day," these particular students said. "We may not have had running water in the house and a few other things, like handy supermarkets, but you don't know anything if you think a shack in the country is not ten times better than an apartment in the city."

Afterward, I talked with one of the students who had been engaged in the dialogue. His family did not have much, he said, but he loved the frosty mornings when the dew glistened on the old water bucket, and the sound of a hoot owl calling at night, and catching minnows in the creek to go fishing in the river, and following a hound dog through the thickets after a coon, and smelling the fresh plowed ground, and burning a pine log on a winter's evening.

There is little to nourish the soul in cities and suburbs. America has often forgotten the trick our ancestors brought with them from Europe, of leaving green preserves in the grid of city streets, oases of living things to give rest from the monotony of pavement and stone and glass. Cities and shopping centers tend to be hard, implacable, nonresilient to human gaze or touch. And it is to these that many children move in the great migration of our times, not to a land gentle with springs or flowing with wheat clean to the wide horizon.

Perry J. is 10 years old. His mother and father have recently divorced, and she has moved, with Perry and his sister Annette, into an apartment. It is a very nice apartment, in a complex of Georgian townhouses. Some very wealthy people live in other apartments in the complex. But there is no grass. From building to building, in the whole expanse of the complex, there is only river-gravel paving. It is very nice paving, and looks much richer than ordinary macadam; but it is still not grass. Perry cannot feel it cool under his feet in the summertime, or roll in it, or lie in it and look up through ancient trees to the blue sky above.

What has happened to Perry often befalls children of divorce. Apartments are easier on the mothers. No lawns to care for. Less trouble with maintenance. The protection of other people living nearby. But what does it do to the children?

"The children miss having a yard," said the overly tan young woman by the country-club pool as she flicked her cigarette ashes into an empty Coke bottle. "They used to play croquet and catch lightning bugs on summer evenings and all that. Now all they do is sit in front of the tube and eat junk foods, unless I bring them out here to swim or play tennis. This is to make up for that. I don't know if it does."

It is even worse for children being taken into older, ghettoized areas of extremely large cities, where, as Silverstein and Krate say, they are daily exposed to "junkies, pushers, winos, hustlers, pimps, prostitutes, and an assortment of other 'street people' in their neighborhood," and where "the high-rise buildings themselves seem to foster a peculiar sense of alienation."[9] Joel S., 12, and his family moved to Manhattan from a town where Joel had been able to wander about in complete freedom. He found confinement in an apartment on Eightieth Street near Central Park too much to bear, and sought to relieve his "cabin fever" by walking the hundred yards or so to the park. Within three weeks, he had been mugged twice in the park and was afraid to leave the building. Benjamin R., 14, also moved from a pleasant neighborhood to Manhattan; he had lived in a suburb of a southern town where there was a small swimming pool in his back yard. He had been in his family's east-side apartment only a few months when he attempted to commit suicide and was hospitalized for depression. He complained of not being able to live "penned up like an animal in the zoo."

The Instinct for Home

Jewell and Loizos, in their study of animals' territoriality and exploration,[10] observe that most mammals rarely venture more than a few miles from their "home range," and then only in extraordinary circumstances such as a fire or a severe shortage of food. Baboons and lions often remain all their lives within a dozen or so square miles of where they were born, and most smaller animals such as voles and squirrels prefer the few hundred square yards adjacent to their homes. Migrating birds, which may travel thousands of miles each year, instinctively select only certain sites along their course for resting and feeding; and many of them return each year to the same place for nesting and reproducing. We speak of this habit, as of the return of pigeons and salmon to their places of origin, as "the homing instinct."

There are good ecological reasons for such an instinct in nature. If a bird or animal remains in a set environment, it always knows where the surest supplies of food and water are, as well as the most protective lairs, not only in normal times but also during the most unpromising seasons. The heron crane of England, for example, has had an exceptionally difficult time in recent winters because of snow and ice, which minimize its food catch and threaten it with freezing. The heron population has dwindled by about thirty percent. But the results would have been much more disastrous had the birds not been familiar with their territories and thus able to stir up food in their best fishing spots.

Bowlby, whose work in attachment and separation we have already noted, supports the theory that human beings also enjoy advantages by remaining in familiar environments. The physico-chemical systems that mediate attachment behavior and fear behavior in an individual, he says, operate more favorably within a recognized and well-defined part of the environment. Leaving the boundaries of familiar territory probably excites stress mechanisms and fosters stress anxiety. Bowlby and others even assume that there is a strong genetic bias in favor of certain territories, and that overriding this produces undue tension in a person.[11]

This suggests that man, like the animals, probably once had a homing instinct, or a home-range preference, and that somehow it has remained in us. Our ancestors had favorite hunting grounds, fishing spots, and sheltering places, and, even in pre-agricultural days when migration was the order of life, returned to those places as long as they promoted survival. Travel as we know it, with the exception of great migratory drives brought about by unusual reasons, is a comparatively modern phenomenon. Even the extensive settlement period of the sixteenth, seventeenth, and eighteenth centuries involved the resettling of no more than three or four percent of the Western populations. The most remarkable era of displacement has been in the years since World War I.

I remember the statement of a middle-aged friend who leads a very hectic life in a managerial position. "I was driving to Chicago one day," he said, "and noticed that I was passing only fifty miles from my boyhood home in Illinois. We had moved from there when I was eight, but I found that I still had a strong attachment to the place. The urge to drive through the little town was irresistible, even though it would cost me an extra half day in appointment time in Chicago. Then I discovered myself parking the car and walking up and down the street where I had played so many times forty years ago, trying to feel the old feelings and recall the old scenes. The pull was so strong to stay there that I almost didn't make it to Chicago that day. It was as if a magnet or something had me in its grip."

Suppose there is that urge to go back, a deep, almost primitive longing to be in the place where one was born and raised, that remains imprinted on the unconscious long after we have gone, after we have traveled many a mile. What does it mean in terms of our own mobility, and of the mobility we force on children before they have a choice? Could it constitute a rape of the emotions, a binding and gagging of certain instincts, the long repression of which can make a child sick, or at least contribute to his patterns of stress and anxiety as he tries to make his way in the world?

Imagine the longing for home progressing geometrically through all the earth, hundreds of millions of people inwardly, unknowingly sighing for where they first came from, their paths crossing and crisscrossing in a hopeless tangle, like a night photograph of traffic patterns in Paris's Place de l'Étoile, resonating and growing, growing and resonating, until space — all the space there is — is imploded with homesickness, with the desire to go back. It may be a pollution secretly corroding the soul far worse than the atmosphere poisons our bodies.

"I like the feeling," said the salesman checking into a Holiday Inn, "of staying in the same place wherever I travel."

Which brings us back to the migrating birds who always feed and sleep in the same spots, year after year.

And to the youngster crying for home.

9

Childhood and Death

When I was three or four years old, I went with my family for a week's visit on my grandfather's farm. One morning my grandfather reported at the breakfast table that one of his horses had died during the night. Timidly, I advanced through the field to see this wonder. There lay a great brown animal, whose power and authority I had been taught to fear, lying inert on its side, not even twitching an eyebrow. I was dumfounded, mesmerized. The enormity of it over-whelmed me. To think that something as big and strong as a horse could suddenly go lifeless!

My grandfather called the glue factory and someone sent a truck to fetch the dead animal. I watched as three men sweated and tugged, winching the beast onto the flatbed of the truck. They gave my grandfather a check and drove away. The check was for a dollar and a quarter. When I asked why they wanted the horse, as it could no longer pull a plow or a wagon or a sledge, I was told they would cut up its body and make glue of certain parts.

The next day I went cautiously out to the pasture again to make sure the horse was not there. I repeated this action for three or four days, I believe. It seemed inconceivable to me that the horse should not return. Eventually I began to realize that to be dead meant to be taken away. I don't think I worried about ever being dead myself, but I did become concerned that either of my parents should ever die like the horse.

I am sure I had been bothered before that moment by occasional brief separations from my parents, especially my mother. My experience of loneliness and anxiety was therefore not entirely new. But there was a new dimension to it now. Now I understood the possibility that separation might be forever.

The experience gave a haunting, cosmic quality to my sense of loneliness. My world was much less stable than it had seemed.

What Children Understand

Rose Zeligs, a psychotherapist who has often dealt with children affected by human death, says that small children cannot really comprehend death's meaning. The ability of children to experience grief is severely limited by their lack of knowledge. She cites, for example, the case of Robert and Louise Brown, ages five and a half and three, whose infant brother had died of a respiratory infection.

"He died and fell asleep," the parents explained to the children. "He is with God in heaven."

Robert could not process the information. "He's not dead! He's not dead!" he screamed, jumping up and down. "I want my baby! I want David! Tell God I want David back!" Little Louise merely repeated, "David died, David died."

The parents told the children they were going to be very busy for a few days and that the children must be exceptionally good. They promised, if the children were cooperative, to get them each a present. At this, Robert dried his tears and said, "I want a Slinky toy."[1]

A woman I talked with remembers attending a funeral with her mother when she was about four years old. "It seemed funny to me at the time," she said, "like a movie. I wanted to laugh. I looked over at Mother and she was crying, and I looked at other people and they were crying, but it wasn't sad to me. I tried to cry so I would be reacting like other people, but I couldn't. I just wanted to laugh."

Jane R. was six when she first became acquainted with death in a human being. The girl next door committed suicide, and Jane remembers sitting on her front porch, swinging, when the body was carried away. "It was all very exciting," she says, "with lots of people coming and going. They carried Susie out in a box. I remember Mama saying that the people were 'tacky', and I supposed that was the sort of thing tacky people did."

Maria Nagy, after a careful study of nearly four hundred children, concluded that those under five have little conception of what it means to die. From ages five to nine, they learn enough about it to be afraid of it. And at ten or eleven they begin to understand it in terms of its reality.[2]

Sylvia Anthony, author of *The Child's Discovery of Death*, agrees. Her study is a correlation of children's mental ages (as opposed to their chronological ages) and their comprehension of the meaning of death. Before the mental age of three and a half, she says, not even the word *dead* has any meaning for children. At the second level, of mental ages four to six, there is some comprehension of the meaning of death, but usually with erroneous ideas. Often, at this age, children confuse death with sleeping or lack of movement. At the third level, of mental ages six to ten, there is increased clarity about the meaning of death, but usually without the child's grasping the emotional impact associated with it. The fourth level, after the mental age of ten, is the one at which children begin to understand death most fully and to fear it as something that will happen to them. At any time after the mental age of ten, children may develop such a complete theoretical control of the concept of death that they can describe it both biologically and logically.[3]

But Anthony admits that children may be deeply troubled even by that which they do not understand. Using Piaget's method of having children complete diverse story openings, she was able to discern clear evidence in younger children of an anxiety about death, even when the same children fell into the first and second levels of understanding.

"Against the background in which it most commonly appeared spontaneously in the children's fantasy," she said, "death is seen as typically a sorrow-bringing thing and a fear-bringing thing, grievous because it involves separation of child and parent, or of parents from each other."[4]

This is the important thing for adults to understand. Even very small children can become deeply disturbed by images of death, whether these occur through the deaths of animals, of human beings, or even on television. The fear of separation, naturally present in the child, becomes greatly enhanced by the encounter with death. The very fact that death is still poorly defined in the child's mind, a mystery, gives it a pervasive power it might otherwise lack; it permeates the child's thinking, his or her entire world. The child may brood upon it, gripped by fear, while not saying a word about it to the parents.

A minister told me that his four-year-old daughter became preoccupied with death after he had been involved in the funeral of a child in his parish. Many people in the parish were touched by the death, and there had been many conversations about it in the minister's home, both by telephone and with persons who came to call. Overhearing much of what was said, the daughter was deeply affected. Somehow, she became afraid her father would die because he was associated with the funeral. For weeks she did not want to let him out of her sight. She cried if he left even to go to the grocery store. Finally he realized that the child's death must have troubled her, and asked if she was afraid her daddy would die. She admitted that she was.

Frances G. Wickes, in *The Inner World of Childhood*, says that adults do not take seriously enough the fears and anxieties of small children. They are too inclined to tease or shame the children, saying, "Oh, you shouldn't be afraid of that!" dismissing the fears as if they had no basis in reality and therefore no reality. To the child, they are enormously real, even though the child's conceptualization of the thing feared is either erroneous or only partially formed. Wickes cites the case of a parent who as a small girl had been seized by an extraordinary fear of a passing funeral procession. Her nurse and parents assured her that funeral processions never left the street and would not come up on the sidewalk to get her, so she need have no fear. It was silly of her to be afraid, they said. "They used to make me feel like a fool," reported the patient, "but they did not touch my fear. By and by I learned to walk past the processions quietly, but I would lie awake at night and tremble at the pictures they called up." The pictures were of vague forms symbolic of death, and of large figures whose meaning she did not know how to interpret.

"As a matter of fact," says Wickes,

> this child was more sensitive to the mysteries of death symbols and to other spiritual symbols than were the adults surrounding her. Death is one of those dark and mysterious forces that has always stood at the background of man's consciousness. It is the urge forever at war with the urge toward living. It is not only the fear of actual physical death but of the regressive element in ourselves. Fortunately the urge toward life, the absorption in the present business of living, is so keen, especially in the young, that these fears rarely break through. Where a child is sensitive to all these inner realities we do not decrease the fear by dwelling on its folly. We only make the child feel different and queer since no one else understands. This child had no fear of being run over or physically injured by the funeral carriages but the sight of them lifted the veil that ordinarily hangs between our lighted world and the world of shadows.[5]

It is the world of shadows, signifying darkness and separation, that really frightens children. Freud said that they cannot distinguish between darkness and death, and they cry when left alone at night because the darkness betokens separation from the major parent.

Thus the woman who at four years of age felt like laughing at a funeral remembers also that she cried, at age six, when she attended her grandfather's funeral, because she understood that his dying and being buried meant she would not see him again. This separation generated such an anxiety that she was afraid to leave her mother to attend school, lest her mother die while she was away and she never see her again.

"I couldn't even bear for mother to shut the bathroom door and take a bath," she says. "I would crouch outside the door the whole time, waiting anxiously for her to come out. When I heard the water draining out of the tub, I would move away from the door so she wouldn't know how upset I was. But I couldn't stand the thoughts of not having her."

What Parents Don't Know

Parents often do not realize that their children are frightened and anxious about death. In the case just cited, the mother was probably unaware of her daughter's reason for crouching near the bathroom door while the mother bathed. Even if she had confronted the girl with a direct question about her behavior, the girl would most likely have fabricated a response to put the mother off, because, in areas where they are inarticulate and believe their feelings to be unique, children resist the naming of their fears; instead, they live in a world of secrecy, generating even more anxiety.

The ways by which children first become acquainted with death are numerous and varied. Sometimes it is through the death of a pet. Then the parent is usually aware of the death and is able to engage the child in a dialogue about the meaning of what has happened. Often, however, the acquaintance comes in other ways and the parent is not aware.

For example, Raymond A. was five or six when he threw a ball bat at a blue jay sitting on the corner of his sandbox. To his great surprise, the bat struck and killed the bird. Remorseful and afraid, he removed a small strawberry carton, one of the old wooden kind, from his mother's pantry, filled it with grass, and laid the bird in it. Then he dug a hole and buried it.

"I was haunted for days by what I had done," he says. "Maybe not for what I had done so much as for what I had discovered — that things die and go lifeless. But I was afraid to tell anybody. I felt terribly guilty. I didn't know what would happen if I told. So I carried the burden of it all by myself."

Today, television is undoubtedly one of the major sources of children's acquaintance with death. Even before they are able to talk, small children often witness hospital scenes, violent accidents, killings, and funerals on television. The horrors of war are brought with only slightly expurgated realism into the family den or living room. People are seen gasping, struggling for breath, collapsing, dying, weeping for those who have died. The so-called experts are unable to agree on the effect this produces in young minds, but there can be no doubt that many children do have their first confused dealings with death-anxiety as a result of what they see on the screen.

"I used to watch all kinds of programs," says Michael G., 14, "and sometimes they scared me, all that bleeding and groaning and all. I would go to bed and pull the covers up over my head and hope I would wake up all right."

"I don't think I was bothered by most of the TV deaths I saw," says Robin W., 16, "except maybe one or two. I remember one show I saw — I must have been five or six — about this family, and the mother died of cancer. I was really into the show, you know, and when it happened I cried just like the kids in her family. It was as real as if it had happened to me. That really shook me up. I think I was afraid it would happen to my mother too. I prayed every night that God wouldn't let anything happen to her."

Zeligs has found that children reared in the country tend to accept death with more equanimity than children raised in urban areas. They are able to see death more easily in nature and animals, she says, and to understand it as a part of the rhythm of all things.[6] If this is true, one can only wonder about the effect of television death on children who live in urban areas, especially in apartment houses and dwelling complexes where they are essentially cut off from nature. Do all things have a rhythm for these children, or does death as they first experience it seem entirely gratuitous and unpredictable?

"I used to feel panicky," says Rick L., 14, "every time I heard a siren at night. You know, those bleepers that go OO-ah! OO-ah! OO-ah! I don't know why, but I thought they were coming after my mother or father. I would listen with my heart stopped, and when the noise would fade away I would be all popped out with sweat."

Did he ever talk to either of his parents about it?

"No."

Why?

"Well . . . I don't know, it's just not something you talk to anybody about."

The Adolescent and Death

As Nagy, Anthony, and others have shown, children emerge from their vague, subjective views of death during the years from seven to eleven, coming gradually to an understanding of it in both logical and physiological terms. In the early years of adolescence, then, they must adjust to a wholly new conceptualization of the way death occurs and what it means when it does.

What are the primary features of this new conceptualization? How does it affect their anxieties about death?

Before the age of ten, most children do not clearly define the difference between animate and inanimate things, but suppose that the life spirit exists indiscriminately in everything. During these early years, therefore, death cannot be comprehended fully as the absence of life. This is why their understanding of the meaning of death is in terms of separation. They can comprehend separation, for they have experienced it.

After age ten, children have acquired a more objective understanding of the way things work. They can begin to explain death in physiological terms as the cessation of pulse beat and bodily function. They can discuss the causes of death in a more rational way. They know death has an etiology, that it doesn't occur without reason.

One of the interesting side effects of this new knowledge in young adolescents is the appearance, in many of them, of a kind of bravado in the face of death. They realize their own vulnerability to death — through car accidents, disease, falls from heights — and instinctively begin to "whistle in the dark" as if they were unafraid.

I. and P. Opie, who compiled the enormous document known as *The Lore and Language of Schoolchildren,*[7] found that British children at about age ten often make jokes about dying. At that age, say the Opies, the outward or material facts of death seem funny to them. They will brazenly inquire of one another, "Are you going to be burnt or buried?" A few years ago, this little song was an obsession with them:

> When I die,
> don't bury me at all,
> Just pickle my bones
> in alcohol.

American children exhibit a similar jocularity at approximately the same age. The reader may recall this bit of doggerel, often sung in a singsong rhythm:

The worms crawl in,
the worms crawl out,
your body turns
to sauerkraut.

There is also a recurring rage, among early adolescents, for "black" humor, or humor that deals cavalierly with
death. For example, this story. Billy rings the doorbell.
Tommy's mother answers. Billy: "Can Tommy come out and
play?" Tommy's mother: "No, Tommy has cancer." Billy:
"Then can I come in and watch him rot?"

Children will tell such stories and then erupt in con-
vulsions of laughter. They may also at the same age engage
in daredevil stunts that seem to bring them right to the edge
of death, such as diving off cliffs, undertaking spectacular
feats on skateboards, or even appropriating an automobile
and using it to play "chicken," a game in which the participant brushes as close as possible to death without flinching.
Graham Greene has told in his autobiography *A Sort of Life*
that he developed at this age a minor passion for playing
Russian roulette with a loaded pistol and on several occasions
actually pulled the trigger.

It is all a kind of bravado, mixed half of failure to
realize the nature of death and half of dawning realization
of its meaning coupled with the fright that accompanies it.
Anthony notes that at this age "the young tend to dispel
solemnity and sentimentality in group mockery of death,"
and at the same time "undertake daring exploits in active
derision of it." She sees in this behavior "an element of de-
fence against anxiety . . . which may persist in many people
through life, so that without the opportunity to dare, life
seems to them hardly worth living." [8]

Beneath this veneer of whimsicality and derring-do,
in other words, there is often a sense of terror about the
possibility of dying. Before, death was vague, mysterious,
and, except for the separation entailed, impersonal. Now,
for the young person who has acquired the facts about death

but not the emotional experience to handle the facts, it may suddenly seem all too personal and threatening. He or she may become abnormally concerned about health, and secretly believe that simple ailments will have fatal results. Or there may be a corresponding fear of almost any potentially dangerous activity, such as diving off a diving board, climbing a tree, or flying in an airplane.

Lars J. is a good example. He accompanied his school principal and three other 12-year-old boys to spend a week at a primitive camp in a wilderness area. The camp, actually a crude log cabin, lay several miles from where the principal parked his car. He and the boys then carried the supplies through the woods and pastures and creek bottoms until they reached the campsite. The first night, after dinner, the principal and the boys were sitting around a kerosene lantern playing cards. Lars developed a headache. First he announced it. Then, a few minutes later, he said, "I think I'd better go home." The other boys protested; he had forgotten the bogs, fences, briar patches, and cow pastures they had crossed to get to the remote place; they would never be able to retrace their way at night.

Soon Lars became panicky, and whimpered about dying. He knew the headache would be fatal. The principal thought he was homesick, but Lars said he had often been away from home, visiting his brother in a western state. The principal ordered him to climb up into the loft and go to sleep, promising to take him home in the morning if the headache had not gone away. On the steps, Lars began to cry. He could not climb into the loft, he said; he would fall and be killed. He clung desperately to the railing, afraid to advance or retreat. The principal and two boys had to force him on up into the loft and get him ready for bed. The next morning, he was fine.

Angela N. was 13 when she shut a car door on her finger and set up a blood condition that resulted in a series of boils and felons. The felons, swelling her fingertips painfully, often kept her awake at night. She reports:

My fingers would throb something awful — so bad I couldn't sleep and would sit up in bed rocking back and forth. Nowadays I guess they'd give you penicillin or a mycin or something for that, but in those days all they had was sulfa, and it didn't work very fast. I remember thinking as I sat up in bed, rocking back and forth to distract myself from the pain, "I'm going to die. And nobody cares, nobody cares." That was the awful part. My parents were in bed asleep. Bobby was in his bed asleep. There I was, dying by myself, and nobody cared. I think I cried more for that than I did because of the pain.

Erikson and others have shown that adolescence is the period when children concentrate most intensely on the formation of their identities. The process at best is less than smooth. It is a time of considerable anxiety, as the nascent self-images appear, recede, reappear, re-recede, and so on, changing perhaps dozens of times in a single twenty-four-hour period. The threat of dying, introduced into such a tentative scheme of things, is extremely upsetting. Children are likely to read far too much into the slightest irregularities in the way they are feeling. Or they are liable to fixate upon any example of death and see themselves dying in the same manner.

It is all a case of a little knowledge being a dangerous thing. Or at least a disturbing thing. Children do not have the emotional maturity to cope with their intellectual understanding of death during the early adolescent period. Parents should be aware of this and help to provide the sense of security in personal relationships that is the only real antidote to the fear of death. Unfortunately, the teen-age years are usually a time of additional stress for parents as well, and they are often less capable of providing emotional security for their children then than at any other period of their lives. Awareness of the children's anxieties is therefore extremely important; it may enable the parents to care at times when they would otherwise withdraw from the relationship in selfishness or disgust.

When Death Actually Touches Children

The loneliness and fear children feel in contemplating death is focused and in that sense intensified when death becomes an actuality for them, either in terms of their own dying or the death of a member of the family. Then complete separation from the family (if the child is dying) or member of the family (if someone else is dying or dead) must be dealt with as realistically as the child is able.

Zeligs says that the most difficult thing dying children must cope with is the sense of alienation that creeps over them. They realize they must be separated forever from their parents, and the realization is like a psychological curtain that drops between them and those who will go on living. Doctors say that even children who have not been told they are dying almost invariably guess that death is approaching, and the fact that the parents are treating it as a secret helps to widen the gap between them. The children fear to be alone, and long for complete companionship with the parents, but normally cannot act to overcome the growing feeling of separation.

Parents often unwittingly contribute to this sense of alienation. Dreading the loss of a child, they begin to develop a kind of self-protection by unconsciously surrendering the child before he or she dies. They may go so far as to actually give away the child's clothes, toys, and other possessions. It is even rather common for parents of dying children to stop coming to the hospital to see them. They do not verbalize the way they have given up the child, but the child senses it and knows what is happening.

Zeligs describes the child's feelings:

> The seriously ill child senses that his family is withdrawing from him emotionally as well as physically. He tends to withdraw from his social environment and concentrate on his own illness and fears. As he becomes more and

more isolated, he feels alone, unwanted, forgotten and abandoned. When death seems imminent he, too, begins to separate himself from his family, and directs his attention to his loneliness and his dying.[9]

Occasionally a child for whom no hope was offered miraculously recovers and is able to return home. Parents must then cope with a new set of emotions, sometimes including resentment that the child is not going to die. They have adjusted their thinking to include his death, and have to rearrange their plans to incorporate his life. This is known among psychologists as the *Lazarus syndrome,* after the Biblical character who was raised from the dead. As the child sensed his parents' willingness for him to die, he may also sense their temporary rejection of his living. It is hardly unusual, in such circumstances, for a child to wish he had actually died.

The death of a sibling is probably the easiest intrafamily death for a child to handle, although such deaths often produce guilt feelings difficult to resolve, especially if there has been a strong sense of rivalry between the two children. And by far the hardest death for any child to adjust to is that of the caring parent. Then the child's whole world seems to collapse. There is a sense of absence or void that can never be filled.

An enlisted man in the U.S. Armed Forces described for me his anguish over the death of his mother when he was only three. He was too young to comprehend the meaning of death, but he soon experienced the meaning of the loss and separation. A year later, the father placed the boy, together with a brother and sister, in an orphanage. "I remember looking out the window every night," says the man, "and crying myself to sleep, hoping my father would return."

During the boy's first year in school, when he was six, his father died of a heart attack. The children were dressed up, taken to the funeral, and then returned to the orphanage.

"It was at this time, I think," says the man, "that the full impact of the events of my life finally dawned on me. My parents were gone and would never return. They would never visit me again and I would never be able to see them again. I remember thinking to myself, even in the midst of all those kids, that I was alone, completely and totally alone."

Unhappy and resentful, the boy became rebellious and difficult to manage. He remembers wishing several times that he could die. Following an unpleasant high school career, he joined the army and eventually, after an experience of religious conversion, came to an acceptance of his unfortunate past. He knows, however, that his entire life has been negatively affected by a sense of loss and deprivation.

The Sense of Guilt

One of the most pervasive problems psychiatrists must deal with in the cases of children who have experienced actual deaths within the family or in the circle of close friends is the feeling of personal responsibility for the death. This is because in an animistic world-view everything happens as a result of the wishes of the person at the center of the world. If the child has harbored resentments, jealousies, or any other form of ill will toward the dead person, he or she naturally feels guilty for what has happened to the person.

The fact that the child supposedly leaves behind an animistic conception of the world at about age ten does not always mean that an adolescent will be exempt from such feelings. Animistic tendencies, being the first way we have of understanding the world, die hard. They frequently remain alive even in adults. A death in the family is often sufficient to trigger them, causing a wife to say, "Oh, my husband would not have died if I had loved him more," or, "Jim would be alive now if I had been more understanding of him."

In *The Child's Conception of the World,* Piaget has demonstrated that the child, especially during the early years, makes no distinction between his or her inner world of thought and the external world of reality; they are assumed to be coextensive and continuous, without interruption:

> During the primitive stages, since the child is not yet conscious of his subjectivity, all reality appears to be of one unvaried type, by reason of the confusion between the data of the external world and those of the internal. Reality is impregnated with self and thought is conceived as belonging to the category of physical matter. From the point of view of causality, all the universe is felt to be in communion with and obedient to the self. There is participation and magic. The desires and the commands of the self are felt to be absolute, since the subject's own point of view is regarded as the only one possible. There is integral egocentricity through lack of consciousness of self.[10]

In other words, if the child has ever envied the father's relationship to the mother and the father dies, the child may actually believe he caused the death by wishing it. Because he conceived of the death, he also thinks he caused it.

Anthony records the case of Bernard N., eight years old, whose father died at work when Bernard was small. Given the Terman-Merrill test (questions and definitions designed to deceive the child's self-censoring tendencies and elicit surprising attitudes or bits of information) and the Story Completion test, Bernard showed definite evidence of an anxiety over disobedience and imprisonment. Even though he was old enough to begin to realize that he was in no way responsible for his father's death, he nevertheless had recurrent fears that he was responsible and would at some time have to pay the social penalty of going to prison for it.[11]

Among primitive peoples, say anthropologists, the question invariably asked by survivors when one of their number has died is not *what* or *how* but *who*. The assumption is that the dead one has been killed, that the death was willful, and that someone was responsible. Anthony sees the same animistic concept at work among children, especially young children and older children of low intelligence. Often, when these children are asked to define the word *dead,* they do so by reference to the words *killed* or *murdered.* This could be the result of what the children have learned from watching television programs in which dead persons were usually killed; but Anthony believes it is related to the child's view of causality in a universe where thought and action are coextensive.[12]

The same sense of guilt that applies to the child whose parent has died applies as well to the one whose sibling has died or been injured. Richard M.'s sister was taken to the hospital for an appendectomy when he was seven years old, and her mother accompanied her, remaining with her for several days. Richard was distraught at his mother's absence and thought it was a punishment on him for having wished his sister out of the way. "I was not unhappy about my sister's having to go to the hospital," he said; "in fact, I was glad to be rid of her. But I believed that my mother had chosen to go with her because I had been bad in wishing to be rid of my sister. Mother was punishing me for my sin. What bothered me most was that I didn't think she would come back. I supposed that she and my sister were going to live together the rest of their lives and I wouldn't see her again. My father was making frequent trips to the hospital to see them, but I was not allowed to go because I was so small. I thought they were all happy but me."

Mitchell records these examples of children's guilt feelings:

"I should have given Tim my bicycle," said a six-year-old. "He wanted it, Mummy. Then he wouldn't have died, would he?"

"Is it my fault that Granny died?" asked an eight-year-old girl. "I didn't carry her bag up the steps."[13]

With respect to the sense of guilt, it ought also to be

recalled that Freud saw very specific connections between children's feelings about animals and their feelings about family members. Small animals, such as cats, rabbits, and house dogs, he said, often figure in their dreams as siblings, and larger animals, such as bears, horses, and elephants, as parents. Thus, when small children are witnessed abusing domestic pets, their actions are not to be divorced entirely from the desire to hurt brothers and sisters. They are much less likely to mistreat larger animals, partly because of the danger to themselves and partly because larger animals represent the authority of adults.

Bertha M., age 8, was one of several children, all under age eleven. When her teacher reprimanded her for putting a hamster in a sink full of water and letting it drown, she said, "It wouldn't stay out of my room." The hamster had of course not been in her home at all. But Bertha shared a small bedroom with two sisters, one seven and one ten. She was probably acting out her hostility for the younger sister, who displaced her as the youngest member of the family. It is much less likely that she unconsciously viewed the hamster as a substitute for the older sister, as the older sister would have partaken of the mystery and authority of a more adult world.

Such matters are not easier on children because they are unconscious. On the contrary, it means that anxiety fills the child's mind like a vapor, seeping into every pore. He cannot keep it out, or begin to cope with it. Like some untreatable malady, it haunts his sleep, erupting in nightmares and bad dreams. It is never far from the periphery of his conscious thinking, but hovers there like some nameless monster waiting to devour him.

Adults to the Rescue

What can we do as parents and adult friends to counteract the loneliness experienced by children who are facing the meaning of mortality? How can we help to illuminate their situations and ease their passage from confusion to understanding, from fear to acceptance?

For one thing, we can talk more about the meaning of death. We can begin to explain the phenomenon to children at an early age, the way we initiate their sexual education at an early age. It is unfortunate that many parents are reluctant to discuss dying in the presence of children. They shush each other when it is mentioned. As Earl Grollman says in his book *Talking About Death: A Dialogue Between Parent and Child,* "The word D-E-A-D has become the new four-letter word of pornography."[14] Everybody steps lightly around it. No one wants to mention it, much less discuss it. It is no wonder the children learn to fear it. It is the great taboo of the technological society.

The viewing of death in television programing can be turned into an advantage if parents watch it with the children and use it as an occasion to discuss what it means to die. Stories that involve the deaths of characters can likewise be used as springboards for discussion. So can the deaths of pets, friends, or relatives. Nor does it hurt occasionally to take children to funerals, so that they may learn about cultural traditions and death, and not encounter them as foreign ways when the death of someone close involves them in a more personal action. These experiences should be thoroughly discussed, so that the children understand them as completely as possible. The children should be told what grief is and how people experience it — why we weep and how we eventually get over it. They should gain the impression that death is not a terrible or forbidden subject, that it is not something pertaining to them alone. In the end, knowledge is one of their surest defenses against anxiety, for anxiety feeds on secrecy and imagination.

A second thing we can do is to encourage and help to implement their relation to nature. As Wordsworth saw so clearly, nature is therapeutic; it soothes the distressed mind and heals the troubled heart. There is something about the rhythms of the natural world that transcends and draws out the rhythms of our own lives. The cycle of existence in nature — spring turning to summer and summer to autumn and autumn to winter — the grain of corn falling into the earth and dying in order that the plant may spring up bearing full ears — gives meaning and beauty to our own living and dying.

Even children in the city can be given vacations in natural settings, where they can see what a year's full seasons have done to the plant life, the river banks, and the farm animals. And, during the year, trips to the parks and zoos will help them to keep in touch with the way things grow and age and die. They will learn, as the writer of Ecclesiastes said, that "there is a time to be born and a time to die," and will gradually understand that dying, when seen in the proper perspective, is not really a bad part of human experience.

Another thing we can do to help the children as they begin to recognize the presence and meaning of death is to give them the advantage of a healthy religious faith. Marjorie Mitchell asserts from her work as a psychotherapist that there is a definite correlation between children's religious faith and their ability to accept a realistic view of death.[15]

Rena L., for example, was 10 years old when her mother was stricken with an advanced form of cancer and died after an illness of only a few days. When an aunt clasped Rena at the funeral and wept, Rena said, "Oh, Aunt Dee, don't cry for Mama. She's in heaven. Do you suppose she already has her wings?"

Even if the religious teachings do not include a picture of the afterlife in such fundamentalist terms, the doctrine of a caring Deity who presides over the interests of human beings is extremely comforting.

"I had just been confirmed in the faith," says Jay M., "when my sister Kate was killed in an automobile wreck. I think my relationship to God, reinforced by the confirmation classes, really helped me to accept her death with a minimum of grief. I remember how I felt at the funeral. I listened to the minister talk about our all being joined in God, and somehow I believed it. It took the edge off of things."

Finally — above everything — we can help the children by caring for them. This is most important of all, more important even than religious faith, for it incorporates what the faith is about.

Elisabeth Kübler-Ross, who is famous for her work with the dying, was asked what could possibly counter the terrible discovery of death in a child's life. She gave a single answer. The most helpful thing in the world, she said, is *one person who really cares.*[16]

We are really back to our chapter on birth, and the importance to the newborn of the mother, the totally caring adult who nurtures, protects, and oversees growth and well-being. In the valley of the shadow of death, when the forms of life melt into evanescence and transience, there is nothing more comforting than that nurturing presence, that one completely loving person who really cares how the child feels and whether the child survives. The awful, unnerving thing about death is its power to separate. But when someone really cares, deeply and faithfully, that power is overcome. *Amor vincit omnia,* as the old phrase had it — love conquers all.

10

Victims of Divorce

The patterns of pain in marital separation or divorce are invariably complex.

At the first level, they affect the two persons who once stood before a minister or civil officer to be joined together. Their energies are probably taxed to the limit by the conflict they are engaged in.

At the second level, separation or divorce involves the parents of the couple, and possibly aunts and uncles and even grandparents — the earlier generations who raised the two. In a sense they have failed too, unless they can lay the blame on the person their daughter or son married.

At the third level are the friends of the couple — neighbors, colleagues at work, fellow club members, church members, golfing partners, an entire social network. It is tricky business for the friends, much more awkward than a death in the family. How does one react at such a time?

And finally, separation or divorce involves the children, if there are any. The children are the youngest and most helpless of all the parties concerned.

It has been estimated by various surveys that between thirty and forty percent of all children in the United States have experienced "family disruption," as sociologists are fond of calling it — the separation or divorce of their parents. It is not an unreasonable figure, considering that more than one out of every three marriages now terminates in divorce. It means that every third child playing in a nursery, sitting in a classroom, yelling at a ball game, or singing in a church choir has gone through the pain and confusion of a divorce in the family.

Correction: *is* going through.

The evidence is that the pain and confusion do not end.

The Pre-Divorce Situation

The suffering does not start at the moment of divorce, of course, either for the children or for their parents. Often it originates years before a divorce actually occurs.

I met a couple who divorced when he was 64 and she 63, after forty years of marriage. "They should have done it thirty-nine years ago," commented their daughter; "it has been forty years of pure, unadulterated hell!"

Louise Despert, a counselor, says in her book *Children of Divorce* that "emotional divorce" — the strain of marital hostility — is often worse for children than actual divorce. It keeps the children in a constant state of turmoil and uncertainty, often without ever ending decisively in "the cleansing surgery of divorce by law."[1]

Even the smallest children are aware of tensions and disputes between their parents, and feel personally threatened by them. Parents may think they are keeping their difficulties secret by not verbalizing them in front of the children. But they forget that small children depend on nonverbal communication more than verbal exchange, and notice subtle things parents themselves may not see.

Despert quotes one 3-year-old who told her: "Today when Daddy came home he didn't pick me up, but he and Mommy started to whisper about something. They were too busy to play with me."

Later, the same child reported: "Mommy and Daddy are not the same as they used to be. When Mommy kisses me good night she's always in a hurry. When Daddy is telling me a story he stops in the middle and looks at me as if I wasn't there. Sometimes he squeezes me too hard when he says good-by. I get scared."[2]

Most children are disturbed by tensions they cannot understand.

"Mother and Dad rarely fought in front of us," recalls a young woman I interviewed. "But they were often surly with each other, especially at the dinner table. I can remember times when Dad didn't speak to Mother for days at a time. You could cut the air with a knife."

Sometimes children try to be peacemakers, as in the case of Julia R., whose parents often disagree and brood for several days. "I can usually tease Daddy into getting over his pout if Mom is willing to make the first step in his direction, but getting her to do that isn't always easy. Sometimes I almost have to fuss at her, you know, shock her, to get her to do it. I'm never going to act like them when I grow up. It's so silly and immature."

It seems to be particularly hard on children if the struggle between the parents takes an overt form, with a great deal of yelling and even physical combat. Mark B. — whose father would sometimes become angry and throw furniture around the room, breaking chairs and table legs and smashing glass fixtures — had a nervous breakdown when he was 15. His psychiatrist attributed it to the sense of powerlessness he felt when his father was in a rage. He wanted to quell the disturbance and compel his father to be quiet; but he was only a child and was afraid to cross the father. When he came under great pressure at school, he succumbed to a breakdown as the solution recommended to his unconscious by the pattern of passivity he had known during the father's periods of antisocial behavior.

It is the children's powerlessness to combat their parents' treatment of each other that is so pathetic.

Laura S.'s parents had terrific arguments before their divorce, and sometimes her father would slap her mother violently. Once, Laura said, he blacked the mother's eye and opened a long gash on her left cheek. The mother collapsed on the floor, weeping, and the father slammed the door and left the house. "I cried too," she said. "I couldn't help it. When Daddy left, I just went to pieces. I shook and shook. Mama held me and tried to get me to stop, but I couldn't. I finally vomited before I got better."

Trevor M. recalls that his mother sometimes brought her male friend to the house when his father was there. Trevor was only 12 at the time.

"They would sit there in the dining room talking about how Mother was in love with Jock and not with Dad. I was so embarrassed and hurt I could have died. Dad was mild-mannered and passive. I could tell he was hurt but he never raised his voice. I wanted to kill Jock and throw Mother out of the house. She had no business doing Dad that way. Dad was such a good man. After they had gone — Jock and Mother — Dad put his arm around me and cried. He said he was sorry but he couldn't help it. Sometimes people don't love each other any more, he said. He still loved Mother, and would have taken her back, but she didn't love him. I couldn't bear to go with her and Jock when they married. She seemed dirty to me. I understand it better now, I guess. But then it seemed like the end of the world to me."

A few years later, when the mother developed cancer, Trevor did not feel sorry for her. He thought she was getting what she deserved. A religious person, he even wondered if it was not a form of divine retribution.

Bobby, Jean, and Miriam were 13, 10, and 8, respectively, when their parents' marital tensions came to a head and the father told the mother he was leaving. The father was a doctor, and he was having an affair with a nurse at the hospital. Bobby and Miriam overheard the confrontation in which the mother accused the father of having a mistress, whom she called "a grade-B whore," and the father said the mother had never cared about anybody but herself, that he was divorcing her and moving to another state to set up a new practice. Two days later, after a drinking binge, the mother took an overdose of pills. Bobby discovered her on the kitchen floor when he came home from school. He ran to a neighbor's house, thinking she was dead, and the neighbor called the emergency squad. The mother was rushed to the hospital and survived. A month later, after the father had left town but before the divorce was granted, she attempted suicide again. Each time, the children were taken in by a neighbor, as the father refused to assume any responsibility for them. All three became highly nervous. Bobby and Jean became noticeably withdrawn and taciturn, and experienced trouble with their schoolwork. Miriam began having nightmares that continued intermittently for two years.

Treating Children as Scapegoats

As helpless as they are, children almost inevitably feel a sense of guilt when they experience hostility between the two people they love. Many psychologists assume that this guilt is related to the Oedipus or Electra complex stemming from the genital period, from ages two to six, when the child feels an erotic attachment to the parent of the opposite sex and is jealous of the parent of the same sex. The feelings are usually repressed, but so is the guilt. The open conflict between the parents, as a fulfillment of the childish wish to be rid of the parent-rival, evokes the guilt again, though without the obvious causal connection. Other psychologists believe a child can feel guilt in the midst of family tensions because he or she would like to do something about the tensions but cannot; it is similar to the guilt experienced by a bystander at a street quarrel who feels powerless to intervene.

Chuck B. was 12 years old when his mother discovered that his father, a minister, was having an affair with one of his parishioners. There was a noisy row one night and the father moved out of the house. Shortly afterward, he left town and took a sales job in another state. A few months later, the parents were reunited and the family moved to another town, where the father received another appointment as a minister. Within a year, however, he was seeing the woman from his old parish again. The wife became angry and told one of the church officials; this led to the termination of the father's ministry.

When Chuck was 16, he and his father took a camping trip together. Alone for several days by a lake, they had several long, intimate conversations about life and the family. Chuck confessed that he had always felt guilty, somehow, about what was happening to his father. He knew his mother was a cool, unresponsive woman. He understood, therefore, why his father might need the companionship of another female. When the mother discovered the affair and became even more withdrawn than ever, he sensed she was punishing the father for something not entirely his fault. This made him feel sorry for the father, and yet, because he was helpless as a boy of 12 to enter into an adult conflict, he felt guilty too.

Many parents are prone, when they are engaged in conflict with each other, to lay guilt upon the children.

Billy Q. was only five or six years old the first time he heard his parents speak of a possible divorce. Realizing he had overheard the discussion, his mother thereafter used his knowledge as a method of controlling his behavior. If he became too noisy about the house, she would say, "Now, Billy, you must be quiet and not annoy your father, or he will go away and leave us." When the parents did divorce, five years later, Billy was certain he had been responsible for the breakup, and had to be treated by an analyst.

Frequently, when a couple are having a marital fight, one will accuse the other of being incompetent with the children, or of having raised them improperly. Without intending to, perhaps, the parent has stated disapproval of the children, and they are implicated, in their own minds at least, in the failure of the marriage. "I never realized," said Tom H., a high school student, "how much my dad despised me, until he called my mother every name in the book for what she had done to me. I was weak, scared of my own shadow, and incapable of seeing anything through on my own, according to him."

When there are two or more children involved, fighting parents often accuse each other of loving one child more than another, raising doubts and fears in the children's minds. Sometimes this is a ploy by one parent to gain the sympathy of the child who is said to be underregarded by the other parent. Either way, the child is victimized by the information that he or she is not loved as much as another child, whether the information is true or not. No protestations of love and care will ever erase the doubt planted in the child's mind.

A child may easily develop feelings of guilt if he or she is made privy to information by one parent that is not available to the other parent. This happened in the case of Sandra M., who was 13 when her parents' marriage broke up.

"Mother would get me aside and tell me she really loved this other man and wanted to marry him. A couple of times she even told me when she was going out to meet him, and once he stopped by the house when Dad was away. I felt like a traitor to Dad. Mother swore me to secrecy, and said she needed to talk to me sort of woman to woman. It was a terrible burden to impose on a child."

Denny P.'s situation was even worse. An only child, he was used as a confidant by both parents.

"Mother would complain to me how Dad was running around with this other woman in town, and how ashamed she was. Once we ran into the woman when we were walking down Harris Street, right in front of the bank. She was as surprised as we were. She started to say something, but Mother just *humphed* and made a sort of sweep around her and we went on without saying a word. Mother said she would like to kill her. But then Dad would talk to me about Mother, and how she liked this man who worked at the school board. They were sweethearts once, when they were young, and my father thought they still liked each other. He said he had seen Mother coming out of the building where the school board office is, and thought she was up to no good. He put his arm around me and told me not to worry, that he would take care of me, whatever happened. I didn't say anything. I never did, either to him or to Mother. I didn't want to take sides."

Irving R. Stuart and Lawrence Abt refer to this kind of practice by the parents as taking the child "hostage." The child is uneasy, because he realizes he is being used as a device for gaining some goal other than his own welfare. "Hostages do not generally feel security or faith in their captors and users," say Stuart and Abt. "They may, if the period of hostaging has gone on for long enough in their lives, accept this as such an unquestioned reality that they adapt submissively, passively, dependently — and thereby lose their psychological lives in a torrent of retreat."[3] In the latter case, it has been shown that children frequently lose their drive for achievement, abandon their previous curiosity about things, and even suffer lowered I.Q.'s.

Occasionally a child's guilt in divorce is the result of an overt accusation by one or both parents that the child is one of the reasons for the divorce. A psychologist friend said that he has had two cases like this, in which a counselee has admitted being told that his parents would not have divorced had it not been for him. In one case, the mother had reportedly sued for divorce in order to take the child away from the father's bad influence. In the other, the father had stated as a reason for leaving the mother that he could no longer stand "the damn noisy brats" she was raising.

As Martin Herbert says in *Problems of Childhood*, children all too frequently "become the battlegrounds for marital warfare and are a tempting target for mutual recriminations about such things as neglect, incompetence or favoritism. Being powerless, children are ideal scapegoats at a time when the parents feel unhappy and frustrated."[4]

Trying Not to Take Sides

Sometimes, when the marital disharmony is obviously caused by a dominant partner who abuses the other, children will openly side with the weaker parent. James M., for example, a 14-year-old, actively took his mother's part against his father, who often cursed the mother, complained of her looks, and threatened to beat her. James sometimes talked back to his father and tried to shame him for the way he treated the mother. Once, when the father struck and knocked him down for interfering in a fight, he told his father that he had better never go to sleep in their house again for fear of what the boy would do to him in the night.

Often, however, the loneliness children experience from marital discord and divorce is a result of their unwillingness to take sides with either parent. Baffled by the unhappiness of their parents, they shrink back from confidence in either parent, and try to hold themselves aloof from the conflict.

Joanna A.'s father was a doctor. During the Second World War, he fell in love with an army nurse. When he returned to the States after the war, she tried to contact him and his wife learned of their affair. Fron then on, until a divorce four years later, their life together was a protracted battle. "It nearly destroyed me," said Joanna. "I could understand what Daddy had done. It was natural, under the circumstances. I could also understand how Mama felt. They were both so lonely and unhappy. I was the oldest child, and they both tried to lean on me for support. I loved them both so very much, and wanted to help them, but I was afraid if I was very friendly to either one, the other would interpret it as taking sides, so I stayed out of it, or tried to. We were all very lonely during those years."

Mack J. was 13 when his parents decided to get a divorce. He had an older brother who was 18 and away at college, and a younger sister who was 9. Because the older brother was not available, both parents turned to Mack as a confidant. They were not angry or demonstrative people, and the household remained remarkably placid through the entire affair. Mack developed a pronounced stutter during this period, however, and still has it today, four years later. The pressure at that formative time of his growth made a mark on him that may never be erased.

One can appreciate the overwhelming sense of responsibility a child must feel when caught in the emotional whirlpool of his parents' unhappiness. At a time when he ought to be receiving love and understanding from them in order to grow freely and happily, they are asking these qualities of him. The energy he needs for maturing and developing within a normal framework of studies, games, and intersexual relationships is being drained into the bottomless pit of a tragic family conflict.

The Loneliness Afterward

There are many agonizingly lonely moments for children in the process of conflict and decision that leads finally to separation or divorce. One 11-year-old boy, Stanley M., told me he could not bear to hear his parents fight, and often went to sleep at night with his pillow doubled around his ears, trying to shut out the noise of their quarreling.

But in most cases the loneliness gets worse after the divorce. The child's energies are no longer spent trying to stay afloat in the sea of constant fighting and bargaining, and can be turned to quiet estimates of where he or she now stands. As soldiers with war nerves often complain, the peace is harder than the battle.

Malcolm A., a hotel manager in San Francisco, was only 12 when his parents divorced. His mother remarried and remained in the small eastern town where she had always lived, and the father moved to San Francisco and bought a restaurant. "I lived with my mother and stepfather during the school year," says Malcolm, "and spent the summers with my father. I loved going out there to be with him. He was wonderful to me. But three months a year wasn't very much to be with someone you loved as much as I loved my father."

Many children, following a divorce, begin to receive far more material advantages than they had before. This is especially true among middle- and upper-class children. Both parents become sensitive to what they have done to the children and try to make up for the emotional deprivation with material supplements. If the parents remarry, their new spouses are also anxious to give the children the kind of attention that can be "touched, tasted, and handled." It seems to soothe the parents' consciences and to guarantee that the children will know they are loved.

Levy S. was only 5 when his parents divorced and his mother moved back from New York to her home state of North Carolina. His father was a teacher. Although the father soon remarried and did not have much money to spare, he frequently sent expensive gifts to the child. When Levy was 8, his mother married a dentist with a well-established practice. They had a child of their own within a year, and a second two years after that. Anxious that Levy not feel unloved or unwanted, his stepfather showered him with presents. Levy had his own pony, a fabulous tree house built by a local carpenter, an extensive layout of model trains, a swimming pool, and, for his twelfth birthday, a small indoor basketball court.

Yet Levy remained quiet and withdrawn, unable to show affection to any of his four parents. He played with his fabulous toys, but without display of emotion.

His stepfather arranged for him to have psychoanalysis.

"He just isn't happy," came the professional report after six months of analysis. "He appears to feel basically insecure because he isn't sure of anybody's love."

Louise Despert sounds the right note in the conclud-
ing words of *Children of Divorce:*

> Beyond nourishing food and shelter from the ele-
> ments, children need little that is material. But their needs
> of the spirit, though simple, are absolute. If these are not
> met, nothing else can serve in their place. If they are met,
> nothing else matters.[5]

Marcia M. was 10 when her mother divorced the army
colonel she was married to and married a congressman who
was also recently divorced. Marcia moved with her mother to
the congressman's home town where they had a suite in an
old family-run hotel. A local girl named Linda was kind to
her at school, and they became friends. Linda says that when
she went to visit Marcia in the hotel suite, she was awed by
what Marcia had — "gorgeous, expensive clothes, big fuzzy
toys, a beautiful room, the kind you see in a movie." She
couldn't understand why Marcia was so quiet and unhappy,
and why she had the nervous mannerism of pulling constantly at her hair.

Later, when Linda had grown up, she knew the reason. "The poor girl was miserably unhappy, living there like
Little Miss Muffet on a satin pillow. She had everything I
didn't have but lacked the one thing I did have — a stable
home life. She probably looked at me and thought, 'Gee,
what a lucky girl she is!' "

The Gesell Institute of Child Development strongly
recommends against the practice of split custody, by which
the children of divorced parents spend part of their time
with one parent and part with the other. It is much better,
they think, for the child to have a definite home and not be
torn between two households.[6] Children are easily confused
by the constant shuttling back and forth between parents'
residences.

"I never know what to do," said Rose, an 8-year-old,
to her therapist. "At my mother's house I never make my

bed. At my father's house I have to make it. And everything is different. I never know what to do where. All that moving back and forth . . . it's bad for a kid. A few days here, a few days there. I just don't understand it. I feel torn apart."[7]

"I always hate it when I go home after a weekend with Daddy," says 13-year-old Maxine D. "Mom gives me the third degree. Where did he take you for dinner? What did you talk about? Did he give you any money? She's so afraid I'll like Dad or something. Maybe she thinks I'll want to leave her and go move in with him. It's a hassle."

Most divorces, fortunately, work out with single custody for the children. The children live with one of the parents and have visiting privileges with the other. At best, this deprives the child of one parent most of the time, and constitutes a situation wherein the child, who needs a constant, almost unconscious, matrix of love during the developing years, is permitted to be less cognizant of the strains of love and of the jealousies the parents continue to feel for each other.

For most children of divorced parents, holidays are the hardest times. Many of them can remember when the family was united for birthdays, Thanksgiving, or Christmas, and that remains the ideal in their minds. After the divorce and removal of one parent, such occasions always seem incomplete.

Ted and Garnet, 13 and 16 years old, had not lived with their father, a professor in a liberal arts college in New England, since they were three and six. Their mother had remarried shortly after the divorce, and they had lived with her in a southern state. When their father took a sabbatical leave and went to England for a year, he and his wife invited the boys to come and live with them for the overseas experience.

Although it was in many ways a rich year for the boys, they greatly missed their mother. We were living near them at the time, and I remember the excitement in Garnet's voice one night just before Thanksgiving when we were attending a concert together. It was his birthday, and he was rushing home to receive a telephone call from his mother. I saw him the next day and asked if the call came through. He didn't try to disguise his disappointment. "I guess the lines were tied up," he said.

It was the same way at Christmas. The mother obviously did not wish to interfere too much in the boys' lives while they were living with their father. The boys, on the other hand, were hungry for home and the love and comfort of their mother. It was an unforgettable picture of the casualties of divorce.

The Stigma of Divorce

Many children are noticeably reluctant to talk about their parents' divorce or themselves as the products of a broken home because they are embarrassed by the failure of the marriage.

I saw an unusually clear instance of this recently when a minister and his wife divorced. The three children in the family immediately became objects of concern and sympathy to the members of the congregation. Many persons went out of their way to show kindnesses to the children. But the children tended to withdraw, displaying embarrassment and, in a few instances, signs of annoyance. When I spoke to one of the boys about this, he replied testily, "I can't help what they did" — "they" being his parents.

Myra Y. is a college student. Her parents have been divorced since she was eight years old, and she and her mother lived alone in a small town until she went away to college. During that entire time, she says, she never once spoke with anyone about the fact that her parents were divorced except to acknowledge, if some teacher questioned her, that yes, they were divorced.

"It was something I just didn't talk about. I don't know why. I guess it was our business and nobody else's. I didn't want people to feel sorry for me. I felt different from other children who had both parents. Even different from a girl friend whose father was dead. My father was living, but he wasn't with mother and me. It was like — I don't know — as if he were in prison or something. I knew people would think he should be with us, not off somewhere else."

Adolescents appear to be more sensitive than younger children about having divorced parents. Perhaps it is because they are more concerned about their own images and identities and are uncertain about how they will be viewed in relation to the divorce. The necessity of pretending or covering up adds an additional psychic burden at a time when life for them is difficult enough, without having to deal with extra problems.

Turning to Rebellion

Research on the children of divorced parents has sometimes provided contradictory results,* but the bulk of it indicates that these children are much more likely to exhibit behavior disturbances than children from normally stable homes. A statewide survey a few years ago of all ninth-grade children in Minnesota showed the highest delinquency rate among the children of divorced couples. The second highest rate was among boys whose fathers had died and girls whose mothers had died.[8]

Figures are often deceiving, because human situations are usually complex and difficult to reduce to mere statistics. But it is obvious that children who have been through the broken-home experience have had a great deal of stress on their personalities and are thus likely to exhibit tendencies to social difficulties. As Dr. Sula Wolff says, marriage breakdown is an index of personality difficulties in one or more of

* Owing to the fact that children in stormy, unhappy home situations also exhibit characteristic disturbance patterns.

the parents, and these not only preceded the breakdown but continue after it.

> Children of unmarried, divorced, or separated parents are children who are being brought up by a parent or parents who have either made an unrealistic choice of partner or who re-enact within their marriage their own neurotic conflicts. Each parent denigrates the other in the children's eyes and when, as often happens, the mother dominates, the father is presented to his children in a poor light. After the break, children from such failed marriages are left not only without a parent, but with an image of a "bad" parent, and this endangers the normal personality development of the child of the same sex who identifies with this same despised parent and *is* often identified with the parent by others. We all have our parents inside us. In part we are our parents. Our self-esteem and our confidence are dependent on our being able to think well of our parents in childhood.[9]

When a parent dies, as Wolff observes, the surviving parent usually speaks well of the deceased partner to the children; if anything, the dead parent's bad qualities are forgotten and good ones remembered, leading to his or her glorification. The child's self-image is thus not only protected but possibly even enhanced through the memory of the dead parent. But in the case of divorced parents the child must live with the continued awareness of someone's failure, and possibly with an elaborate description of personality faults or aberrations.

Occasionally, if the child's life has been relatively secure and happy most of the time prior to the divorce, he or she may react rather maturely to the breakup of the marriage and determine to do well despite the hardship.

Harold V., for example, was 14 when his parents decided to separate. The marriage had been a happy, prosperous one until the father contracted polio and was left, after a year's illness, mobile but impotent. His attractive young wife thereafter became involved with another man, and, when the father learned of it, he decreed that they should get a divorce. Harold was doubtless chagrined and embarrassed as well as hurt by the development, but bore it admirably. Instead of letting his studies go, he dug into them with new determination and won the praise of his high school teachers for his conscientiousness and consideration. When he graduated, he won a scholarship prize and a citizenship prize.

Harold's example, unfortunately, is the exception, not the rule. Most children whose parents are in the pre-divorce or divorce patterns of existence become listless about schoolwork and tend toward real neglect or failure. David N., for example, was a 13-year-old boy when his parents divorced. He had an I.Q. of 119, well above average. Prior to seventh grade, he had made all A's and B's and had been considered a top student. In his seventh-grade year, which was the year of the divorce, his work fell to C level. The following year he was reprimanded for receiving D's in some courses and for not turning in portions of his work.

Doing poorly in school is only a part of many children's reaction. They go even further and become problem children in their behavior.

Mary P., for instance, had been a pretty, well-adjusted child before her parents' divorce when she was 12. Her father moved away and she and her mother moved into a small apartment. Her mother took a job and was away from home until six in the evenings. Mary soon began to associate with a crowd of wild youngsters, most of whom had difficult home lives too. By the time she was 14, she had become promiscuous and was having relations with many men much older than she. Her mother, because she spent so much time working, felt powerless to control Mary's actions.

Boys are normally more problematic than girls after a

divorce, because they often live with their mothers and lack an intimate male model of behavior, as well as fathers to discipline them.

Terence G. was 9 when his father and mother, who were both doctors, divorced. His mother left Canada, where they had lived, and moved with him and his sister, who was 7, to the States. In order to continue her professional life, she hired a series of live-in babysitters to care for the children and do the cooking. Terence professed to hate his father because he felt betrayed by him. By the time he was 12, he had become a constant nuisance to other people living in the apartment complex, and the landlord, after repeated warnings, finally asked his mother to move. Terence was generally quiet and well-behaved in school, possibly because his teachers were mostly males. Even after his mother obtained a house with a yard large enough for Terence to play in, he continued to be a terror to other children in the neighborhood, and his mother frequently had to go out in the evenings on peacemaking missions. She understood that he had special problems because of the absence of a male parent, and, apart from an occasional scolding or desperate plea, did little to curb his misbehavior.

Robbie T. was the son of upper-class parents. His father was a banker and his mother a professional model. After several years of stormy life together, they decided to divorce, but, because of extensive family connections, to remain in the same city. The mother had many boy friends following the divorce, and continued her active social life. Robbie and his sister, who were 12 and 9 years old, were cared for by a maid and cook. Soon after the divorce, Robbie grew noticeably ruder and rougher with other children in his classroom at school. Although he often asked children to accompany him home after school or to come for a weekend, few were willing to accept the invitation because of his aggressive behavior. Those who did rarely returned a second time. Generally they complained to their parents of Robbie's manners and physical roughness toward them.

By the time Robbie was 13 and in the seventh grade, his behavior at home had carried over almost completely to the schoolroom and playground, and teachers and school officials found it necessary to discipline him frequently for mistreating other students. Under pressure from the school's headmaster, the mother finally sought psychoanalytic help for Robbie, but that did not seem to improve his behavior. I lost track of him when the mother remarried and moved to another state as he was about to enter the eighth grade.

Later Problems

Not all of the problems falling to the children of divorced parents occur immediately; some have a long fuse and show up only in later life. Numerous investigations have correlated parent loss in childhood with various kinds of psychiatric and social disturbance in future years. High on the list are mental breakdown and suicide. It has been clearly shown, in fact, that a larger proportion of children from broken homes commit suicide than from any other classification.

Joanna A., whose case was discussed earlier (see page 197), tried to end her life before she completed her high school education. She had been going steady with a boy in her class. They had a fight and he began dating another girl. Joanna took a bottle of pills from her father's office, drove to the boy friend's house, found no one there, entered, and swallowed the entire bottle of pills. The boy's mother returned from the store, found Joanna unconscious on the kitchen floor, and called an ambulance. She was rushed to the hospital and her life was saved.

"Life didn't really seem worth living," she said. "Mama and Daddy were both so miserable. They had made a mess of their lives. When Bill walked out on me and started going with Nancy, it seemed that I had made a mess of mine too. I didn't want to go on."

Lila M. was 10 years old when her father deserted her mother. Lila's mother had to go to work to support the two of them. An older sister was married but was not in a financial position to help. Lila appeared to adjust bravely to the new situation. Throughout high school she was popular with both girls and boys. She married shortly after graduating from high school, and had three children in rather rapid succession. In her early thirties, she became very depressed and unhappy. One day when her husband and children were away she started the car in the garage with the door shut and attempted to asphyxiate herself. A neighbor discovered her and called the rescue squad. She was given psychiatric care for a year and has not attempted suicide again.

"Everything just seemed empty," she says. "I couldn't shake the feeling. I thought of poor Mama all those years, working so hard to put me through school and buy me nice clothes and all. And for what? My life wasn't worth it. My children would be as well off without me. Ray [her husband] would marry again. I just wanted to end it all. I was tired of fighting."

In both these cases, and in many others that could be adduced, the persons lacked a sense of self-validation. They had expended so much emotional energy on their parents' situations at a critical period of their own growth and development that it left them depleted for the ordinary tasks of living. The evidence is that children simply cannot be deprived of natural, relatively unselfconscious home relationships during latency and adolescence without paying for it later in some form of psychological disturbance.

As Ira P., who was 12 when his parents divorced, says, "You always feel that there is something missing inside you — some security, some time of innocence, some experience of wholeness and joy. You think, when other kids were playing and enjoying life and just growing up, I was struggling with my family's destiny and worrying about how I was going to make it in the world. It leaves a mark on you. Sometimes when you're tired and not thinking about anything in particular, you slip up on yourself and realize that your mind is picking over that period of your life again, trying to make sense of it, trying to discover some important bit of evidence you never saw before. You get so you hate it. It's like a bad dream that won't go away."

11

The Struggle for Independence

John Holt tells in his book *Escape from Childhood* about visiting a large group of ninth-graders in a Midwestern suburban school. It occurred to him, when some time was left after his talk to the students, to ask them what they were thinking and feeling about the institution of childhood. He posed three questions. The first was, "If you could legally vote in political elections, how many of you think that at least some of the time you would vote?" The response was slow; about two-thirds of the students raised their hands. The second question was, "If you could legally work for money, how many of you think that at least some of the time you would work?" Again, a two-thirds show of hands. Finally, almost as an afterthought, Holt asked the third question: "If you could legally live away from home, how many of you think that at least some of the time you would do so?" This time he was amazed at the response:

> Every hand shot into the air, so quickly and violently that I half expected shoulders to pop out of joint. Faces came alive. Clearly, I had touched a magic button. I thought to myself, "If only I had thought to ask that sooner, how much I might have learned." But the period was at an end. I thanked the students, wished them luck, and they filed out of the room. My hosts and I continued our tour of the schools. No one mentioned that last response, and I thought it better to let it drop.[1]

Reflecting on the incident, Holt supposed that many people would read it as the wish of rebellious teen-agers wanting to get away from nay-saying parents so they could live it up on their own. Yet he did not think that was the case. It might have been with some of them. But most of them, he believed from his experience with American children, were only saying that they wanted to live, at least for a while, among other people who might see them and treat them as people, not children. He knew children well, and he knew that the majority of them are not resentful toward their parents.

The careful studies of psychologists support Holt's impression. E. Douvan and J. Adelson, in a survey of over three thousand young people in the early sixties, found surprisingly little of "the turmoil, the conflict and instability normally attributed to this group." On the contrary, these investigators expressed concern at the absence of "the passions, the restlessness, the vivacity" that they considered a healthy requisite to normal maturation.[2] W. W. Meisner, who asked over one thousand boys age 13 to 18 to describe their attitudes toward their families and home life, found that the majority of them were proud of their parents and liked to be at home; 84 percent spent more than half their leisure time at home until they neared the end of adolescence, and showed little inclination until this age to get away from their family situations.[3] And, in a poll reported in *Life* magazine in 1971, 57 percent of both younger and older adolescents reported that they got along well with their parents and had no trouble communicating with them. Of those who said they had such trouble, only 18 percent thought it was the parents' fault; 6 percent said it was their own fault; and 74 percent said it was "both our faults."[4]

These figures help us keep a proper perspective in our discussion of the storms and stresses of adolescence. Most young people are not out to "get" their parents and most of them do not give their parents bad marks. It is just that adolescence is an unusually difficult time. It is a *no time,* actually, when they are neither fish nor fowl, neither kids nor adults. Except for the first three years of their existence, there is no time of life when they are changing so quickly and radically, both physically and psychologically. Recently a father who had been away from home for six months returned in time for his daughter's thirteenth birthday. "My God," he said, "I left a little girl and returned to find a woman!" She had developed small breasts, started menstruating, and become very conscious of her femininity. A few nights later, the girl became upset at something her mother said at the dinner table. She got up angrily, went out, slammed the door, and pouted in her room all evening. The father was nonplused, for he had never before seen her in such a mood; her disposition had always been sweet and temperate. But she had entered puberty and adolescence, which are as baffling to children as the children are to their parents. As Irving Weiner says, there is such unanimous agreement among psychologists and analysts about the normality of adolescent disturbance that its *absence* may be more a source of concern than its presence.[5]

I was at a party where several adults fell into a discussion of the topic, "If I Had My Youth to Relive." At first there was some serious grappling with the idea. "I would study harder," said one. "I would have dated a lot more," said another. Finally, the entire discussion fell into a single chorus as everyone, men and women alike, gave thanks that they did not have to relive their youth. "I couldn't stand it," "It was bad enough the first time," "What a wretch I was," constituted the tone of these last remarks. Everyone remembered the agonies, the helplessness, and the sense of loneliness during those years of rapid change and growth.

The Search for Identity

Erik Erikson characterizes the child's years from the onset of puberty to the end of adolescence as a time of "Identity vs. Role Confusion."[6] It is the period when the child really undertakes and, it is hoped, tentatively completes an objective assessment of who he or she is in the light of all the biological, social, and psychological evidence. The process of understanding this has been going on since infancy, but it becomes keenly focused during adolescence. During these critical years, the future seems to bear down more and more on the youngster, and he or she feels an increasing pressure to be prepared to say, "This is who I am and here are my credentials for living."

"The integration now taking place in the form of ego identity," says Erikson, "is . . . more than the sum of the childhood identifications. It is the accrued experience of the ego's ability to integrate all identifications with the vicissitudes of the libido, with the aptitudes developed out of endowment, and with the opportunities offered in social roles." [7]

In other words, the child must now do a juggling act, trying to integrate whatever he knows about himself from childhood experiences with the new biological urges coming to bear upon him, with other latent interests and abilities beginning to come to the fore, and with whatever skills he is able to master for interacting with other persons in his world. It is a tall order, considering that the left hand doesn't know what the right hand is doing and that new ingredients keep intruding unexpectedly into the act as it goes on. This is why Erikson labeled it a time of identity versus role *confusion* — the process is so halting, distracting, and uncertain as to seem at times overwhelming, both to the person going through it and to the parents, teachers, siblings, and others who stand near enough to experience the fallout.

John Conger, a psychologist at the University of Colorado School of Medicine, cites the case of one adolescent girl who had three distinctly varying styles of handwriting. When asked why she did not have a single consistent style, she answered, "How can I only write one way till I know who I am?" [8] It was a fair question. She sensed that handwriting is an extension of personality, and she was still utterly confused about which aspects of personality she was experiencing were really hers.

In a similar vein, budding adolescents frequently experiment with different ways of signing their names. A boy named Conrad Dwight Tillington III may go through such permutations as Connie Tillington, Conrad Tillington, Conrad Tillington III, Conrad D. Tillington, Conrad D. Tillington III, Conrad Dwight Tillington III, and even C. Dwight Tillington or C. D. Tillington III.

At this stage girls especially are likely to undertake a series of changes in their hair styles, trying to find the one most attractive and that seems to fit best with the present stage of personality development. One 13-year-old went from a pony tail to a side part to a center part to a dry-blown, Farrah Fawcett style, to a short style in only eight weeks. "I couldn't decide," she said, "which was me. Now I guess I'll have to be me with short hair for a while, because my hair doesn't grow quickly."

Parents are often confused and annoyed by their children's weathervane attitudes and uncertainties at this age. After all, as Piaget has pointed out, their children have been quite happy with the autocracy of the parents. They have dressed, bathed, eaten, and slept at the parents' commands. Suddenly, now, they have entered a new phase of existence when what *they* think and feel matters a great deal. No longer happy with autocratic parents, they want the governing of their environment to be cooperative and participatory. Some parents are simply not prepared for this. They have been too accustomed to giving orders and imposing "the way it will be" on their children, and cannot easily shift into the new gear of relaxed regulations and government by consensus.

Adolescents are particularly concerned about peer-group fashions. This is one way they try out a new identity, one separate from that of their parents. When the parents thwart the child in his or her attempt to identify with others in the peer group, the child feels an almost unbearable inner constraint. Some children, who experience constant thwarting from their parents, feel totally isolated and alienated within their private worlds, for they feel both unloved by parents and unaccepted by peers.

"I will never forget," one college student told an interviewer, "how terrible I felt the time my dad refused to let me get my hair styled. He said it cost too much and looked stupid. But one Monday morning two of my best friends came to school with new styles. I felt like two left feet. Everybody who mattered to me had a mod style. Everybody but me!"

Often it is over such superficial things as hair or clothing styles that parents and children have some of their most crucial disagreements. Probably the parents are reluctant to witness the changes taking place in their children. They prefer a certain congruence between the *image* of the children they have developed through the years and the *actual appearance* of the children in the present, and consent to changes only grudgingly, if at all. The children, on the other hand, find superficial alterations the easiest and most convenient method of experimenting with personality possibilities. If a style doesn't suit, it can be changed. Their psyches are going through a revolving door at top speed, and they are not concerned about permanent images.

During the sixties and early seventies, one of the biggest fashion flaps was over the styles of eyeglasses. "I'm the veteran of many a battle," one optometrist told me, "between Mama and her kiddos who had to have new specs. Mama was always on the side of status quo, or at least said that Papa wouldn't like the new styles. But the kids almost invariably opted for the big new frames that sprawled across their faces like TV screens." It is reasonable to assume that glasses were a sorer item of contention than shoes, because families could sit at the dinner table without looking at the children's shoes, but they could not avoid seeing the flamboyant spectacle frames.

Some of the saddest cases of child-parent conflicts I have heard have been from youngsters whose parents refused to recognize the biological changes in their children. One girl's mother refused to buy her a brassiere, even though the girl's breasts had expanded so much that she felt self-conscious about them and tried to keep her arms held in front of her whenever possible. Another girl's mother would not purchase sanitary napkins for her when she began her periods; the girl wadded up toilet tissue and used that until she was old enough to get a babysitting job and purchase napkins herself.

Parents can be especially cruel at the onset of puberty when children begin to feel attraction to persons of the opposite sex and want to be with them either on dates or in casual settings. One father was completely intolerant of his daughter's behavior during this time, and resembled a medieval tyrant in the strictness with which he attempted to guard her purity. He forbade her to have dates and cross-examined her if he even saw her speaking to a boy on the street or at church. Once, when she was 12, he took her to a movie. Being farsighted, he sat at the rear of the theater. She begged to be allowed to sit nearer the front, and he relented. During the show, a boy came in and sat beside her. The father accused her of having prearranged to meet the boy. She denied it, insisting that nothing had been arranged and that they had not even spoken to each other. When they reached home, the father adamantly demanded that she confess her "sin," and beat her with a whip cut from a tree, raising great welts all over her back.

Many parents would, if they could, arrest their children's development, freeze them forever at the stage they perceive as "sweet and innocent." Perhaps they see something of themselves in the growing adolescents, and, reminded of their own adolescence, which may not have been very pleasant or satisfying, wish to repress that something, to stop it from emerging.

In any event, it is a very difficult time for most young people. Those whose parents are not sympathetic to the strains upon them have probably never before felt so alien-

ated and lonely. Some are tempted by the promise of peace
and tranquillity they knew during earlier years, and so either
feign capitulation or actually accede to their parents' desire
to keep them as children, suffering inwardly because the
urge to self-recognition is temporarily halted or obstructed.
Others, unable to dam the tide of changes occurring within,
spiritually say good-by to their parents and set sail for whatever fantasy islands may lie in their futures.

One of the most pathetic documents in all literature
must surely be Franz Kafka's "Letter to My Father," an actual
letter of over one hundred pages that the famous author
wrote in an attempt to declare his independence from a
domineering, insensitive father. The elder Kafka, a strong,
boisterous man who had been a soldier and a successful en-
trepreneur, constantly derided his physically weak, psychologically introverted son, and assured him he would never be
a success at anything. Disappointed in the son he saw emerging through adolescence, the father apparently determined
to destroy him as a person. Poor Franz, neurotic and dependent on his parents, took the abuse meekly, often beseeching
his mother to intercede with the father on matters that were
most important. He finally wrote the extremely long letter as
a catharsis for himself and, he hoped, a corrective for his
father.

But he never had the courage to send the letter.

The Unfortunate Clash

It is most unfortunate that parents are usually passing
through a critical stage of their own lives at the very time
when their children are undergoing their adolescence. A
man in his forties often begins to wonder if he has chosen
the right vocation, married the right woman, pursued the
right goals. His wife, similarly, sees the children growing up
and wonders what will become of her in the future; she feels
superfluous at a time when her energy reserves are still
strong and her sex level high. Enormous psychic energy is

necessary for coping with day-to-day existence at this time of life. All one can see, as Gail Sheehy puts it, is "the dark at the end of the tunnel."

It is not the most propitious time, in other words, for the children in the family to be hitting a period of great stress in their lives, when what they require is more patience, love, and understanding from their elders. In the natural paranoia of weakness and confusion they experience, the elders may well interpret the identity probing and testing of their youngsters as ultimate challenges to their integrity and authority as parents. At another period in their own lives, they might receive their children's problems with more kindness and resourcefulness, and help them ride out the storms they are experiencing; but, under present circumstances, they often feel attacked and called to account, and respond with constricted spirits, resentfulness, or even meanness.

Most domestic friction brought about by adolescence is over the authority model by which relationships are governed. The children, developing biologically and psychologically into pre-adults, must begin to assert more and more independence in their behavior. The parents, if preoccupied by personal concerns about career, self-worth, and other matters, may thoughtlessly respond to acts of assertion as though they were acts of rebellion to be put down at all costs. With things moving toward such an impasse, even the smallest, most insignificant disagreements can easily escalate into an all-out war between the generations.

I saw an example of this not long ago while visiting in the home of friends. The friends had made a recent trip abroad and were telling me about it. The 17-year-old daughter of the family was sitting on the floor by the fireplace, animatedly listening to the conversation and joining in to share her impressions of places they had visited. At one point, after her father had made a remark about a certain city, she said, "Oh, no, I don't think so at all!" and proceeded to say how she felt. "Elizabeth!" the father's voice cracked like thunder, "*we*'re talking!" Humiliated and hurt, Elizabeth said almost sotto voce but loud enough to be heard, "I thought I was part of the 'we.'"

The father is normally a thoughtful, considerate parent. I am sure that if he thought back on the incident he regretted having cut his daughter off so curtly. He did not realize, apparently, that she was a fully blossomed young woman, with definite opinions and feelings of her own, and that she felt she had entered the adult world sufficiently to be included as an equal in conversation. To him, she was still the little girl he had rocked on his knee and thrown into the air over his head, and he was not prepared to treat her as an equal, especially when she offered any disagreement with his own statements of opinion.

I happen to know that the father, in his mid-forties, has been experiencing the pressures of mid-life crisis for two or three years, for we had often discussed the fact that his present job was not really commensurate with his abilities or the level of his creative energy. Although he has continued to be a much better than average parent through it all, there is no doubt that his psychic reserves are often depleted by the inner struggle with his own problems, and that he does not always permit the latitude to his children he would otherwise give. The two of them, father and daughter, were at odds over something that should have been overlooked by the stronger and older of them, but he was unable at the moment to do so.

Where this kind of conflict between parent and child is frequent or constant, a habitual bitterness of attitude develops and normal, relaxed conversation becomes impossible. Every discussion seems to end in rancor, name-calling, and recrimination. "You *never* listen to me," the child may say, "you don't care about me!" To which the enraged parent is liable to retort, "You mind your tongue, young lady!" or "Go to your room this minute, young man!" The language of exchange, once characterized by cooing and softness, has become harsh, brittle, prickly.

Almost every subject of interest to the growing child

becomes incendiary: schoolwork, clothing, sex, marriage, money, friends, drugs, smoking, alcohol, cars, grades, television, all are volatile topics.

If the parent is not liberalized and prepared to recognize that his or her child is growing up and experimenting with life, he or she is likely to come down on the negative side of each and every issue. The adolescent, after all, only recently wore the clothes provided for him, played with the children he was encouraged to play with, had no interest in drugs or alcohol, and did his homework on command. Why should he suddenly expect to know his own mind about all these matters, much less exert his own authority in them?

The case of Eddie M. is fairly typical. Eddie is 16 and a junior in high school. He has been shaving for a year, and recently obtained his driver's license. He is a clean, pleasant-looking lad who dresses in suntans, polo shirts, and sneakers, his school "uniform." His hair is a little long for some people's tastes, but he keeps it clean and neatly combed. He speaks politely and appears to be considerate of others. His grades are in the B range generally, and he takes homework with moderate seriousness. He plays the drums and is part of a combo that occasionally performs for dances and parties. On Saturdays he works as a sackboy in a grocery store to earn money for records and dates. He doesn't have a steady girl, but seems to be well liked by most of the girls and boys who know him.

In my book, Eddie is a well adjusted teen-ager, in touch with himself and the world he lives in.

To hear his parents talk, he is a demon. Or, to be fair to them, he often *seems* to be a demon.

"I don't know what will become of him," declares his mother. "We simply cannot socialize him. He stays up till all hours listening to that awful music. His daddy finally got a pair of earphones for his stereo so the rest of us didn't have to listen, thank God. Then he doesn't want to get up in the morning. He drags into breakfast with his eyes half shut. And the car! We have the awfulest rows over the car when he wants to use it. He seems to think that because he has his license now he is entitled to use it whenever he wants to. Sometimes he stays out till midnight, and Jim [her husband] won't go to sleep till he hears it in the garage. He hasn't banged it up yet, but Jim expects him to. Teen-agers don't know the price of things. They drive as if nothing could happen to them."

Earlier, the mother said, there were arguments about the length of Eddie's hair and about his staying out late to play in the combo. It was finally agreed that he could play on weekend nights and for one mid-week engagement each month if he made no grades lower than C on his report card. "One D," his father said, "and it's all over — for good!" The only thing Eddie did that aroused no criticism was to get a job on Saturdays; both parents apparently took pride in that, and it inspired the father to talk about his first job and how it was a sign of assuming proper responsibility.

It is hard for the mother to believe Eddie is a normal youngster doing the things most boys do. She and her husband are serious parents, but in their seriousness they are not able to relax and allow Eddie to emerge into pre-adulthood. The home is unnecessarily in a constant state of edginess, which only makes it harder for Eddie to explore the possibilities open to him and arrive at his self-identification.

John Byng-Hall and Marilyn J. Miller, in a perceptive article on "Adolescence and the Family,"[9] cite a similar instance involving a family named Hardy and their 14-year-old daughter Jane. Against her parents' wishes, Jane has remained out until three o'clock in the morning on a Saturday-night date. She comes in late to Sunday dinner wearing a filmy nightgown. Her mother slams a plate of food in front of her, and relations at the table are obviously strained. When 4-year-old Mandy picks at Jane, repeating one of the mother's criticisms of her, Jane gets up to leave the table. Her mother orders her to sit down and eat. Jane flounces away to the record player and turns it on as she says, "I didn't want any anyway." Mr. Hardy looks at his wife and says, "Oh, let her alone; it's Sunday, can't we have some peace?" Mrs. Hardy retorts that she went to a lot of trouble to prepare the meal and that if she is not appreciated she will simply leave. Tension fills the room. Satisfied with her new tack, Mrs. Hardy begins to criticize Jane for staying out half the night. The music grows louder and Mrs. Hardy shrieks at Jane to cut it off. She begins nervously clearing the table, despite 13-year-old Peter's protest that he has not finished. The music becomes even louder as Mr. Hardy orders Jane to help her mother with the dishes. Jane finally goes sulkily to the kitchen, but leaves the music blaring.

It is a simple story, but there are numerous points to ponder in it.

First, Jane is the center of the tension because she is growing up and leaving the family at times when her parents think she should be at home in bed. Her budding sexuality is further underlined by the fact that she came to the table in her gown and by her father's not being willing to join with the mother in persecuting her. There may even be sexual jealousy on her mother's part.

Second, the mother apparently feels like a Cinderella; she has prepared the meal and served it while her young competitor remained in bed. Jane's coming late to the table was particularly annoying in this regard, and her wearing the gown was only a further insult.

Third, Jane's playing the record and leaving it on when she left the room is an assertion of her independence and identity as a young person who likes a kind of music her parents don't seem to appreciate. Psychologists are widely agreed that the whole rock music mystique is in large part successful with teen-agers because their parents do not like it; it belongs all the more to *them*.

Byng-Hall and Miller interpret the episode as one of Jane's challenges to what they call the Hardys' "family myths." Every family has such myths. In this case the myths may be the idea that theirs is a tranquil, peaceable family, the idea that the family members all love one another, the idea that the parents have pure thoughts and want only the best for their children, and the idea that they never take unfair advantage of each other or of their children. Such myths evolve spontaneously through the years, and provide a fabric of superficiality or unreality to the family's dealings, both with one another and with outsiders.

Adolescents often intuitively attack these mythical structures as a mode of self-defense. They have lived with them for years, but are more immune to their fantasy power than the adults, who have come to understand and re-enact their daily existence with their help. In the same way that the developing children puncture their own fantasy images in the search for themselves, they also turn and puncture the family images.

Byng-Hall and Miller see this in a very positive light:

> These family encounters can provide important pivotal points in a family's history. Adolescents are particularly likely to provoke scenes and rows. In this way they discover what parents are really like. They uncover fears, anxieties and prejudices and they challenge myths. The family may negotiate new, fresher life-styles in a row, but sometimes there is a backlash. From our point of view, family rows are interesting because repudiated themes may surface, old myths may crumble and new myths crystallize.[10]

The language reminds us of Prometheus and his defiance of the gods, who chained him to a lonely rock where the ravens daily ate at his liver for punishment. Myth-assailers have always been Promethean in their daring and courage, and young people across the centuries have tended to identify with the original fire-stealer. We can see in the image the stark loneliness and even misery of their position; those in authority never want to share the possession of fire with upstarts, for it diminishes their pre-eminence.

Theodore Clark, who has worked with many young persons and their families, accuses most parents of resorting to what he calls "oppression dynamics" to maintain their supremacy over the young. They consciously or unconsciously foster fears and anxieties in their children that will not only make the children subordinate at the moment but teach them to submit to societal oppression all their lives:

> Through oppression dynamics, the family as a social institution builds into the development of the young person the basic conditions necessary for him or her to be continually oppressed and exploited by society. The only reason people do not immediately perceive the nature of their condition is because the process of oppression is aimed not only at their behavior but at their consciousness as well. Therefore, the function of the family is also to communicate the values, assumptions, and despair that dominate and shape the consciousness in such a way that few individuals want to perceive, or are actually capable of perceiving, their oppression. Finally, because people *experience* oppression, the family must invalidate emotions and perceptions or persuade the individual that the experience of oppression is actually due to something wrong with him. Since the process of conditioning an individual for society is continuous from birth, most young people come to accept oppression as a natural state.[11]

This is a terrible accusation, all the more frightening because it is so true. Parents do not realize that this is what they are doing to their children because they are simply doing what was once done to them. The chain of oppression is thus passed on unwittingly from generation to generation.

Bruno Bettelheim's study of children reared on Jewish kibbutzim, which I have mentioned previously (see page 108), is interesting in light of this. Not wishing to perpetuate the traditional model of the Jewish family, kibbutz couples early decided that their children should be raised in an objective nursery setting with a *metapalet* or caretaker in charge. The mothers therefore wean the children at six months and they are surrendered to the *metapalet* to grow up in the company of peers, with parents visiting only a few minutes each day.

When the parents visit with their teen-agers, says Bettelheim, there is little tension in the encounters, for the parents do not feel under any pressure to rear the children; that is taken care of by the commune. They are free instead to chat with the children, to talk about whatever occurs to them, to visit with them more as equals than as subordinates. There is a negative aspect of this too, as there is not any real intimacy between parents and children, as there often is in non-kibbutz homes; sometimes the children complain that when they try to discuss problems with the parents, the parents shrug them off too easily, as though it were not their affair. But, in the main, the children are relieved of the pressures of adolescence because their parents expect nothing of them and they are able to develop freely within their peer groups.[12]

An 18-year-old boy named Jesse told me what he thinks the root of the adolescent problem is, and I think he may be right. "Parents can't stand having more grownups in the house," he said. "It freaks them out."

Jesse has a 16-year-old brother and a 5-year-old sister. He came to his conclusion about too many grownups from watching the difference between the way he and his brother were treated by their parents and the way their little sister was treated. It was always "Honey this and honey that" with the small child, but "Watch out!", "Stop it!", "You can't do that!" with the teen-agers. The parents often had overnight visitors in the house, and the boys observed that this too made their parents tense and nervous. They decided it was the presence of additional adults that raised the anxiety level.

This is a very perceptive observation. More adults in the household diffuse the power. It is no longer in the complete control of the parents and puts added demands on the mother's and father's nervous systems, because they have not learned to live with diffused authority and like to have things exactly their way.

The tragedy is that it makes children feel as unwanted as overnight guests who have outstayed their welcome. A psychological survey of approximately two thousand children across all age, sex, and social brackets showed that more than forty percent of them felt unwanted and rejected by their parents who were autocratic in the relationship.[13]

"If I had had the guts," a graduate student told me, "I would have either run away or committed suicide, so that my parents did not have to deal with me. In either case, I have no doubt that they would have thrown a party and celebrated all night."

The Importance of Peer Groups

Today many adolescents turn to peer groups for the help and support they need during identity formation. This is a relatively recent phenomenon that owes its existence to certain changes in the societal structures. With the breakdown of the integral community and the extended family, and the concomitant development of what is known as the nuclear family, consisting of only two generations, parents and children, the adolescent has had to solicit the feedback and relationship he needs from fellow adolescents.

How important the peer group has become in youth culture today is evident in a report issued by the Harvard Laboratory of Human Development. In a poll the HLHD took of both American and Danish adolescents, three out of five persons interviewed stated that if they had serious personal problems of any kind they would discuss them not with a parent, teacher, or other adult counselor but with other adolescents. They admitted they would probably turn to an adult with such practical problems as finances, career decisions, and certain kinds of school matters. But for other concerns they believed they would receive more sympathy and help from contemporaries.

Armed with this poll, I asked some youngsters about it.

"Yeah, I guess so," said Gary W., a 15-year-old freshman. "I mean, sure my parents care, I know they do. But it's like they're a lot older and don't understand as well as my friends do."

Seventeen-year-old Steve C. agreed: "Your friends are closer to your problems. One or two of them are bound to have experienced what you're going through, and they really care. They may horse around a lot, and act like a bunch of dodos, but when the chips are down they really come through for you."

"My parents are divorced," said pretty Gail R., 15, "and Mom and I are pretty close, probably closer than most moms and daughters. But there are some things I wouldn't bring up to her. I don't know why. I guess I just think there are some things you talk over with your friends, not your parents."

Perhaps this is the kind of solidarity that has contributed most to the formation of a subculture among the young people of our time, with its own heroes, literature, fashions, music, language, and mythology. It is true that the subculture is often manipulated by entrepreneurs who will produce and sacrifice pop idols at an astonishing rate in order to turn a few dollars, and it is true, as Erikson has said, that young people often "overidentify" with their cultural models.[14] But the young have needed the support of such a widely based culture to replace the support adolescents formerly received from the network of community and family relationships.

Sociologically speaking, it has been interesting to witness the dramatic confrontation of the adult culture and the adolescent subculture in recent years. Youth movements are no longer local. With the advent of television and jet travel, they have become strikingly universal, with the result that unrest among the young people of France, Germany, Japan, and the United States tends to converge and multiply geometrically. A youth life style, marked by long hair, unisex clothing, and the use of drugs, encircles the globe. Adolescents have discovered they can effect both social and political change through a variety of tactics, including sit-ins, demonstrations, draft-card burnings, rock festivals, underground publications, embarrassment of authorities, and mass defiance of adult "law and order."

At the heart of the youth movement of the sixties and early seventies was an attempt to expose the double standard of values held by the majority of adult leaders in Western society. It was an enactment on a national or international scale of the challenge to "family myths" of which we have spoken. The conflict over Vietnam proved especially embarrassing to American politicians, for it revealed the hypocrisy of American policy that pretended to be altruistic, when it was in fact geared to the benefit of an industrial economy.

Consciously or unconsciously, the ritualized use of drugs may well have been part of youth's challenge to the Establishment. John Conger thinks it was. He sees the use of psychedelic drugs, particularly, as a frontal attack on "a society dedicated to the Protestant ethic, with its emphasis on activity, competition, aggressiveness, delayed gratification, and material success."

> Drug users were seen as, in effect, telling the Establishment that its fundamental values were wrong, and that the struggle was not worth the candle. This threat was, of course, heightened by the nature of psychedelic drugs. Marijuana, by far the most popular, tends to induce passivity, pleasure for pleasure's sake, and an introspective awareness of the self, rather than external action. In contrast, alcohol, despite its many casualties, has tended to be accepted by our society "because it lubricates the wheels of commerce and catalyzes social intercourse." In short, adolescent drug use, particularly of marijuana, was seen by the society at large as an uncomfortable symbol of the alienation of a significant portion of its young.[15]

It is interesting to note that now drug usage among the young appears to be waning and is being replaced by an alarming increase in the consumption of alcoholic beverages, and that this is happening at the same time college students are clamoring for more order in their curricula and there is a more general acceptance among the young of the Protestant work ethic. There is also a growing repudiation of hard rock music in favor of softer, more romantic music and a general turning away from the extremes of hippy styles of a few years back.

The reversion is comparable to what occurs in the adolescent after a hard attack on the family myth: having made his point, he tends to fall back, uncertain of his power, and to become for a period a more docile, contributive member of the family group.

Troubles with Peers

While the peer group seems to be well established in modern culture, it also poses new problems for certain adolescents who do not fit readily into group molds. It is a societal expectation that everyone function within his or her appropriate group. Parents and teachers alike worry about certain youngsters who do not fraternize easily with their peers, and often bring psychological pressure to bear on them to enforce conformity.

Daniel M., for example, is a 15-year-old high school freshman. His mother worries that he does not get invited to any of his classmates' parties and never shows any interest in having friends into his home. She has spoken with some of Daniel's teachers about this, and two of them have expressed similar concern in response. "He doesn't seem to get on well with the other boys," said one teacher; "he appears to be a loner." Mrs. M. has questioned Daniel several times about this, and warns him that he may be establishing anti-social habits that will make him just like his father, who has never gotten along well with his colleagues at work.

Daniel protests: "I don't dislike the fellows. It's just that they're so silly. They're always cutting up. I do have friends, sort of. But I also enjoy being by myself. What's so wrong in that?"

What is really wrong is the adult expectancy that every child should be associated with a peer group. Fifty years ago, being a loner was not the socially reprehensible thing it is today; in fact, it often betokened a serious, well-intentioned child who would grow up to become a respectable person in the community. Now, with the advent of the nuclear family that provides little relational support for the child, we have come to believe there is something wrong with a child who does not turn to other children for support and friendship.

Marjorie H. is not popular with her classmates and thinks it is because she does not go to many parties. She has reasons for not going to the parties:

> I really don't like the music. I can't dance well either. I went to a dance class for a year, but, well, I suppose I'm just not rhythmical or something; I never could get the hang of it enough to enjoy it like some of the others. And, well, the boys are so stupid most of the time. They like to clown around and have a good time on their own, and usually the girls end up dancing by themselves, which I don't think is such a hot idea. So I don't go. Why use yourself doing something you don't want to do?

Other youngsters report that they don't get along with many peers because they don't use drugs, won't drink beer, don't like to "talk dirty," aren't allowed to ride around in other kids' cars, don't like to listen to records all the time, or won't pet to orgasm or go all the way sexually. A 16-year-old girl complained that most of the boys and girls in her class made fun of her for not making out with the boys. "I'm the only one who hasn't, they say. But I told them I have other things on my mind besides sex, and there's plenty of time for that. Mother used to fuss because I didn't spend more time with them, but she shut up real fast when I told her why I don't. I haven't heard any more of that!"

The conformity issue is a big one, precisely because of the identity problem among young people. There is terrific pressure on the average boy or girl to be like the others in the group in order to belong. Those who use drugs or alcohol and indulge in free sexual activities are already contending with inner guilt, both privately and collectively, and therefore lean all the harder on potential friends who challenge their values by refusing to participate.

It is easy to see how many students with an aversion to membership in such groups become even more confused in their search for identity, for, in addition to the problem of developing maturity in the world at large, they are afflicted by self-doubts about their ability to get along with others and find acceptance in peer relationships. With peer groups ranged on one side of them and parents and other adults on the other, they walk a lonely middle path, wondering what is wrong with them that they don't fit anywhere.

It is a hard thing to be a teen-ager.

Is It Harder Today?

Historians and sociologists believe it is harder to be an adolescent today than it was in any previous age. To be sure, teen-agers in earlier generations went to work earlier — many by the time they were fourteen — and enjoyed fewer educational benefits. They also tended to marry sooner, often assuming full adult responsibilities by the time they were 16 or 17. As Philippe Aries has shown in his book *Centuries of Childhood,* adolescence is a segment of the life span that was little emphasized before the eighteenth century. Children before that time went almost directly from swaddling clothes to being small adults. They lived in the same rooms with adults, swore like adults, drank wine and beer like adults, and, in most ways, lived like adults.

Many of the problems faced by today's teen-agers, however, spring from the fact that they do not become adults soon enough. Prevented from earning a living until they are at least 18 or 20, they cannot establish their own homes and escape from constant encounters with their elders. They cannot enter into marriage relationships until several years after the advent of sexual desire. They must contend with the expectations of peer groups and the added pressures these create. And they also have to cope with cultural shock waves unknown to young persons three or four generations ago.

Think of the shock waves that have hit their young psyches in the last forty years: the explosion of the atomic bomb and subsequent development of nuclear science; the threat of global annihilation; the struggle for racial integration; the assassinations of national leaders; the youth movement; the drug culture; Watergate; the emergence of Third World nations; space shots and moon landings; hijackings and terrorism; heart transplants; sensitivity groups; biofeedback; stereos, transistors, and memory chips; the energy crisis; the feminist movement; and, along with all of these, the growth of media coverage, so that they have not only heard about the shocks but have seen them on television with their own eyes!

Anthropologist Margaret Mead says that events and developments have begun to transpire so quickly in the modern world that no generation is able to absorb them into its cultural mindset. Consequently the torch passes constantly from the young adults to their children, as frequently as possible. More and more pressure is put upon the young to understand their culture and to assume responsibility for it. This despite the fact that they are kept in an overlong adolescence and given little real responsibility in the home! They move almost directly from being children to taking control of the world.

> Even very recently, the elders could say: "You know, I have been young and *you* have never been old." But today's young people can reply: "You never have been young in the world I am young in, and you never can be."[16]

This puts an incredible burden on the young, says Mead. They are thrust into responsibility before they are ready and are at the same time divided against their parents who must relinquish responsibility. And we have seen only the prelude, thinks Mead. Because the elders have never been young in this kind of world, they must surrender the future to those who have. The young are at home in this time. They have never known a sky not filled with satellites, a home not linked to the world by television, a world not threatened by nuclear or pollutive destruction. They do not anthropomorphize computers or romanticize political arrangements. They know instinctively the necessity of rational planning for population, food supplies, and world order. They recognize what their parents never did, that distinctions based on race and caste are anachronistic. They are no longer bound to the linear expressions of the printed page; their world comes to them with the fullness and immediacy of the electronic image.

The young belong to another country of the mind. Like the children of immigrants, they can no longer learn from their forebears. They find the language and fashions of their parents gauche and embarrassing. Even the ability of the two generations to communicate is soon lost. There is nothing for the children to do but turn their backs on the elders and create their own world.

And, with change increasing in the world at exponential rates, the young realize they cannot hope to program the future any more than their parents did. The best they can do is to steer the course of life for a little while and relinquish it to their children, who will be better educated and prepared for the task than they were. The whole course of life and education is thus reversing; transmission that once moved from parent to child is now turning in the other direction, and parents are dependent on children.

Does this all sound fantastic? Is Mead overdrawing her conclusions? I think of the dialogue at dinner with our own teen-age sons. My parents used to explain the world to me. Now my sons explain it to me. Oh, I fancy I teach them some things about values and moral choice and all that. But they tell me about new developments in computers, biochemistry, automotive science, rocketry, communication, and dozens of other subjects. I am afraid they do not find me an apt pupil. My old mind is tired, or else preoccupied with dreams of the past, so that I often cannot remember all they tell me and I am frequently chided, "But I told you that before and you didn't remember!" I have mentally resigned the future to these boys — my future as well as theirs. I am glad they appear to love me. Otherwise I should be quite alone and frightened. I must believe that they will take care of me in this puzzling new world, as my parents took care of me in the puzzling old one. Somehow, in the passage through, it was never *my* world. Not for very long, at least.

But what a burden it places on the young! They have their identities to discover, and, at the same time, the responsibilities for creating and governing the world. Baffled by the biological urges beginning to explode inside their bodies, they must nevertheless be assuming the moral leadership of the very race that produced them!

How Adults Can Help

I believe Mead has probably exaggerated the picture, despite what I said about my children educating me. Her notion of a culture totally dependent on the young is extrapolated from the idea that cultural developments will proceed along the same line they have been following. But history has a way of fooling us. It often moves ahead five paces, then back three, instead of continuing to go forward. And there are signs today that the rapidity of change we grew accustomed to in the sixties and early seventies is moderating.

But there can be no doubt we have moved into an age that puts much greater strain on adolescents than the one in which their parents grew up. Their childhoods may be longer than those of preceding generations, but they also become aware much earlier of the importance of performing well. The sheer pressure of testing is enormous. Every high school student is faced with a battery of College Boards,

SAT's, and Achievement Tests. More demanding schools expect the preliminary PSAT's as well, and some of the really tough independent schools, intent on a good showing, require students to take the SAT's and ACH's not once but twice!

"I was so nervous on my SAT's that I twisted my glasses in my hands and broke them," said Lynn R. "I knew how much was riding on my making a good score. All the colleges I wanted to get into had a six hundred fifty score as their bottom line of admission, and doing well was important even in getting a scholarship to the state university, if I end up going there."

A student in Sussex, England, where highly competitive A-level exams are the deciding factors between a person's going on to university and dropping out to enter another kind of life, recently broke down during his exams and wrote his name thousands of times on the papers, thinking he was answering the questions asked.

Some intelligent adolescents simply balk at proceeding through the maze of pressures, and opt out at lower levels of ability. Geoffrey R. has an I.Q. in the "bright normal" range, putting him in the top twenty-five percent of America's young people. He did well in school until his sophomore year in high school, then began to slide. In the second half of his junior year, he was put in a special curriculum with disadvantaged children, which included easy academic courses and work in manual training. During his senior year he failed most of the academic courses and had to attend summer school before receiving a diploma. He refused to apply for college admission, electing to attend a trade school and take a job as an auto mechanic. His parents, who were both professional people, were embarrassed and hurt that Geoffrey didn't have more, to use his father's words, of "what it takes." But Geoffrey had his own opinion about what he had done:

"I know I disappointed my folks, but, after all, it's my life and I have to live it. I probably could have done better.

I know I could. But why? What's the purpose? So I can be like Dad? He has to pop tranquillizers all the time just to keep his hand from shaking when he's drinking his coffee. He'll have a heart attack by the time he's fifty or I miss my guess. No thanks. I'd rather work with my hands and not worry about so many things. Life's too hectic today. I like simple things."

These bastions of civilizations, the bringers-in of the new society, are after all children, not hardened men and women.

I could not help being touched recently by this observation. Our 18-year-old, who sails through problems in calculus, writes essays on Hamlet's Oedipal complex and the current economic situation, and collects books of literary criticism the way I once collected comic books, had a day off from school. How did he spend it? Listening to records? Reading a book of poetry? Taking a girl friend to the movies? No. He did none of these things. He got out a box of toy soldiers he had owned since he was a child of six and spent the day playing with them just the way he did ten or eleven years ago.

For all their cleverness and education, today's teenagers are often scared and puzzled by the maze they are trying to thread on the way to adulthood. They are consistently inconsistent. One moment they are defying the world by writing a new symphony or experimenting with pulsating waves, and the next they are down on the floor playing with toys or coloring a picture. Sometimes, when things get too tough for them, they run away and hide. Some even commit suicide.

Adults can help, if they have a secure sense of their own identities and are willing to exercise a little patience.

There are two things to avoid: too much restriction and too little restriction. If we try to draw the boundaries too tight, young people will rebel and crash against them every time. As psychologist Paul Upson says, "the more we allow ourselves to become angrily preoccupied with an extreme of attitude or behaviour in an adolescent, the more likely we are to ensure its continuation."[17] But, at the opposite end, complete nonrestriction is invariably interpreted by a child as the parents' failure to care. The girl whose mother and father permit her to stay out until two in the morning without even a question or a reprimand thinks she is unloved, and may engage in anti-social behavior to determine whether there are any limits at all to her parents' tolerance.

The secret is similar to that employed by a good fencer, who treats the handle of his foil as though it were a bird: "If you hold it too tightly, you kill it; if you hold it too loosely, it will fly away from you."

Children need the security of limits, the feeling of care that good boundaries give them; and they also need the sense of ease and flexibility afforded by their parents' love and understanding. A good father or mother learns to adjust between the two to suit the child, and to share authority as the child is able to be responsible for it. After all, the child will not always be a child, or should not be; it is unfortunate if he is treated in such a way as to impede his maturity, so that he is unable to stand responsible for himself when he is 20 years of age. It is our task as adults to help him negotiate the curves in the road but to let him take over more and more of his own driving as he heads toward the goal of independence.

It is really quite wonderful, as your teen-agers grow away from you, to find that you lose your children in order to gain new friends; for that is what they will be, if you have been a wise parent: friends. All your life they will be persons you will enjoy seeing, visiting with, laughing with, reminiscing with, and planning with. It is a relationship worth waiting for.

12

The Biological Limbo

There is nothing more natural in children of any age than sexuality. I once heard Dr. William Masters, of the Masters-Johnson team, say that the very first baby he helped deliver came from the mother's womb with an erection. Sexual fantasies, masturbation, experimental lovemaking are all a normal part of each child's growing up and becoming a mature human being.

Yet there is no area of development that causes children more anxiety about themselves, or leads to more repression from parents, than sexuality. It is still, despite today's liberalized attitude toward sex, a subject of uncertainty and debate, and one in which parents try to exercise a fretful and often unhealthy kind of control. It is a topic many children never broach except in the company of their peers, for they learn at an early age that it is taboo in family circles. Caught between growing sexual urges and the prohibitions of parents and society, they feel guilty and lonely. Their bodies are sending them one message, the environment another. All they can do is build up more anxiety.

Crusty old A. S. Neill, founder of the famous Summerhill School in England, said he had never had a student who did not bring to Summerhill "a diseased attitude towards sexuality and bodily functions." He could only conclude that the corruption occurs in infancy:

Early in life, the child learns that the sexual sin is the great sin. Parents invariably punish most severely for an offense against sex morality. The very people who rail against Freud because he "sees sex in everything" are the ones who have told sex stories, have listened to sex stories, have laughed at sex stories. Every man who has been in the Army knows that the language of the Army is a sex language. Nearly everyone likes to read the spicy accounts of divorce cases and of sex crimes in the Sunday papers, and most men tell their wives the stories they bring home from their clubs and bars.[1]

There is, in other words, a double standard at work. Adults take a great, sometimes even lurid, interest in sex, then act as if sex were abnormal in their children. They punish their children for the guilt of their own obsessions. The cycle then repeats itself, with the children feeling guilty about sex all their lives and punishing *their* children for it.

Sears, Maccoby, and Levin agree. In their widely respected book *Patterns of Child Rearing,* they give the following summary of the goals of childhood sex training in the United States: (1) to inculcate the taboo against incest; (2) to teach the child not to masturbate; (3) to train the child to avoid sex play with other children; and (4) to maintain control of information about sex, in the illusion that the adults thereby retain control of the child's sex life.[2]

The major emphasis of sex training in our country, in other words, is repressive. It is aimed not at explaining sexuality to children and helping them to understand how it is a natural part of their development as human beings, but at curbing all forms of sexual expression before marriage. The training does not even have to be explicit. Many parents convey their message by avoiding the subject of sex altogether and by shushing the children when they mention it in any way. Thus a child reared in a home where sex is never overtly mentioned can nevertheless become convinced at an early age that it is dirty, perverted, and wrong, and that some great, unnameable punishment must surely befall the child who succumbs to its temptations.

The Sense of Guilt

Parents can hardly be blamed, of course, for children's earliest worries about sex, which apparently occur without provocation from the parents. Freud identified these as becoming vaguely conscious in children between the ages of three and five, which he called the *genital* stage of life. During this period children become aware of their genitalia, recognize sexual differences between males and females, and begin to have erotic feelings about persons of the opposite sex, especially parents. Such feelings inevitably involve a sense of anxiety, if for no other reason than that the child is threatened by the fear of competition from the parent of the same sex.

Freud attributed to this secret fear the origin of the castration complex — the anxiety in male children that centers on the removal of their genitalia. My own earliest sexual memories confirm this basic Freudian insight. My mother and father slept in separate bedrooms and I had a crib in my mother's room. I was about three years old, I believe, when I awakened one night and discovered that mother was not in her bed. Frightened, I climbed out of the crib and went searching for her. I found her sleeping with my father in his room. Ordered back to bed, I began to cry. I was overcome by feelings of anger and jealousy. Sometime afterward I was ill and a doctor came to the house to see me. I lay helpless in my crib as he poked and pressed on my body, lingering inordinately, it seemed to me, upon my genitals. I had the definite impression that he was going to remove them, and suspected it was a punishment because of my feelings for my mother. She and my father stood chatting amiably with the doctor, and I supposed they were all in collusion about what was going to occur. I felt betrayed by my mother and conquered by my father.

My parents could not be blamed for the guilt and fear I experienced, as these were in no way articulated to them. I bore them silently, as children always do, and suffered inwardly.

Erikson has described both the irony and the depth of similar feelings in every child:

> The "oedipal" wishes (so simply and so trustingly expressed in the boy's assurance that he will marry his mother and make her proud of him and in the girl's that she will marry her father and take much better care of him) lead to vague fantasies bordering on murder and rape. The consequence is a deep sense of guilt — a strange sense, for it forever seems to imply that the individual has committed a crime which, after all, was not only not committed, but would have been biologically quite impossible.[3]

Eventually, says Erikson, the sense of guilt becomes translated into initiative and aggression, so that the child learns to make things instead of "making" people (i.e., having them sexually). The stronger the sense of guilt, the more aggressive the child, both in childhood and in later life. Thus the consciousness of guilt is sublimated into a sense of achievement, though it is never totally eradicated.

Bettelheim, in *The Uses of Enchantment,* says that children's fairy tales are filled with veiled allusions to sexual guilt and castration anxieties, and that this is one reason the stories have such appeal. In "Jack and the Beanstalk," for example, the beanstalk symbolizes the almost magical power of the penis to rise and lead Jack into a wonderful paradise; but Jack finally chops down the beanstalk — renounces erection — lest the ogre come down and devour him.[4] An earlier version of the story, "Jack and His Bargains," had Jack trading the family cow for a wondrous stick; all its owner had to say was "Up stick and at it" and the stick would beat all enemies senseless. When Jack returned home without any money, the father became so furious that he took a stick and began to beat Jack. In self-defense Jack called on *his* stick, which beat the father until he cried for mercy. This, says Bettelheim, represented Jack's Oedipal conflict with his father and the dream that he could vanquish the father with his own stick or phallus.[5]

The implication is that children "recognize" motifs in such stories unconsciously and enjoy them without knowing why. The stories provide vicarious outlets for deep-seated feelings of guilt and unworthiness.

As the children grow older, these feelings are substantially reinforced by parents' attitudes toward sex, both in what is said and what is left unsaid.

Mark H., for example, remembers his initiation into sex when he was four. A little girl friend reported that she had seen her parents doing something strange. Mark asked what it was. She pulled down her panties and had Mark pull down his trousers. Then they rubbed their nude bodies against each other. "I sensed the danger in what we were doing," says Mark, "but I enjoyed it — so much so that we did it several times, until my mother caught us doing it. She walloped the daylights out of me. She also told the girl's mother, and she walloped the girl. They didn't tell us what we were doing wrong. They just beat the hell out of us."

"I have often wondered," says Mark, "exactly where I lost my innocence — whether it was in rubbing bodies with the girl or in being whipped for what I'd done. I think it was in the latter. It *made* what we'd done wrong. Before that it didn't seem half as bad."

Martha L. says that she knew nothing about sex as a child but that her mother's warnings against it turned it into a fascinating mystery for her. "She was always saying, 'Don't get into a car with a strange man,' 'Don't let the boys touch your legs,' 'Don't ever look at anything a boy tries to show you.' I didn't know what she was talking about, so I would ask her what she meant. But she never explained. I was a teen-ager before I had any idea what she meant."

The result of parents' unwillingness to be open and

specific about sexual warnings leaves children with both ignorance and apprehension. Sex acquires such an air of for-
biddenness that they feel guilty at the mere encounter with
it. William S., a college student, says that he entered a public
restroom when he was seven or eight and saw a man masturbating in a urinal. "I felt disturbed and unhappy for weeks,"
he says, "as though I had done something I shouldn't." Another boy, Robert R., was ten when he stumbled upon two
boys engaged in a homosexual act in a locker room. "I didn't
know what they were doing," he says. "I didn't understand
about such things. But I felt terrible. I couldn't get the picture of that thing out of my mind for several years. I felt
somehow involved. It really threatened me."

The Hardest Time

Sexual anxiety is normally at its peak for children entering puberty and adolescence. It has been present all
along. But the time between the genital stage, which ends at
about age five, and puberty is generally a time of latency;
children have become more or less accustomed to sexual
differences between males and females, and turn their attention to such practical matters as getting along with peers and
learning to live in the world of school. With the onset of
puberty, biological changes occurring in their bodies reassert
the potency of their sexual natures and compel them to become interested in sexual activity. Girls begin having men-
strual periods and developing breasts. Boys discover the
wonder and the embarrassment of erections. Children of
both sexes realize they will not be children much longer.
They begin to think of the day when they will be adults, and
to ponder their identities. Life becomes much more complex
for them.

If they have not been made to feel comfortable about
themselves as persons and as sexual beings, and have been
kept in a state of relative ignorance about sexual information, they may during this period become extremely dis-

traught about what is happening in their lives. The enriched level of their fantasies, coupled with a lack of reliable data, often results in mental and emotional agony. Bill C., a 10-year-old, for example, broke down in tears and confessed to his minister that he had committed adultery. The minister questioned him gently and learned that Bill had been in a peeing contest with two other boys slightly older than he. In a similar case, an 11-year-old told a priest he had committed adultery and the priest discovered that the boy had merely spent several hours looking at the ladies' underwear section of a mail-order catalogue. A psychologist counseled a boy who, after his first ejaculation, had become so terrified that he scraped up as much of the semen as he could and swallowed it. He was afraid it might be vitally necessary to the functioning of his body and that he would die for his "sins" without it.

None of these children would have experienced such acute anxiety if they had been taught by their parents about the nature of the body and its functions and had been led to expect strange new sensations during the onset of puberty. They were all unfortunate victims of the conspiracy of guilt and silence that surrounds the subject of sex in our culture.

G. Stanley Hall, who is often called the father of American psychology, once wrote of his own terror and loneliness during the years of puberty. He was so disturbed by his involuntary nocturnal emissions that he rigged bandages to his penis to try to control them. When he yielded to the temptation to masturbate, he said, the occasion was invariably followed by great waves of guilt.

> I suffered intense remorse and fear, and sent up many a secret and most fervent prayer that I might never again break my resolve. At one time I feared I was abnormal and found occasion to consult a physician in a neighboring town who did not know me. He examined me and took my dollar, and laughed at me, but also told me what consequences would ensue if I became unchaste. What an

untold anguish of soul would have been saved me if someone had told me that certain experiences while I slept were as normal for boys in their teens as are monthly phenomena for girls. I did not know that even in college and thought myself secretly and exceptionally corrupt and not quite worthy to associate with girls.[6]

For a long time Hall believed he should never marry. It was a great relief when he finally learned that his experiences had not been abnormal or even exceptional.

A woman who is a concert artist describes the agony she felt because of her sexual feelings and the sense of repression in her puritanical home:

> Sex was never mentioned in our home. Upon observation, it would appear that all eight children were the result of immaculate conception! Oh, we knew sex existed from listening to our relatives gossip. But it was obviously distasteful, sinful, and filled with dire consequences. The worst thing that could happen to a girl was to be raped and the worst thing that could happen to a family was a daughter with an illegitimate child or a "shotgun" marriage.
>
> But, as with so many children, solitary investigation proved to me that, sinful though it might be, sex was pleasurable. And for a few moments the whole world of loneliness and rejection could be blotted out.
>
> Thus began a vicious cycle of indulgence, guilt and disgust that was to mar so many years of my life. I knew instinctively even though the subject was never mentioned that what I did was not approved of. That it must be hidden. The loneliness this produced went deeper than mere isolation. It was a bereavement of my soul. I withdrew more and more into the world of fantasy. A world where I was clean and beautiful and everyone loved and admired me; where I was valuable and really counted for something.

In her childish effort to reject her sinful body, the woman attempted to kill it with food:

This was brought out unmistakably during analysis. My obesity was the only way my mind could deal with the anger against what I thought I was. Obesity was also the protection I gave myself against the fear that if I was slim and attractive I might be sexually promiscuous. From old parent tapes I had gotten the idea that any woman who was attractive was automatically more inclined to be more promiscuous. And with my history of compulsive behavior what else could I expect? So strong was that tape and the one of bodily rejection that even after I had faced them, I was powerless to change them.

The Escape into Fantasy and the Vicious Cycle

Withdrawing more and more into the world of fantasy — that is precisely what confused and lonely youngsters do. Convinced that their developing sexuality cannot be openly accepted, they do not accept it themselves. Yet they cannot resist self-stimulation and the erotic fantasies that accompany it. They become caught in a vicious cycle, condemning themselves and feeling morally lonely, then assuaging their loneliness by indulging in more fantasy.

Peter Dally, senior consultant psychiatrist at Westminster Hospital in London, says that most unhappy children engage in masturbation because it is pleasurable and relaxing. The constantly unhappy child uses it as a substitute for an unsatisfactory relationship. Masturbation becomes the child's main outlet for his loneliness, anger, and sense of deprivation.

> He discovers that through his fantasies he is virtually omnipotent, that he can control and provide for himself what he cannot obtain in real life. And at the same time he re-creates for himself the person for whom he longs and whose love he craves. . . . Through his fantasies he becomes the master of his world, is transformed from a helpless being into an all-powerful emperor. All his sensual and emotional needs that have been searching for an object now become displaced onto masturbation and its fantasies.[7]

As guilt frequently follows masturbation, the cycle is enjoined. Fantasy becomes masturbation becomes guilt becomes fantasy again. Children who become locked in the circle never escape from loneliness, frustration, and a destructive self-image. Salvation must generally come from without, as love is given and self-worth is established. Otherwise the guilt drives a wedge further and further between the self and the external world.

The sheer range of sexual experimentation during puberty is amazing. It is obviously a time of feverish exploration, when the anxiety of guilt is outweighed only by the ecstasy of sensual discovery. One man reported that he felt nearly as sensitive in the area of the anus as he did about the genitals, and often excited himself by inserting into his rectum a glass test tube onto which he had rubbed some soap. "I was always afraid it would break while it was inside me," he said, "and I would have a devil of a time explaining it. But I enjoyed it so much I couldn't stop doing it." Another man, who lived on a farm, said that in his "ranker" days of adolescence he sometimes inserted his penis into a hole in an old fencepost and tried to achieve orgasm with the post. A college girl said that when she was twelve or thirteen she discovered the pleasure of inserting a large marble, nearly an inch in diameter, into her vagina and then expelling it by the contraction of her muscles. For the first few times, she said, she had a "mortal dread" that the marble might not come out of its own accord and she would have to be operated on for its removal, but she soon learned that there was no danger. Each of these persons considered himself or herself "weird," "strange," "unique," or "sinful," and had a lower opinion of self because of the experimentation.

R. C. Sorenson, in *Adolescent Sexuality in Contemporary America,* says that guilt feelings and anxieties about masturbation are "mostly of another era." Yet the figures he cites hardly corroborate such a statement. Forty-five percent of all boys questioned admitted they had guilt feelings either "sometimes" or "often," and among girls currently masturbating the figure rose to 57 percent. Only 17 percent of the boys and 22 percent of the girls said they never have guilt feelings associated with self-stimulation. Among younger girls who masturbate the guilt level is much higher than among older girls — 76 percent admit to guilt feelings "sometimes" or "often." [8]

Marjorie Proops, reviewing the thousands of letters she received as an advice columnist for the London *Daily Mirror,* says that masturbatory anxieties are far and away the greatest ones boys have, and that for many girls as well they are a tremendous source of guilt, depression, and insecurity. Most of the letters revealed obsessive concern with old wives' tales and moral prohibitions.

> The astonishing myths still abound: "Will hair grow on the palms of my hands?" "Will the habit damage my penis?" "Will I ever be able to have normal sex if I don't stop doing it?" "Will it make me impotent?" "Will it stop me having babies?" "Will it give me heart disease?" "Is it, as my mother says, a sin against God?" [9]

It is perhaps worth noting that early adolescence is the time when most children are ripest for religious conversion and commitment to future religious vocations. It seems probable that the guilt associated with new sexual experiences leads directly to spiritual searching. Countless references in the literature about masturbation are similar to G. Stanley Hall's confession that he always prayed fervently after masturbating, promising never to engage in the act again; and numerous examples from both medieval religious writings and contemporary counseling journals suggest that many persons never outgrow the tendency to associate sexual desire with spiritual unworthiness. The connection is ingrained from childhood on.

The Limitations of Learning

Many school systems now offer at least a modicum of sex training for adolescents, and there can be no doubt that students generally benefit from such training. The primary service it renders is in the demystification of sex. Youngsters who see well-prepared booklets and films on the physiological aspects of sexuality are no longer held in bondage by ignorance and by the incorrect descriptions of sex provided by other children. For some, the mere fact that sexual acts are openly described helps to normalize them and assuage the sense of guilt.

"It was wonderful for me to see those films," reports a 16-year-old girl. "I found out I wasn't the only kinky person in the world. I used to lie on my bed and listen to old *Let's Pretend* records, the ones where princes and heroes rescued girls in locked castles and all that, and I would find myself rubbing my thighs and getting very excited. I didn't know about me. I thought I was terrible or something. But the films explain what's happening to you — you know, puberty and everything."

But it would be a mistake to think sex education is able to solve every adolescent's sex problems. It isn't, for some very obvious reasons.

First, it is not always possible to translate mere information into flesh-and-blood realities. Sexual experience — including guilt and fear — is a very personal matter. While an adolescent may see excellent films and study well-designed books about sex, and acquire a fundamental understanding of human bodies and procreation, there is no guarantee that he or she will be able to integrate the information into the self's understanding of its sexual pilgrimage. Sexual knowledge is not always retroactive — it may not enable the student to forgive himself for offenses he believes he committed before the knowledge was imparted. Thus, there are many young people today who have been liberated from ignorance of the technical aspects of sex, yet remain inwardly tormented by the ghosts of childhood sexual experiences.

It would be helpful if courses in sex education were always accompanied by counseling sessions in which students learned to discuss sexual matters with their parents and with school counselors. Few schools, however, attempt such a program. The material is presented, students are asked if they have any questions, there are a few titters, and the sessions are concluded. Nor do many students, once they have had a sex-education course, approach school counselors or teachers about sex-related personal problems. Consequently the newly acquired information about sex often remains at the information level.

Many psychologists agree that giving adolescents basic sex information without counseling them about the moral or spiritual applications of it is like teaching them the rudiments of driving a car and turning them loose on the highway. Both teen-agers and their parents, they say, derive far too much confidence from the fact that the teen-agers have had a course in sex education; it is assumed that the young people know what they are doing when in actuality they cannot possibly comprehend the powerful social and psychological dynamics involved in all sexual behavior.

Sometimes young people themselves realize this. "I'm not about to do it [have sex] until I'm older," said Melissa L., 15. "You can't possibly understand what you're doing at my age. I'm still a kid!" Lane B., a college freshman, agrees: "You've been breezing along having sex for two or three years and one day you wake up and say, 'Hey! What's all this about? Am I making love because I have to or because I know how?'"

Like any complicated emotional matter, sexuality simply cannot be learned overnight. It is a process of self-understanding, a pilgrimage, and children need to know this. There are many physically mature persons in the world who have never matured in sexual self-understanding. As welcome as sex-education courses are — or should be —

they cannot foreshorten either the time or the effort required to reach fullness of understanding.

The second reason sex-education courses cannot solve every adolescent's sex problems lies in the unpredictable growth patterns of adolescents themselves. Adolescents do not mature in a straight line. There are ups and downs in their progress toward adulthood. Many psychologists speak of early adolescence, middle adolescence, and late adolescence. Yet even these categories are too precise to capture the forward-backward movements of most adolescents. The years of puberty are such stressful years that a child in middle or late adolescence may suddenly appear to revert to early adolescence.

Simon Meyerson says:

> Adolescent sexuality is like an evolving, complex, kaleidoscopic jig-saw or crossword puzzle in which the pieces, the clues, the questions, the struggles and explorations, and the answers may change shape and colour before the full pattern is formed. Changes in one area influence another. There are causes and effects, actions and reactions, expected and unexpected. There are obsessions and digressions, progressions and regressions. There are times of clarity and times of obscurity; times of failure and of triumph; glow and gloom. There are times of excesses and interactions; times of stillness and reflection. Sexual feelings may arise, respond and influence the gestalt in different ways at different times.[10]

All of this is very confusing to adolescents. They themselves cannot understand why they do not develop constantly, without periods of regression and depression. They do not yet know that all growth is characterized as much by dormancy as by active progress. Parents, instead of chiding them for inconsistency, should encourage them by reminding them to be patient with themselves, and not to expect to mature too quickly.

Sex education, although often viewed by adolescents

as the superhighway to all their goals, can never take the place of sexual learning within the family. There is where the child's earliest fantasies occur, where guilt is most often experienced, and where forgiveness must be made real. Only as caring adults help the child to understand himself or herself in the context of social interaction, and to integrate information and feelings, can the child come to perceive the true form and function of human sexuality. If our society is sexually sick, it is not because of the failure of sex education in the schools, but because sex and love have not been nurtured together in the home.

Sex as Communication

If sex education in schools has achieved one thing, it has made young people much freer about sex in middle and late adolescence. No longer afraid of pregnancies, many of them engage in sexual activities to an extent that can only be alarming to their parents. Approximately 75 percent of all adolescents agree with the statement that "When it comes to morality in sex, the important thing is the way people treat each other, not the things they do together." Eighty percent of boys and 72 percent of girls believe that "It's all right for young people to have sex before getting married if they are in love with each other."[11]

The most interesting factor, however, is not the abandon with which adolescents now engage in sex but their emphasis on caring relationships. Adults often overlook this in assessing the morality of the younger generation. Today's adolescents may be a lot freer about sex than were their parents, but they are also more concerned about the quality of interpersonal feelings.

"Sure, I like to make out," says Doug A., 18. "But not with just anybody. I have to care about a girl first. I mean really care. Not to get married, I don't mean that. But as a friend, as somebody I trust and believe in."

One of the most significant discoveries made by Sorensen in his interviews with teen-agers concerns the way they use sex as a means of communicating with one another:

> Some adolescents find it very difficult to make friends and tend to be loners. They find meeting people difficult and the development of a friendship even more so. They lack the ability to put their reactions into words, and they do not always know how to extract opinions and ideas from other young people. Small talk comes hard for many young people who need to know others well before they have anything much to say; but they do not know how to know others well.
>
> For some, having sex with another is the ideal means to introduce meaningful communication. A sexual relationship frees some of their inhibitions, and in the happiness of their emotional and physical reactions ideas come and words flow.[12]

"It's like getting inside a girl's head," said one 15-year-old boy. "It isn't that you just know a girl better after you've had sex with her. It's that you open up to each other, and you trust each other, and you find yourself saying things that maybe you never even thought out for yourself before. I get to know a girl a lot better after we've balled, better than I used to think I had a right to know anybody."[13]

It is wrong to think of most young people who have sex freely as sexual experts who thoroughly enjoy what they are doing. On the contrary, few of them become adept enough at lovemaking to relax and savor the experience; it is often marred by anxiety and self-consciousness. They frequently prefer to smoke marijuana or get a little drunk before having sex, because they find that this reduces inhibitions and makes the act more pleasurable.

"I like to smoke a joint and then screw," said one 16-year-old girl. "Smoking always makes me want to screw. Then, afterwards, we lie there and smoke some more, and we talk. You say things you'd never have the courage to say under other conditions. You feel warm and good and loved.

Not just by the other person, but by everybody, by the world. It's wonderful!"

What it all comes down to is a shift in the place of sex. For most adults, sex was viewed as the acme of a relationship, the moment two persons waited for; when they had been together a long time, done a lot of talking, gotten to know each other well, they might then proceed to go to bed together, either before or after marriage. Many young persons now view sex as a more natural occurrence *on the way* to knowing the other person. Instead of talking, they make love. Then they find they can talk better, that the relationship is easier.

The latter viewpoint is probably the result of sex training in schools and a more open attitude toward sex in all the media by which society disseminates sexual understanding. Sex has been desanctified. It is no longer the Holy Grail of the boy-girl relationship. The relationship itself is the primary object, with sex as a means to an end.

Many parents do not like this. Not only does it differ from the tradition in which they were raised, it removes from them the control over children that parents once exercised because they were the keepers of sexual information and the ordainers of sexual activity. What they really fail to see and take responsibility for, though, is the fact that their children use sex as an aid to relationship because they have not learned how to relate in the family. Sexual freedom became a big issue among the young of the sixties because it was their way of saying to parents all over America, "You never taught us how to relate to one another in love and acceptance but now we are doing it!" In other words, sex is as much an answer to loneliness and rejection for the kids who make out all the time as it is for the ones who stay at home and indulge in autoeroticism. They too are hungry for relationship, for acceptance by others.

One reason sex becomes such an obsession with some teen-agers is that it is their one big hope after years of loneliness and self-doubt. Burdened by unhappiness in the fam-

ily, pressures at school, and failure in other social relationships, they accept the biological changes taking place in their
lives as the thing they have been waiting for, the magic moment when they will be transformed from ugly frogs into
powerful princes and ravishing princesses. They have to believe the metamorphosis will occur, because they have waited
for it so long. They cannot bear it if it fails — which of
course, in many cases, it does.

"I thought when I went away to college," says Rob T.,
now a young stockbroker, "that I had it made. Co-ed dorms,
pot parties, chicks every night. It was a blast at first, but it
soon simmered down. Now it seems like a dream, like it
really didn't happen. It didn't change things the way I
thought it would. I'm still Rob T. and I still have trouble
knowing who the hell I am and what I'm doing in this
world."

The point is, kids *are* looking for answers in sex —
because they have not found them in life.

The Agony of Role Diffusion

Add one more problem that many children face in
adolescence today — the changing roles of the sexes. Advo-
cates of role reform naturally insist that this is not a problem
but an advantage enjoyed by young people today — they no
longer have to conform to stereotypes of male and female
established in ancient times. This is true, in some cases. But
there is often confusion in an era of change like our own,
and no one is more uncertain than a child still trying to
resolve his or her identity questions.

Take the girls, for example. On one hand they are
encouraged to be as free as boys; the strong ideological message they receive from the feminist movement is that they
are no longer to think of themselves as objects in the sexual
relationship, but as subjects and even as pursuers. On the
other hand, most girls realize that sexual stereotypes have
not actually changed as radically as libbers would like them

to, and that the sexually free or aggressive female is still, in most boys' eyes, a "loose" woman. As Elisabeth Henderson says, it is still, whatever girls would like to think, "the old choice between the virgin and the whore":

> These alternatives are reflected in the boy's attitude to girls. Most people accept that most boys will experiment with sex, if not actually go through a period of promiscuity. The girl with whom he experiments is an object — her significance lies in "how far he can go" with her, in what he will be able to report to his peers. His feelings are likely to be reserved for the ideal and maybe untouchable girl. It is as though the adolescent boy approaches sexual encounters in the spirit of the Oedipal boy who has two attitudes to the same mother. One is of anger and denigration towards the sexual mother who goes off and leaves him; the second is of love for the beautiful, ideal mother who stays with him.[14]

In other words, girls will not be completely liberated sexually until boys have been freed from their Oedipal attachment to mothers. Therefore they are caught in the bind between the generally freer attitudes toward women and the single area of exception to those attitudes, in the minds of young men who are seeking "pure" women for serious attachments.

Actually it may not be in a single area. Judith Bardwick and Elizabeth Douvan have done research suggesting that girls' fears of traditional stereotypes in the way they are perceived lead them to conform to those stereotypes in such matters as grades and athletic ability as well as sex. That is, they perform less freely than they might if they were not concerned about appearing feminine and subordinate to males. Say Bardwick and Douvan:

> While boys are often afraid of failing, girls are additionally afraid of succeeding. So the adolescent girl, her parents, her girl-friends and her boy-friends, see success as

measured by objective, visible achievement, as antithetical to femininity. Some girls defer consciously, with tongue in cheek, but the majority . . . internalize the norms and come to value themselves as they are desired by others. The only change from childhood is that the most important source of esteem is no longer the parents but the heterosexual partner.[15]

A college girl told me she feels much freer to excel in her studies now that she is married and doesn't have to cultivate the "weaker sex" identity. She is in fact making much better marks than her husband, who is also in college. I asked how he feels about this. "Oh, I think it hurts his pride," she said, "but he's very good about it. Now he even asks me to help him organize material when he's facing a test, and he seems to realize that my competition in this area doesn't affect our personal relationship."

A survey conducted by *Psychology Today* indicates that females also have difficulties today adjudicating between their liberal ideals of manhood and the more traditional machismo views. While new role diffusion values suggest that quieter, gentler boys who are less aggressive and athletic make better partners than rougher, manlier types, sexual desire is still more often stimulated by the latter than by the former. One respondent said:

> I had tended to idealize traits such as gentleness and warmth, indicating that they were vital to masculinity. But when I reflected on one intense relationship, it was the traits I had minimized on paper that had aroused me in fact: pride in physical strength, competition in sports, and his constant awareness of being masculine. I think what I've found is that my feelings still lie in the deepest of traditions. While I will continue to assert myself as powerful in my own right, I'll always revel in my dreams of someone tall, dark, and handsome, to open doors and protect me forever.[16]

Again it is the problem of trying to rewrite infantile sexuality in adolescence and beyond. As the young man still longs for the mother pure and undefiled, the young woman desires the protective father. The strain of trying to mediate between instinctive desire and contemporary ideology is very severe on the younger generation.

The adolescent male does not fare much better than the female when it comes to the matter of role diffusion. He reads and hears constantly about the androgynous ideal, the man who is poised and self-assured in his masculinity, yet tender and sentimental as a woman, gentle with children, and willing to do housework. For some boys, to be sure, such an ideal is a godsend, providing a shield for aversion to athletic contests and other symbols of machismo. For others, it is much more difficult to achieve than the simpler black-and-white-role models of yesteryear. It is particularly damaging to the All-American-Boy type who excels on the gridiron or the basketball court but is deficient in tenderness. Statistics indicate that he still makes out as well as ever with girls in short-term relationships, but is troubled by the girls' new expectancies of him in longer relationships.

Boys appear to be more often troubled than girls by the open dissemination of information about homosexuality, and to have fears that they may be inclined toward becoming homosexuals. Perhaps one reason for this is the fact that people commonly believe male homosexuals are revealed more easily through physical traits than lesbians, although this belief has never been substantiated by evidence. Sorensen's study concludes that there has been no increase in adolescent homosexual activity in the past twenty-five years. Yet the dramatic growth in the amount of publicity given to alternative sexual habits has contributed enormously to the number of adolescents who suspect themselves of being deviant because they have had normal experiences of homosexual experimentation during puberty or before. The newspaper and magazine columns of doctors, psychologists, and advisors to the lovelorn frequently carry anguished letters from teen-age children confessing such experimentation and wondering imploringly about their sexual futures.

The Leisure to Worry

The sum of it is that children in our society experience a great deal of anguish because of their sexuality. Whereas in more primitive societies young people are ushered rather quickly and peremptorily from childhood into socially approved sexual relationships — usually marriage and the establishment of a home — in ours they are given several years to search for their identities, largely on their own, and then left to themselves to resolve the matter of mating, trying to bring the whole thing off under an elaborate system of taboos and penalties. As a result, many of them become confused, accumulate a lot of guilt feelings, develop poor philosophies about sex and about themselves, and carry with them into adult relationships the kind of immature attitudes that are bound to endanger their marriages.

As Eleanor Hamilton, author of *Sex With Love,* said on a Today Show program,[17] our children arrive at puberty earlier than the children of any previous generation and must wait until later to get married. Once children entered pubescence at about 14 and were married and on their own by the age of 18. Now they generally arrive at puberty by 12 and marry at an average age of 22. Somehow they must negotiate a ten-year passage of their lives in which sex is exploding in their veins and they must delay its complete gratification.

Moreover, not since the days of ancient Greece and Rome has there been an age more devoted than our own to sexual stimulation of every kind. Clothing, hair styles, perfumes, shaving lotions — all are designed with sexual attractiveness in mind. Madison Avenue markets more items in terms of sex appeal than any other motivating factor. Newspapers, magazines, and television keep sex before us constantly. Young people could not, even if they wished, avoid the continuous bombardment of sexual suggestion and innuendo aimed randomly at the public.

It is no wonder that many teen-agers feel as if they are living in a pressure cooker with the heat turned up. "I don't understand adult thinking," said one 15-year-old boy. "They wave that stuff — pornography and all — in front of us like a red flag, then they complain that all we seem to think about is sex!"

Bettelheim says we must either re-examine the time-table by which our children are presently raised or else accept more and more accommodations to early sexual needs than we have already seen in the sixties and seventies.[18] Perhaps he is right. The waiting period is inordinately long and the pressures are considerable.

But there are ways in which we can help.

The End of the Tunnel

Secure sexual identity, as Arthur Hyatt Williams says, is "the epilogue of adolescence, not its prologue."[19] In the beginning is fear, excitement, guilt, trepidation. At the end, ideally, is hope, confidence, a healthy understanding of the workings of sex, and the ability to relate wholly to persons of the opposite sex, in love and responsiveness as well as in physical passion. In between is the long, dark tunnel of adolescent groping and guilt feelings, of experimentation and discovery, of frustration and occasional ecstasy.

Parents can play an important role in helping their children see the light at the end of the tunnel. They do this in three ways. *First,* they do it by having a healthy, positive relationship with each other, in which sex is treated as a beautiful, natural part of life and marriage. Despite the Oedipal period through which every child passes, there is nothing quite like this kind of relationship for saying to the child, "Sex is good, and, in the proper context, ought to be enjoyed." *Second,* parents help their children by being sensitive to their erotic nature even as infants, and by always providing responsive hearts for freely dealing with the anxieties either openly or cryptically expressed by them. It is never too early to begin real sex education, and there is no substitute for the home as a place to teach it. And, *finally,* parents can enormously ease the pressures of adolescent sexual anxieties by carefully and lovingly reassuring teen-agers, sympathizing with them, and supporting them as they negotiate their fuller social and sexual identities. There should never be, as there all too often is, a jarring disjunction between the way the young child was accepted by the parents and the way the adolescent is accepted; that is, there should never be a point at which the child-become-adolescent is able to say, "Gee, they seemed to love me when I was little; what's happening between us now?"

The pressures adolescents feel are enough to guarantee times of depression and loneliness. Such times are occasional in the happiest of children and more or less continuous in others. The adults in their lives should know this, remembering similar times in their own adolescent experiences. If they are mature persons, secure in the knowledge of their own sexuality and love, they will be able to "temper the wind to the shorn lamb," meeting fear with tenderness and abrasiveness with a calm spirit. And the reward for them, if they are constant and uncalculating, will be receiving their children at the other end of the tunnel, not as mere children, but as young men and women in the full joy of their sexual being.

13

What You Can Do

Ronald P. Rohner, an anthropologist, has made a comparative study of the child-rearing practices of two different societies, the Papago Indians in the southwestern U.S. and the Alorese, a tribe in the string of islands east of Java.[1] The Papagos love children. Although they rarely display affection toward one another, they constantly fondle and play with their babies. They swing them in hammocks, talk to them, and pick them up whenever they cry. In the Alorese culture, on the other hand, women work in the fields and are usually unhappy about the coming of additional children. They often try to miscarry, or undergo abortions. Mothers normally return to their work two weeks after giving birth, leaving the infants with a variety of caretakers.

The contrasting results among the two tribes are eye-opening. Papago children are happy, placid, and agreeable. They develop with a minimum of hostility and aggression, and take their places easily and naturally in the adult world. They marry and look forward to having children of their own to love and cuddle. Alorese children, at the other extreme, are almost invariably resentful, hostile, and unhappy. They rebel against parental authority and are unreliable in even the smallest responsibilities. They are hypersensitive to slights, and fight or throw temper tantrums at the least provocation. Their principal goal in life is usually to get rich by trickery or cleverness in order to lord it over other people. There is little real self-esteem among them.

The cycle repeats itself. What children become is largely determined by how they are treated during their most formative years. If they are loved, they will be loving. If love is withheld, or given only inconstantly, they will have difficulty with their affections. If they are encouraged and given signs of their parents' belief in them, they will believe in themselves. If not, they will never be able to accept their own worthiness, regardless of how admired and respected they may become in the eyes of the world.

It is vitally important, therefore, to understand as much as we can about children and to try to be thoughtful, caring adults. The trouble is that we are rarely ready for the responsibility of raising children at the time when we are doing it. Like getting married and choosing an occupation, it is one of the major tasks of life we always understand better when it is too late to make alternate choices. As someone once put it, "Isn't it too bad we can't be grandparents before we are parents? Then we would know how to treat our children."

The following suggestions are not the complete answer to children's loneliness or unhappiness. As we noted much earlier, there are metaphysical or ontological dimensions to loneliness, some stemming from the birth trauma itself, and these are not always responsive to treatment. But there are aspects of loneliness that *are* responsive, and it is for this reason that I list some of the things that "successful" parents and other child caretakers have found to be helpful in dealing creatively and lovingly with children.

Provide "Touch Security"

From their earliest experience, it is important for children to be aware of the touch of those who love them. Long before they are able to understand verbal communications, they can feel "acceptance messages" through the handling and loving of the adults around them. And long after they have become adept at verbal communication, they still need the assurance of these nonverbal messages.

We discussed in an earlier chapter the significance of the mother's cradling and fondling her infant so that the safe, enclosed feeling of the womb is not entirely lost at birth. There is no reason for the fondling to cease once the child is weaned or has begun locomotion. Continued touching can be very reassuring to a child through latency and adolescence, as well as to young and older adults.

In Western culture, there has been a tendency for fathers to cease offering physical displays of love at very early ages of the children, and for mothers to desist gradually from such displays, especially with their sons. One reason for this is the developing sexuality of the children and the puritanical heritage opposed to sensual feelings. But peoples of Mediterranean and Latin American origins continue to display physical affection to their children even after the children are grown, and to witness them in action is to realize how much families in our own traditions have missed.

Some people's fondest memories of their parents focus on moments when the parents broke their usual reserve and reached out to the children in physical gestures. A middle-aged woman whose mother had died said that when she went home for the funeral her father embraced her for several minutes: "It was the first time he had touched me since I was a little girl, and, I hate to say it because I don't mean it as cruelly as it sounds, but it was almost worth Mama's dying to feel his arms around me." A man who could not remember his father's ever kissing him or putting an arm around him recalled the single occasion when he was eight years old and his father took him sledding: "If I live to be a thousand, I'll never forget how good it felt to cling to my father's neck, lying on his back, as we plowed down the hill into the snowbanks. I still remember the warm, good smell of his clothing as I held on."

Don't hesitate to be physically responsive to children. Snuggle them, carry them, roll on the floor with them. Dance with them, embrace them, kiss them. And don't stop when they become three or six or twelve years old. Let physical touch continue to be a major form of communication with them until they become adults and can freely touch and fondle their own children. It is a case of the medium's being the message — they will learn deep down, where it counts most, that they are loved in ways no words can say.

Listen to the Children

How easy it sounds: *Listen to the children.* And how difficult it really is, how few of us really do it. Oh, we *think* we listen, but it is so easy to assume that one is hearing their real thoughts, their innermost desires, when what one is actually hearing are his or her own thoughts and desires projected onto the child's face, even into the spaces between his words, and echoed back again, like sayings shouted in a mountain cavern. Once we have made the assumption that we really hear and know what the child is feeling, it seals us off all the more from him, because he sees that we only *assume* to hear and know and despairs of true communication. This is when he shrugs his shoulders and slips into the argot of his peers, knowing he will not be understood by despotic adults. It is a moment of deep loneliness.

Robert A. Fein, in a study of men's experiences with childbirth and their young children, cited an illuminating time in the life of a rising lawyer who had an operation and was forced to spend several weeks at home recuperating. He found himself playing each day with his four-year-old son. "Billy really took good care of me," he mused to a friend. "He knew when I felt sad, and when I wanted to be alone. And I learned a little of what the world looks like through his eyes. It's a different world than mine, and it's pretty nice. You know, I had no idea what's on the underside of a parking meter. And I'm not used to watching people's faces the way he is. I really like my work but I'm considering trying to change my schedule so I can spend more weekday hours with my son."[2]

The lawyer's desire was commendable, but the chances are he never again had such a valid sense of the way the world looked to his son. Like most adults, he probably went back to his workaday world, became preoccupied with it, and didn't bother to lie on his back and really listen to the ticking of his son's mind.

We don't take the time or make the effort. We assume we know, and we don't. We don't even concern ourselves enough with feedback — with how our own sayings are heard and digested in the minds of the young. And we rarely listen with real openness to imperfectly formed thoughts and ideas from our children's mouths.

The message to the children is that they are incidental, that they are peripheral to our real concerns, that they do not matter very much in the overall scheme of things. And when they get it at home, at school, in church, from the clerks in stores, from society as a whole, they feel pretty rejected. If enough of them feel it at once and communicate with one another about it, they can easily decide the adult culture is hypocritical and tyrannical and they want nothing more to do with it. Then their songs and poems and newspapers begin to speak of alienation and counterculture, for they see no place for themselves in the world from which they've come.

Friends of ours have always made mealtime a time of being with their children. Not superficially, in the sense that they are all physically together. But emotionally and sympathetically. They try to hear what the children are seeing and feeling and coping with in their lives. The children share on equal footing in all conversations. Over the years, they have talked about everything — animals, books, work, play, theater, music, art, cooking, crime, drugs, games, war, people, vacations, and hundreds of other subjects. The children are amazingly well informed. They can carry on discussions just like adults, because they have never known a time when they were not treated as serious participants in family talks.

The beautiful thing, say the children's parents, is what they have learned from the children through the years. They feel they have been immeasurably enriched by letting the children's world be *their* world.

It is not easy, if you have not spent time with your children and grown up with their world, so to speak, simply to jump in feet first and become real participants with them in the things that interest them. It will require patience and kindness — a willingness to experience some disappointments, perhaps even some rebuffs, until they have accepted the idea and found it meaningful. The secret is to really care about their perspectives enough to be willing to leave the safety of your own. It is a little like putting yourself in the trust of a person in another country or another culture and saying, "I want to experience the world as you experience it, not as I have always known it."

Give Them Psychological Roots

Children who hurt and have anxieties often feel they are the only persons who have ever felt that way — that they are psychological voyagers in uncharted seas.

One reason they feel this way is that adults don't share with them meaningful information about their own frustrations and anxieties in life. "Shield the Children" is a game parents play. Thus the children fail to realize that their parents have gone through agonies similar to their own. They do not know Dad felt rejected as a child or Mom was ashamed of her acne. They do not see that to suffer and be lonely is a normal human problem. If they did see this, they would have a healthier perspective on their own unhappiness.

It is important to give children psychological roots — to help them acquire a historical context for dealing with their anxieties. Share with them the negative feelings as well as the positive feelings from your own childhood. Tell them about your problems with parents and siblings, with teachers and bosses, and with fellow students. Talk about the sense of inadequacy you felt, or the resentment you nursed, or the period of alienation you went through. Let them see, when their world seems to be in lousy shape, that it was in lousy shape for others before them.

This in itself will be helpful. It will assure them, when things get bad, that they will come out on the other side of the mountain, and aren't in an endless tunnel.

But you can go one step further, if you're anything of an amateur psychologist. You can talk about solutions to your own problems you wish you had seen as a child — how it would have helped to have realized your mother had an inferiority complex that made her lean on you to succeed, or half your friends were as worried about their appearances as you were about yours. Teach them to think in terms of problems and solutions instead of only in terms of problems. Then they're halfway home. They can begin to attack their loneliness and frustration in an adult manner.

Show Love and Kindness

It is impossible, in relationships with children, to overestimate the importance of love. Children are destroyed by quarreling and bitterness. Some of the most pathetic interviews I have had have been with youngsters whose parents often drank to excess and then fought loudly and angrily with each other. An associate who interviewed children from troubled homes reported that more than half the children complained of their parents' fights and said they would not return home even if they could. Silverman and Krate say that the children in Harlem are aggressive and anxiety-ridden because their parents are always fighting, shouting, and beating them with sticks, bed slats, belts, ropes, and ironing cords. There is little hope for children in homes like these.

Children need love and gentleness if they are to feel loved and accepted and to grow up with a sense of self-worth. They need firmness too; when there is no discipline, no setting and enforcing of boundaries, they also feel unloved. But with the firmness they require a constancy of affection and tenderness assuring them of the basic goodness of their world and of their own integral, responsible part in it.

In her book *The Needs of Children,* Kellmer Pringle sets "the need for love and security" in the very first place, as the sine qua non of child rearing. "The basic and all-pervasive feature of parental love," she says,

> is that the child is valued unconditionally and for his own sake, irrespective of his sex, appearance, abilities or personality; that this love is given without expectation of or demand for gratitude; and that the constraints imposed upon parental freedom of movement, upon time and upon finance, are accepted without resentment or reproach. . . . Parents communicate this unconditional affection through all their relations with him: from physical care and handling to responding to his first smile and sounds; from protecting him from, and then gradually initiating him into, the social world; and from restraining to eventually punishing him for going beyond the limits they have set for acceptable behavior.[3]

The emphasis on unconditionality is important. Not even the child's behavior should be made a condition of love. Threats of withholding love or of sending the child away for misbehavior are extremely disturbing to children — far more than adults can ever imagine. Affection should be given freely and constantly, the way the sun shines on us whether we plant sweet peas or saw briers.

It is easy to sound rhapsodic about love. But nothing can take its place in a child's life. It is the one real antidote to self-doubts, fears, anxieties, and unhappiness.

Children who do not have love dream of having it. Some even scheme to achieve it, like 10½-year-old Anthony in Mira Rothenberg's *Children with Emerald Eyes.* Anthony tried to drown himself. He locked himself in the bathroom and held his head under water until he passed out. Rothenberg asked why he did it. Anthony lowered his eyes. He said it was to make his father sorry — then the father would love him.[4]

If only parents would remember this hunger for love in their children. It is a hunger fully as real as any physical appetite — and as important to feed.

"Whenever I think about my childhood," said a friend of mine, "the thing I recall most of all is my parents' love and devotion. It isn't any one thing I remember, but the look of patience and affection I always saw shining in their eyes. Once, when I did something naughty, my father had to spank me. He had tears on his cheeks. That broke my heart. I knew there was nothing in the world I could do that would ever put me beyond his love. I cannot tell you what that has meant to me through the years."

Go Places with and for the Children

One special way of showing love and concern for children is to take them places where they will enjoy themselves — places you visit for them as well as for yourself.

Trips are fun. They remain as bright spots in the memory. Most adults love to recall the trips they made with parents when they were children — trips to the ballpark, to vacation spots, to relatives' homes, even to restaurants and shopping malls. "I remember when my father would sometimes take me to the movies," says one woman. "Once we went to a Betty Grable picture and sat through it twice. Dad really liked her. It's a wonderful memory. We didn't have a car and didn't go many places." "I love to think about the times we went to visit my grandparents in Kansas," says a middle-aged man. "We would get up and leave our home in Tennessee about one in the morning. I slept on a mattress on the floor in the rear of the car and my brother slept on the seat. Sometimes we would stop down near the Mississippi and eat at one of those old-fashioned watermelon stands. You sat at big wooden tables and ate all you wanted for about ten cents. It was a marvelous time. My father was always so relaxed. He loved to be going home. We would sing and carry on in the car in a way we never did at home."

There are vast extremes in children's travel experiences. Many children, in this day of jet travel, have been all over the world by the time they are ten or twelve. Others have never been out of the part of the city in which they live. But nearly every city abounds with things for parents to do with their children and places they can visit together — movies, plays, zoos, art galleries, specialty shops, restaurants, planetariums, parks, lakes, riverfronts, unusual buildings, exhibits, churches, synagogues, factories — the list is virtually endless.

The important thing is for adults to think of the children and take them on trips that will be fun and exciting for them. This gives children a sense of their importance to the adults in their lives, and it also gives them pleasant memories to think about when they tend to feel lonely or depressed. Even adults need the recollections of special trips together to reinforce their sense of meaning to each other. But children especially require such memories.

Ironically, it is often the parents who can most afford to take their children on really special trips and vacations who tend to leave the children at home in somebody else's care while they take the trips. "Oh, we like to get away from the little people," said a well-to-do lawyer's wife about her and her husband's frequent journeys to international gatherings, "and they're quite content to stay at home and watch TV while the maid opens a can of ravioli for their supper." It is true that parents do need time alone in order to continue their courtship well after marriage; but this particular couple have never taken their children anywhere except to the grandparents' homes.

They don't know what they're missing, actually. Some

of our finest hours have been spent on trips that were under-taken for the children's sakes and turned out to be wonder-ful experiences for us adults as well. We have laughed at the antics of monkeys in zoos, caught our breath in the fast-rising elevators of numerous skyscrapers, told ghost stories in sleeping bags on camping trips, hiked into ravines in search of hidden waterfalls, eaten too much fried chicken at Knott's Berry Farm, laughed at the clowns at circuses, ridden glass-bottom boats at Silver Springs, looked at seven states from atop Lookout Mountain, rowed a boat in Hyde Park, watched Punch and Judy shows in the Tuileries, and thrown coins into the fountain of Trevi. Without all these experi-ences and hundreds of others undertaken originally for the children, our lives would have been considerably duller and less memorable than they have been.

And, more significantly, our children would have far less a sense of security in their parents' affection and interest than they have.

Encourage the Children

On the subject of encouragement, there surely is nothing finer than a very short story by Sarah Orne Jewett called "Miss Tempy's Watchers." The scene is a wake — two ladies in a small northeastern town are sitting up with the body of Miss Tempy, an elderly spinster who has died. Qui-etly and quaintly, they talk about the qualities of the de-ceased. Eventually the talk gets around to the wonderful quince jelly Miss Tempy made and distributed to friends each year. The marvel of the annual jelly, as the ladies recall, was that Miss Tempy had only one quince tree, and it was so old that everybody thought it would quit bearing fruit years ago. But Miss Tempy had had a way with the tree. As one of the women said: "She just *expected* that thorny old thing into blooming!"

There is many a thorny old thing that will bloom when expected to — and many a thorny young thing as well.

There is nothing most people can't do — especially children — until they think they can't.

If we want children to blossom into healthy, happy, adaptable young adults, we will take care to encourage them all along the way, praising them for the good things they do and affirming them for the good persons they are. It is unnecessary for children to grow up as many do, feeling that they can do nothing right and that there is something innately wrong with them that makes them less successful than other persons. Parents are simply too thoughtless about withholding their approval. So are teachers, in many instances. A. S. Neill found that this was precisely the trouble with many of the "problem children" brought to him at Summerhill — the natural goodness of the children had never been praised or rewarded and so they were confused about how to relate to society.

"To every child," says Neill, "adult approval means love; whereas disapproval means hate."[5]

How true. Children who receive little approval feel neglected and disliked. They may even build their identity around disapproval, as Jean-Paul Sartre says Jean Genet did; raised as a foundling by foster parents, Genet was treated as a thief and an intruder; he decided that that was who he was and so became a criminal. Years later, when Genet had been in and out of a dozen prisons, Sartre raised the question about who the real culprits were. He suggested it might be "the decent folk" who had made a moral scapegoat of a child. Perceiving himself as unloved by the adults in his life, Genet simply reified the existence he thought they were projecting upon him.[6]

We have always tried to show as much interest as possible in whatever interested our children at particular phases of their lives, believing that this encouraged them to continue their absorbing adventure of exploring the world around them. We have aided in the collection of postcards, stamps, shells, coins, medallions, Rolls-Royceiana; praised countless paintings, drawings, and designs; listened attentively to oral recitations and musical renditions; chauffeured for ball games, piano lessons, drum lessons, violin lessons, and dates; eaten cakes, cookies, and even, on one or two occasions, a meal prepared by them; and auditioned many records and watched a great many TV shows selected by them. Other parents of our acquaintance have suffered through innumerable dance recitals, pulled ponies around half the country to riding competitions, nursed broods of kittens and rabbits and gerbils, and fought their way through Armageddonish scenes to fetch the autographs of TV and musical personalities.

It is easier, admittedly, to let the children pursue interests on their own while adults do likewise. Children *are* often fickle, turning from one interest to another as if they were going through revolving doors. But there is something important though intangible about really being present to your children in their interests — something that goes far beyond the unfinished collections of butterflies and rocks that lie taking up space in dresser drawers. It has to do again with a feeling of love and security, of being truly wanted by the parents.

We cannot but admire the parents in Michael Deakin's *The Children on the Hill,* who not only shaped their lives but even designed their living space to accommodate the children they loved. As Deakin says, the prepared environment permitted experiments of a kind most mothers would find intolerable in the average home.

> Thus, by the time he was a year old, Christian was experimenting with water toys, pouring liquid into containers of different sizes and shapes, working out the volumes needed to fill one bottle from another. It was perforce a very messy game, sometimes the table or floor would be swimming in water, but Maria never forbade him, never did anything to curtail his experiments, till he was satisfied that he had discovered what his curiosity demanded and stopped them of his own accord.[7]

All parents probably need to give more thought to having "childproof" rooms, attic spaces or basements, where children can experiment with paints, woodworking, metalworking, and other messy enterprises. It would save a great deal of scolding and reminding.

What we are really trying to encourage, in the end, is the child's sense of positive identity and self-worth, so that he or she is able to live confidently and happily with peers and develop into a sociable and productive young adult.

"I am not especially gifted at anything," said a young banking examiner, "but I am a very contented person. My mother and father were always good to tell me I could do anything I set my mind to, and then to lavish praise on my efforts. I know my limitations, but I can live with them quite comfortably. My greatest talent, I think, is for relationships. That's what my parents really taught me."

Give Your Children a Sense of Humor

George Meredith called it the "comic spirit" — seeing the world from a perspective that enables one to bear big troubles and laugh away the little ones.

Children obviously need such a spirit; we all do. If we can "see ourselves as others see us" and manage a chuckle at the sight, it saves us from a lot of things — among them, embarrassment, pompousness, and loneliness. There is a great deal of paranoia in a world as crowded as ours. People often feel they are being laughed at, attacked, put down, or treated prejudicially. The ability to see things in perspective, and even to kid ourselves about our irritability, is an effective antidote.

It is important to teach children from an early age how to have a sense of humor about themselves and the world around them. It will save them from many of the minor frustrations of life that have a way of growing, if unchecked, into a major habit of complaining or of feeling "picked on." If a child is not invited to a party, he can learn to say, "Oh, well, they probably didn't want to see me do my imitation of W. C. Fields trying to swim upstream in a water spigot!" It will help relieve the sense of neglect and loneliness he feels. If he doesn't win a speech contest, he can say, "I guess pig-Latin just isn't in right now," and not take the loss as a personal rejection.

Three things are helpful in imparting such a spirit to children. The first is a general sense of security and well-being; it is much easier for children who feel loved and accepted to be generous and self-accepting about their faults and failures. The second is for adults to exhibit a good sense of humor in themselves; children can get the hang of it much easier if they first see adults they trust mocking and spoofing themselves about disappointments and shortcomings. And the third is an actual explanation of the significance of humor, in which children are helped to understand that a good spirit not only makes defeats and disappointments more acceptable to the person who experiences them, but makes the person more likable to others who see him handling them.

Admission of one's vulnerability is after all the best defense. No one enjoys hearing another person trying to rationalize a mistake or defend himself for a shortcoming. A cheerful acceptance of the self's problems nearly always seems endearing in a person. The child needs to understand that we often like other persons more for their shortcomings than for their successes.

One of our sons once came home from field day at his school without having won a single ribbon. He had run the 440, the 220, and the 100-yard dash, had participated in the broadjump, and had been a member of two different relay teams, and was defeated in everything he attempted. He came home long-faced and embarrassed, on the edge of tears. It was at a period when he was extremely fond of root beer, and would drink a giant bottle at a single sitting if permitted to do so. My wife had returned from the store that morning with the groceries for the week, and had bought an oversized bottle of root beer that she had intended rationing out for several days. On learning of our son's bad day, she slipped into her sewing room, fashioned a large blue ribbon, printed on it the words "Root Beer Champ," attached the ribbon to the bottle of root beer, and put it in the refrigerator. When our son, hot, tired, and dejected, went to the refrigerator for a drink, his eyes lit up and his whole attitude changed. Perched on a chair with a half-empty bottle in his hand, he looked as happy as if he had won every event he had entered that day.

It was a valuable lesson to him and a useful metaphor to all of us. Now, whenever anyone in the family is defeated in something and feels tempted to make an excuse for it, all someone else has to do is to say "Root Beer Champ." Then there is a burst of laughter and the whole atmosphere is transformed.

Teach Skills and Abilities

I have spoken earlier of the importance of work to children in their adolescent period, and of the unfortunate conditions that now often make it difficult for them to find rewarding jobs in their communities. The lack of outside work may be offset, however, by various kinds of work young people can do around the home if taught proper skills and abilities early in their lives.

One father I know, for example, makes it a point to teach his children how to garden. The raising of flowers and vegetables, he feels, is an art that no longer flourishes as it should since our country has become urbanized and industrialized. His children are learning to share his pride in marigolds and forget-me-nots, cucumbers and tomatoes, and to feel they are contributing to the family's sustenance by digging and planting in the earth.

Another father is imparting a knowledge of tools and woodworking. His son has helped him build a garage and a toolshed, as well as several small items of furniture. The boy has a sense of real accomplishment in what he has done, and points out his work to friends and neighbors. Throughout his youth he will be able to see the tangible fruits of his labor, and their existence will be part of his feeling of belonging in his home.

Many mothers happily teach their children to cook, beginning with simple things like Jell-Os and salads and cookies and progressing to harder ones like cakes and casseroles and entire dinners. My wife has even taught our sons the rudiments of cooking, so that they are self-sufficient when we are away. With the new emphasis on sensitivity and caretaking in males, it is no longer considered "sissy" for boys to learn such formerly feminine arts.

Sewing is another skill that gives a child a feeling of self-importance and helps to avoid boredom. One woman said: "My mother taught me to use a needle when I was five and a sewing machine when I was ten. I was always proud as a peacock of what I could whip out in a few hours. I made all my own clothes and some of my sister's as well."

There are two interesting chapters in John Holt's *Escape from Childhood;* one is entitled "Competence in Children" and the other is called "The Right to Work." Although separated by intervening material, the two chapters belong together. Children can be very competent, if given a chance to perform, and they do have a right to work. Moreover, they have a right to do the kind of work that requires competence.

One of the reasons some children appear to be lazy is that they rebel at the thought of sweeping carpets, dusting furniture, and carrying out trash. They can hardly be blamed for this; adults often rebel at such tasks too. Children can be both industrious and helpful when given work that involves skill and care, especially if it is the kind of work in which results are readily visible. They will learn soon enough to do routine tasks, and will have plenty of years in which to do them.

In the meantime, it is a good idea to encourage them

to do the kinds of work that are exciting and meaningful to them. Then they will feel they are a vital part of the family economy and learn to take pride in their achievements. They will also find, as do most adults, that work is one of the best ways of overcoming a sense of loneliness or isolation.

Be Interested in Their School Lives

From the time children are six years old until they are eighteen, they spend nearly half their waking hours in school.

If you are a parent, you are probably your children's best interpreter of many of the things happening to them at school. They are too young, too inexperienced, to understand what is happening without some guidance. They are too close to the events to see them properly. They need someone to talk to about how they get along with other children and with teachers, about the significance of certain courses ("If Latin is a dead language, why should I study it?"), about their academic performances as these relate to their future lives, about the talents and interests unearthed in the course of their studies, and about dozens of other matters. You, as a parent, are the logical person to guide them, to listen to their complaints, to help them get on course again when they have strayed.

As we have talked with our children about their school lives, I think one of the most important things we have imparted to them is some understanding of why teachers behave as they do. When one of the children had a teacher who was extremely harsh and unpleasant and came home complaining about the unfairness of the teacher, we did not counsel getting out of the teacher's class. Instead, we asked a lot of questions about the teacher, involved the child in observing her behavior over several weeks' time, and then tried to help the child to assess the teacher's personal situation that made her the way she was. The child arrived at a conclusion himself: the teacher felt insecure and threatened by some of the brighter, more articulate children in the class, and she compensated by trying to seem hard and tough. Soon the child felt sorry for the teacher and was going out of his way to be nice to her. Sometimes he chided classmates who he thought were being unreasonable in their actions and thus provoking unpleasant reactions from her. The result of this kind of interpretive role was to turn a difficult situation that the child found grating and intolerable into a learning experience in its own right, and one in which the child may have received a lesson far more valuable than anything being offered in the curriculum. Instead of being bored and unhappy in the class, and perhaps occasionally feeling lonely because the teacher seemed so bearlike, he discovered something about the excitement of human relationships and how they work.

If you have a good relationship with your children and exhibit a strong interest in their schools, you will inevitably find yourself knowing their classmates, many of them by reputation and some in person, and will surely have opportunity to participate in the actual life of a class or classes from time to time. Many schools welcome the activities of parents, especially in helping to prepare special parties for the children, doing remedial teaching with slower youngsters, sharing personal experiences and travels through talks, slides, or movies, and assisting in various school programs to organize meetings, fundraisers, festivals, and other events in the school's life.

Robert Fein relates the story of a truckdriver named Mack whose 4-year-old son's enterprising nursery-school teacher invited Mack to come to school with his son and play with the children. One morning Mack showed up, feeling very shy and awkward. Under his arm was a book about trucks. "What are they going to do today?" he whispered nervously to one of the teachers. His son went on playing quietly on the other side of the room, ignoring Mack's presence. One of the teachers began building a road with some blocks, and soon the children were pushing little cars and trucks along the road, making sounds of "brrrmm" and "beep-beep." They played that way for about half an hour. Then Mack sat in their midst and read his truck book to them. They were captivated.

> Mack emerged from the classroom at the end of the hour slightly dazed. "Thanks," he mumbled to the teacher, "that was . . . uh . . . really great." Then, going down the steps, the young father turned with a puzzled, almost anguished look. "What'll I tell the guys at work about this?" [8]

Children never forget this kind of involvement in their school world. It is an interlacing of school and home that says to the children that the adults in their lives care about them, and that they are not alone in facing any problems that may arise in this world away from home.

Encourage Your Children's Religious Interest

I have purposely avoided discussing children and religion until now, for it is easy to provoke controversial feelings by anything one says on such a personal subject. But I have found in interviewing children that many of them derive considerable consolation for their loneliness or isolation from the religious faith they espouse. Several of those I talked to above the age of ten or eleven spoke of praying when they feel despondent or neglected, and felt this was usually helpful.

Religion has also been used as a means of moral discipline in some children's lives, and this has often produced fear, anxiety, and even a sense of estrangement. One woman testified:

"I was scared nearly out of my mind by religion when I was a little girl of eight or nine. It was at one of those tent meetings, where the preacher shouted and ranted. He said that everyone who didn't read the Bible all the time was going to hell, and he was very graphic about what hell was like. I went home and was afraid to go to sleep, afraid I would wake up in hell. It affected my brothers that way too, even though they were older than I was. One went around quoting the Scriptures for months after that, like he was crazy. I couldn't stand it. It's a wonder I ever became a religious person after that. It was a terrible thing to do to a child."

A college student recalled:

"My mother used to appeal to Jesus as an all-seeing eye whenever she thought I was doing anything I shouldn't do. She would say, 'I may not be able to go with you everywhere and see what you do, Jim, but Jesus can.' It gave me the willies. I don't know what she thought she was doing, but I felt awful strange when she talked that way."

These are negative examples of the use of religion in a child's life. Religion should not be used manipulatively, to gain an adult's will over the child or to punish a child who has done wrong.

But religious faith that is gently and lovingly taught can be an enormous support to children, for faith invariably leads them to look beyond the vicissitudes of human affairs to a more permanent sense of care and justice, and helps them to align themselves with this sense in such a way that they have more confidence in their self-worth and their relationships with other persons. Moreover, spiritual commitment normally puts the individual child in contact with a body of believers who hold a similar faith, and these persons can be extremely supportive of the child during the difficult years of latency and adolescence.

We have never insisted upon a specific framework of beliefs for our children, knowing that one generation's framework can become another generation's prison. But we have taken care to set before them both religious precepts and examples and to see that they have had opportunity at every stage of their development to be in the company of good, devout people who would exhibit to them the finest virtues of spiritual thought fleshed in day-to-day activities.

And from time to time they have mentioned to us that they "really prayed" about something troubling them. They are appropriating the real values of the religious life, I believe, without having to be committed to specific forms that their growing minds might challenge and reject with embarrassment or repulsion.

I am in firm agreement with R. S. Lee when he says, in *Your Growing Child and Religion,* that "Religious ideas can be taught, but the truth of religion can only be discovered," and that it is far more important to foster the spirit of discovery in children than it is to persuade them to accept without question what their teachers tell them.[9] Religious ideas, important as they are, usually become objects of contention, and the salty young teen-ager who is testing the merit of all kinds of ideas he or she came up against in earlier years is bound to have a whack at a few of them. But once the *spirit* of religion has been tasted — which, after all, animates all the worthy ideas of a religion — there is no forsaking it.

Therefore it is important to put children in the way of religious discovery without insisting on their conformity to certain truths; the peace and consolation they find will become an integral part of their lives.

Play with Your Children

We are only now discovering, after several centuries of practicing the Puritan work ethic, the great importance of play. Johann Huizenga may have initiated the discovery by saying in *Homo Ludens (Man at Play)* that we are most truly ourselves when we are playing; in the relaxation of games, dancing, or just having fun, we permit the masks to drop from our faces and appear as we are when we are happiest and most childlike. Now there is a whole school of child psychologists who say that the only way to really know children is to observe them at play, for there they do not bother to dissemble or try to fool us. As D. W. Winnicott, a leading British psychoanalyst, says in his study *Playing and Reality,* play is the medium in which both creativity and therapy are able to occur, and we cannot ignore it, either for our children or for ourselves, and remain healthy.[10]

Parents who truly desire to be with their children soon learn that play is the medium in which this is most possible. Children cannot enter the adult world; they try, almost from the first, but it is a transition they cannot accomplish. Adults, however, have been children and, to the extent that they are able to divest themselves of adult cares, responsibilities, and perspectives, can readily slip into the role of childhood again, imagining hobgoblins, stirring up mud pies, and playing the thousand and one games children love to play. The children enjoy adult companions at play; there is a magical, Gulliver-like quality about having a large, warm body to touch, struggle with, or hover near. It is assuring and confidence-building to them, because their world has always seemed safer when there were loving adults present than when they were alone or with their peers.

One of the most important by-products of physical playing, I have discovered, is the amount of touch-loving that goes on in it and then lingers afterward. This has been especially true in basketball and football, where body contact is inevitable; we tumble together, crash into each other, become enmeshed, and often hug as an expression of the fun we're having. The physical familiarity carries over to other sports. In the summer when we are swimming the boys constantly pop out of the water from nowhere, often behind me, to touch or hug and then dive off to another part of the pool.

Not all our family's playing is physical, by any means; it goes on frequently, almost continuously — in the house, the car, wherever we are. My wife is a great one to initiate word games; she and the boys began doing this once when I was away on a trip, and the boys have insisted on playing them from time to time ever since. Often the games are quite simple: Name a song beginning with A, then B, then C, and so on, with each player taking the proper turn until he cannot think of one and must drop out; name a bird whose name begins with A, etc.; name a girl's name beginning with A, etc. A favorite in the car is to find the consecutive letters of the alphabet in road signs, car licenses, and advertisements. Punning, repartee, joke contests, and insult contests are part of the constant fare. Dreaming aloud about trips we have made or plan to make, about Christmas, about birthday parties, about redecorating a room, or about something one of us is working on is a lot of fun when shared; enthusiasm builds until someone says, "Oh, I can't stand it, it's too exciting!" and the conversation terminates on that high note, or comes down to more basic matters of planning.

There is something about play that lubricates life, preventing its hardening into mere habit or routine. Its spontaneity allows for novelty. Creative impulses arise, making connections between ideas and actuality and cementing relationships between persons. The quality of all life is affected, so that work itself is not drudgery but a more sober part of life's playfulness. Attitudes are softened, and there is less harshness among people. Anxiety levels are lowered, and homes become more wonderful places for children to grow into healthy, enthusiastic adults.

Accept Your Children's Sexuality and Celebrate It with Them

In the chapter on "The Biological Limbo" I talked about the problems of loneliness, frustration, and identity-confusion many children experience during puberty, when the whole matter of sexual potency becomes dominant in their lives. There is nothing more important, in connection with this aspect of their development, than for the adults around them to provide an aura of grace and love in which they can accept without guilt the natural evolution of their bodies and physical desires, and even learn to exult in what is happening to them.

It is true that children today have much more exposure to sexual information than the children of previous generations. Many of them have sex education courses in school. Those who don't have multiple access to sexually explicit materials in newspapers, magazines, movies, and TV programs. As one mother of teen-agers said, "They can get a liberal education just standing at the paperback book rack in the grocery store."

But knowledge is not enough. Children also require the feeling of acceptance, of belonging, of pride in their development. And this means that the adults in their lives need a secure sense of their own sexual identity so they may gladly welcome younger family members into the fraternity (or sorority!) of sexual awareness and fulfillment. Hesitant, fearful, or even jealous adults can easily cripple the sexual blossoming of their offspring, thereby forcing them into lonely psychological exile and secrecy. When the grownups are happily adjusted in their own sexual roles, however, they can greatly ease and expedite the physical maturing of the children. Mothers can help their daughters understand menstruation as a welcome, not a dreaded, phase of the body's development. Fathers can remove their sons' fears of erection, masturbation, and emission. And both parents can conduct their children into a responsible, satisfying understanding of sexual functions with a sense of joy that the cycle of life is fulfilling itself in the coming of age of those who were born of the parents' own sexual desires.

In our family, the process of pubertal growth has been noted and celebrated at each step of the way. The discovery of the first pubic hairs and subsequent growth of hair under the arms and on the legs was duly heralded in family discussions, and the children congratulated. Discussions of sexual instincts, erection, masturbation, and relations with the opposite sex, which had been broached well in advance, became intensified. Every effort was made to insure that our children felt comfortable in themselves with what was occurring to them, and that they knew they could trust the child-parent relationship for any question or problem they might wish to introduce for counsel.

As our boys have become young men, we have made an open matter of their erotic relationship to their mother. Anne and I have permitted them to see more and more that we are not just parents but lovers, and that we have a sexual relationship that both predates and will postdate their period with us. We have gently teased them about their love for their mother and the competition they offer their father. "Hey, that's my wife you're hugging," I may call to one of them, or "Find your own girl," my wife may say when one of them tries to break in upon our embraces. Everything is accepted as a natural part of human sexual development, without friction, without moralizing, without complaint, and is made to appear as it is, a stage in an evolutionary process that will one day arrive at its climax in their own marriages and having children.

In this way anxiety levels are kept low and sex is seen for what it is, a beautiful aspect of human life, which, in all its complexities, problems, and enigmas, is a tender and holy gift, one to be revered and cherished and lovingly passed on from generation to generation.

Encourage Children's Relationships with Others

Much human loneliness is the result of a failure in the socialization process. Individuals do not learn, for one reason or another, how to relate to other persons in a creative, ongoing way. If we do not want our children to feel isolated from others and grow up timid and introverted, then it is important that we begin early in their lives to encourage their interaction with persons outside the family circle. It is best whenever possible to see that this interaction occurs with adults as well as with the children's peers, giving them a broad spectrum of age levels and personality types to which they may relate in various ways.

We have never tried to create artificial relationships between our children and their peers, hosting parties for them or planning outings that would bring them together.

But we have always been careful to support the tentative relationships in which they have shown interest, suggesting they invite their friends to play and have refreshments after school, take a meal with us, or spend the night or make a trip with us.

Our greatest efforts have probably been in the direction of helping our children to have adult friends, for we have found that the presence of significant "other adults" is much harder for children to come by in urban settings than it was in the small towns where we grew up. My wife and I both remember the importance of several caring adults during our adolescent years, and feel that our children should have similar opportunities in their lives. Consequently, we have a number of friends whom we try to share with the children — mostly older persons whose own children are grown and gone or single persons who have never had children — in the hopes that the exchange will be mutually enriching. The children have always dined with us when these persons were in our home as guests, have exchanged birthday cards and other greetings with them, and have had a chance to see themselves through the eyes of adults other than their parents.

Children do not automatically know how to stimulate and maintain friendships, and we have attempted to provide instruction on this subject at the various stages of their relationships, emphasizing such matters as really caring for people, taking an interest in their interests, tolerating differences of opinion, initiating and sustaining conversations, being thoughtful at special times in others' lives, and responding graciously to the overtures of friendship made by others. There is nothing more pathetic than seeing a lonely child hanging about on the periphery of a group of children or adults because he or she simply does not know how to approach inclusion in the group.

Teach Children the Importance of Doing *Something to Overcome Loneliness*

Loneliness has a hard time coexisting with activity. I have found that children themselves perceive that much of their loneliness occurs in moments when they think they have nothing to do and time is hanging heavy on their hands. At other times they rarely consider their feelings of alienation.

If they have been taught skills and abilities, as I suggested earlier, they will soon learn on their own to turn to the practice of these whenever their anxiety levels are rising and they feel a sense of loneliness or boredom coming on. If they have not acquired such skills as playing a musical instrument, making furniture, cooking or sewing, however, it will be helpful to teach them the simple fact that any kind of interesting or demanding activity is an effective antidote to negative feelings.

A vigorous ball game will soon take children's minds off themselves and their problems. So will cutting the grass, building a model, going to a movie, having a milkshake, studying a catalogue, reading a book, running, going for a bicycle ride, and dozens of other things.

It seems amazing that children will not recognize this themselves or, having done so, will forget it. But adults are prone to forget it too. Therefore it is good to remind them from time to time. Or, at a time when the child shows signs of being in "one of those moods" — what we in our family call the "can't-help-its" — the wise adult may simply assign the child something to do, knowing the performance itself will have the desired effect and banish the blues. This avoids the child's difficulty in overcoming inertia and getting started at something. "Roger, the grass needs cutting" or "Sally, I want you to vacuum the house" can be a lot more charitable than either appears on the surface, especially if it is thought up to combat boredom or melancholy.

And of course there are all the things we can do *with* the children that will dispel their gloom. We can say, "Hey, Bev, get your coat and let's catch the movie at the Globe," or "Come on, guys, I feel like a game of basketball," or "Jeanie, honey, I'm going to teach you to make this fabulous cake I found the recipe for the other day."

Talented children may even be challenged to transmute their feelings of loneliness into some kind of art. Writing a poem, an essay, a short story, or a piece of music expressing these feelings often leads to the dissipation of the feelings and gives a sense of pride in the achievement of the art form. Many famous writers, artists, and musicians, including Emily Dickinson, Vincent van Gogh, Thomas Hardy, Frédéric Chopin, and James Baldwin, began their careers as an escape from an extreme sense of loneliness or depression. While their work did not always banish the loneliness for very long, it was invariably an effective anodyne while the work was going on, and it did give them an important outlet for communicating and thus coming to grips with the deep and sometimes contradictory feelings within themselves. To be able to express something — to *name* it — is part of the battle against it.

Give Them Freedom but Keep the Net Handy

Children grow up. They are supposed to. Many adults don't like this; they want to keep them small all their lives. "Why do they have to get beyond the *sweet* stage," said one mother, "when they accepted your word as law and tried to please you all the time?" It is a narcissism in parents that desires this. But parents should buy pets if what they are after is stability and unchangingness. Children do grow up and they do develop interests and ideas of their own. As adolescents, they go through a period of rigorously testing the logic, sanity, truth, and desirability of nearly everything they have been taught since they were born. It is all part of the process of becoming mature, responsible citizens who know what the world is about at first hand and not by mere hearsay.

This can be uncomfortable for parents and other adults. None of us likes to be challenged or threatened by a younger generation. Some of the great stories of mythology are concerned with this rivalry between the young and the old. There is a very ancient antipathy to the idea of surrendering leadership to those who will inevitably supplant us.

But one generation must give way to another. We may naturally feel threatened, but the young are naturally bursting with energy and the desire to make a place for themselves under the sun. A collision is inevitable.

Unless.

Unless the adults are wise enough to see the inevitability of change and to recognize it as part of the pattern of human life.

Then perhaps we can behave more gracefully, not only accepting the efforts of the younger generation to break away from the confines of our teaching and domination but actually welcoming those efforts and congratulating the ones who make them. This is, after all, a happier response to make to what is inevitable anyway. It is perhaps a little like the Biblical injunction that "Whoever takes your coat, give him your cloak also," or the Zen story about the master who returned to his simple hut to find that a thief had stolen his possessions but soon noted with rejoicing that the moon still shone through the window, for it had not been taken.

Children must have freedom, and we should grant it to them willingly as they are able to accept it. When we give it only grudgingly and sparingly, they are made to feel frustrated and guilty about taking it. It is best to give it generously while keeping the net of security under them for them to fall back on if they need to. The disappearance of the net should in fact occur so gradually and silently as to go unnoticed by both children and parents, and probably should not occur finally until well into the children's young adulthood.

I like the emphasis of Rapoport, Rapoport, Strelitz, and Kew, of the Institute of Family and Environmental Research, who move in their book *Fathers, Mothers and Others* from a discussion on "Parenting with Adolescent Children" to a chapter on "Parenting with Adult Children and Grandparenting." As they say, the *active* role of parenting may have ended and the great outlay of energy in raising children may be over, but the connection is never severed; we are still our children's parents, even if they have families of their own and live thousands of miles away, and they ought to be able to feel that in an emergency of any kind they still have parents to call upon.

It is immature of parents to say to their children such things as "If you marry, don't count on any support from me" or "If you decide to become an actor, you can forget about looking to me for help"; that is an attempt to control the children's lives beyond the line of rightful control. It is all right to say, "My advice is this," but that ought to be followed by a reaffirmation of parental care and your willingness to be there for the child whenever he or she needs you.

After all, you need your children's independence as much as they need it; it is a part of your growth cycle as well as theirs, that having had children and raised them to an age of responsibility, you will then become free to enter a new and exciting phase of your own existence, when you can renegotiate your future according to present experience, interest, and desire. If you bind the children to your way of life, you are also binding yourself to it. The realization that your children have themselves become responsible for their lives can be exhilarating, especially if you have loved them and helped them to achieve healthy, mature outlooks on life. It means that you have arrived at a new rung on the ladder of experience and can look down proudly and happily on the one on which you formerly stood.

It is difficult to put the beauty of the life cycle into words. Sidney Callahan has attempted to do so:

From playing peek-a-boo to supporting career plans, the good parent entices and encourages the child into social life. As the first human partners in playing all games, learning all skills, and meeting all problems, good parents initiate and sustain an ongoing dialogue. There may be many different styles of parent-child dialogues which succeed. Since satisfactory human dialogue is a joy, a good parent introduces his child to the goodness of life.[11]

That is precisely what good parents do for children: they introduce them to the goodness of life. And, in the process, the parents discover the goodness of life themselves. There is no benediction on child-rearing like the one felt in the heart when you see your grown or nearly grown children happy and excited about living. When it happens to you, you will understand, and you will find that your own life is fulfilled in your children's. That is what life is about, and how to find it. There is no easy road. It takes constant vigilance and self-exertion. But when you arrive it will all seem worth it — abundantly.

NOTES

CHAPTER 1: *The Ordeal of Infancy*

1. Otto Rank, *The Trauma of Birth* (New York: Harper and Row, 1973), pp. 4-5.

2. Arthur Janov, *The Feeling Child* (New York: Simon and Schuster, 1973), p. 41.

3. Ibid., p. 43.

4. Ashley Montagu, *Touching: The Human Significance of the Skin* (New York: Harper and Row, 1972), p. 18.

5. R. A. Spitz, "Hospitalism: An Inquiry into the Genesis of Psychiatric Conditions in Early Childhood," in O. Fenichel et al. (eds.), *The Psychoanalytic Study of the Child*, Vol. I (New York: International Universities Press, 1945), pp. 53-74.

6. Hiag Akmakjian, *The Natural Way to Raise a Healthy Child* (New York: Praeger Publishers, 1975), p. 73.

7. John Bowlby, *Attachment and Loss, Vol. II: Separation* (New York: Basic Books, 1973), pp. 26-27.

8. Urie Bronfenbrenner, "Nobody Home: The Erosion of the American Family," *Psychology Today*, X, no. 12 (May 1977), pp. 41-47.

CHAPTER 2: *The Threat of Separation*

1. Bruno Bettelheim, *The Uses of Enchantment: The Meaning and Importance of Fairy Tales* (London: Thames and Hudson, Ltd., 1976), p. 15.

2. Stuart Sutherland, *Breakdown* (London: Paladin Books, 1977), p. 10.

3. Bettelheim, op. cit., p. 146.

4. Sigmund Freud, *A General Introduction to Psychoanalysis* (New York: Permabooks, 1953), p. 414.

5. Ibid., pp. 414-415.

6. Ibid., p. 416.

7. "Crisis Points: Is the Family Really Dying?", *The London Sunday Times*, May 28, 1978, p. 14.

8. Benjamin Spock, *Raising Children in a Difficult Time* (New York: W. W. Norton, 1974), pp. 236-237.

9. Bronfenbrenner, "Nobody Home," loc. cit., p. 41.

10. Bowlby, *Separation*, p. 30.

11. Ibid., pp. 226-227.

12. Ibid., pp. 227-228.

13. Ibid., p. 230.

14. Ibid., p. 220.

15. Martin Herbert, *Problems of Childhood* (London: Pan Books, Ltd., 1975), p. 133.

16. Ibid., p. 138.

CHAPTER 3: *An Agony of Helplessness*

1. Rollo May, *Power and Innocence* (New York: W. W. Norton, 1972), pp. 19, 23.

2. Adele Faber and Elaine Mazlish, *Liberated Parents/Liberated Children* (New York: Grosset and Dunlap, 1974), pp. 25-26.

3. Madeleine L'Engle, *A Circle of Quiet* (New York: Fawcett Publications, 1972), pp. 171-172.

4. George Dennison, *The Lives of Children: The Story of the First Street School* (New York: Vintage Books, 1969), p. 24.

5. Jean Piaget, *The Moral Judgment of the Child* (New York: Penguin Books, 1977), p. 216.

6. Barry Silverstein and Ronald Krate, *Children of the Dark Ghetto: A Developmental Psychology* (New York: Praeger Publishers, 1975), pp. 21-24.

7. Michael Deakin, *The Children on the Hill: The Story of An Extraordinary Family* (London: Quartet Books, 1973), p. 62.

CHAPTER 4: *The Damage Done by Schools*

1. L'Engle, op. cit., p. 170.

2. Don Dinkmeyer and Gary D. McKay, *Raising a Responsible Child* (New York: Simon and Schuster, 1973), pp. 203-204.

3. Theodore N. Clark, *The Oppression of Youth* (New York: Harper and Row, 1975), p. 63.

4. Ibid., p. 73.

5. Ibid.

6. Rocco D'Angelo, ed., *Confrontations with Youth: A Critical Analysis of Process and Proceedings of Ohio's Youth Flight Conference,* College of Administrative Science Monograph No. AA-11 (Ohio State University, 1976), p. 24.

7. Ivan Illich, *Deschooling Society* (New York: Harper and Row, 1971); Paulo Freire, *Pedagogy of the Oppressed* (New York: Penguin Books, 1972).

8. Edward Blishen, *The School That I'd Like* (Harmondsworth, England: Penguin Books, 1969), p. 10.

9. Gisela Konopka, *Young Girls: A Portrait of Adolescence* (Englewood Cliffs, N.J.: Prentice-Hall, 1976), p. 112.

10. John Holt, *How Children Fail* (New York: Dell Publishing Co., 1964), p. 157.

11. Ibid., p. 142.

12. Nicholas Hobbs, *The Futures of Children: Categories, Labels, and Their Consequences* (San Francisco: Jossey-Bass Publishers, 1976). See also Marvin R. Koller and Oscar W. Ritchie, *Sociology of Childhood* (Englewood Cliffs, N.J.: Prentice-Hall, 1978).

13. Holt, op. cit., p. 125.

14. Dennison, op. cit., p. 74.

15. Holt, op. cit., p. 91.

CHAPTER 5: *The Cruelty of Peers*

1. Neal Silver, "Lonely Children Virtually Invisible to Their Peers," *Nashville Tennessean*, February 6, 1977, p. 13-A.

2. Erving Goffman, *Stigma: Notes on the Management of Spoiled Identity* (Harmondsworth, England: Penguin Books, 1968), p. 43.

3. Silverstein and Krate, op. cit., p. 217.

4. See Thomas Kochman, "Rapping in the Ghetto," in Lee Rainwater, ed., *The Black Experience: Soul* (Chicago: Aldine, 1970); Roger Abrahams, *Deep Down in the Jungle: Negro Folklore from the Streets of Philadelphia* (Chicago: Aldine, 1970); and William Labov, *Language in the Inner City: Studies in the Black English Vernacular* (Philadelphia: University of Pennsylvania Press, 1972).

5. Bruno Bettelheim, *The Children of the Dream: Communal Child-Rearing and Its Implications for Society* (Frogmore, England: Paladin, 1972), p. 89.

CHAPTER 6: *The Kingdom of the Jocks*

1. James S. Coleman, *The Adolescent Society* (New York: Macmillan, 1961).

2. Neil D. Isaacs, *Jock Culture, U.S.A.* (New York: W. W. Norton, 1978), pp. 34-35.

3. James Michener, *On Sport* (London: Corgi Books, 1977), pp. 134-135.

4. Ibid., p. 21.

5. Cf. H. Webb, "Professionalization of Attitudes Toward Play Among Adolescents," in G. S. Kenyon, ed., *Aspects of Contemporary Sport Sociology* (Chicago: The Athletic Institute, 1969), pp. 161-178; Brian M. Petrie, "Achievement Orientations in Adolescent Attitudes Toward Play," *International Review of Sport Sociology* (Warsaw: Polish Scientific Publishers, 1971), pp. 88-89.

6. Robert Lipsyte, *SportsWorld: An American Dreamland* (New York: Quadrangle Books, 1975).

CHAPTER 7: *The Unattractive Child*

1. Herbert, op. cit., p. 188.

CHAPTER 8: *Childhood and Mobility*

1. Vance Packard, *A Nation of Strangers* (New York: David McKay Co., 1972).

2. Michael Young and Peter Willmott, *Family and Kinship in East London* (Harmondsworth, England: Penguin Books, 1962), p. 14.

3. Packard, op. cit., p. 248.

4. Alvin Toffler, *Future Shock* (New York: Bantam Books, 1971), p. 75.

5. Robert Coles, *Migrants, Sharecroppers, Mountaineers*, Vol. II in *Children of Crisis* (Boston: Little, Brown and Co., 1967), p. 64.

6. Robert Coles, *Privileged Ones*, Vol. V in *Children of Crisis* (Boston: Little, Brown and Co., 1978), pp. 321-322.

7. In *Ladycom*, September 1977, pp. 14-15, 26-27.

8. Coles, *Migrants, Sharecroppers, Mountaineers*, p. 61.

9. Silverstein and Krate, op. cit., p. 10.

10. P. A. Jewell and C. Loizos, eds., *Play, Exploration and Territoriality in Mammals* (New York: Academic Press, 1966).

11. Bowlby, *Separation*, pp. 148-150.

CHAPTER 9: *Childhood and Death*

1. Rose Zeligs, *Children's Experience with Death* (Springfield, Illinois: Charles C. Thomas, 1974), pp. 3-5.

2. Maria H. Nagy, "The Child's View of Death," in H. Feifel, ed., *The Meaning of Death* (New York: McGraw-Hill, 1959).

3. Sylvia Anthony, *The Discovery of Death in Childhood and After* (Harmondsworth, England: Penguin Books, 1973), pp. 50-55.

4. Ibid., p. 23.

5. Frances G. Wickes, *The Inner World of Childhood* (London: Coventure Ltd., 1977), p. 203.

6. Zeligs, op. cit., p. 27.

7. I. and P. Opie, *The Lore and Language of Schoolchildren* (Oxford: Clarendon Press, 1959).

8. Anthony, op. cit., p. 241.

9. Zeligs, op. cit., p. 117.

10. Jean Piaget, *The Child's Conception of the World* (Frogmore, England: Paladin, 1973), p. 188.

11. Anthony, op. cit., pp. 97-100.

12. Ibid., pp. 19-20.

13. Marjorie E. Mitchell, *The Child's Attitude to Death* (New York: Schocken Books, 1967), p. 107.

14. Earl Grollman, *Talking About Death: A Dialogue Between Parent and Child* (Boston: Beacon Press, 1976), p. ix.

15. Mitchell, op. cit., p. 41.

16. Elisabeth Kübler-Ross, *Death: The Final Stage of Growth* (Englewood Cliffs, N.J.: Prentice-Hall, 1975).

CHAPTER 10: *Victims of Divorce*

1. J. Louise Despert, *Children of Divorce* (New York: Doubleday and Co., Dolphin Books, 1962), pp. 256-257.

2. Ibid., p. 170.

3. Irving R. Stuart and Lawrence Edwin Abt, *Children of Separation and Divorce* (New York: Grossman Publishers, 1972), p. 11.

4. Herbert, op. cit., p. 481.

5. Despert, op. cit., pp. 297-298.

6. Frances L. Ilg and Louise Bates Ames, *The Gesell Institute's Child Behavior* (New York: Dell Publishing Co., 1962), p. 352.

7. Stuart and Abt, op. cit., p. 201.

8. I. Gregory, "Anterospective Data Following Childhood Loss of a Parent: 1. Delinquency and High School Drop-Out," *Archives of General Psychiatry*, XIII (1965), 99.

9. Sula Wolff, *Children Under Stress* (Harmondsworth, England: Penguin Books, 1973), pp. 119-120.

CHAPTER 11: *The Struggle for Independence*

1. John Holt, *Escape from Childhood: The Needs and Rights of Children* (New York: E. P. Dutton Co., 1974), p. 30.

2. E. Douvan and J. Adelson, *The Adolescent Experience* (New York: John W. Wiley Co., 1966), pp. 351-354.

3. W. W. Meisner, "Parental Interaction of the Adolescent Boy," *Journal of Genetic Psychology,* CV (1965), 225-233.

4. L. Harris, "Change, Yes — Upheaval, No," *Life,* January 8, 1971, pp. 22-27.

5. Irving Weiner, *Psychological Disturbances in Adolescence* (New York: John W. Wiley Co., 1970).

6. Erik Erikson, *Childhood and Society* (New York: W. W. Norton, 1950), and *Identity: Youth and Crisis* (New York: W. W. Norton, 1968).

7. Erikson, *Childhood and Society,* p. 261.

8. John J. Conger, *Adolescence and Youth: Psychological Development in a Changing World* (New York: Harper and Row, 1977), p. 95.

9. In Simon Meyerson, ed., *Adolescence: The Crises of Adjustment* (London: George Allen and Unwin, 1975), pp. 54-72.

10. Ibid., p. 60.

11. Clark, op. cit., p. 31.

12. Bettelheim, *The Children of the Dream,* pp. 132-136.

13. G. H. Elder, Jr., "Structural Variations in the Child Rearing Relationship," *Sociometry,* XXV (1962), 259.

14. Erikson, *Childhood and Society,* p. 262.

15. Conger, op. cit., p. 464.

16. Margaret Mead, *Culture and Commitment: A Study of the Generation Gap* (London: Panther Books, 1977), p. 88.

17. Paul Upson, "Adolescents and Groups, Subcultures, Counter-cultures," in Meyerson, op. cit., p. 180.